DO YOU KNOW . . .

—What style bathing suits were worn during the *Summer of '42*?

—How long a letter took to make its way from Washington, D.C., to Houston in 1890?

—What San Diego, California, was like during World War II?

—What programs were being broadcast on the radio in 1959?

—What it was like to be a woman in Germany in the 1600s?

Fiction writers need to be confident about the authenticity of their stories' settings, time periods, and background details. Their research needs are special, and now, for the first time, they have a reference book designed just for them. Clear, easy-to-use, and time-saving, this valuable resource tells novelists and short story writers of every genre where to go . . . who to ask . . . what to read . . . how to find the information they need.

THE FICTION WRITER'S RESEARCH HANDBOOK

MONA McCORMICK is Librarian in the Reference Department of UCLA's University Research Library. She is the author of *The New York Times Guide to Reference Materials*, available in a Signet edition.

THE FICTION WRITER'S RESEARCH HANDBOOK

MONA McCORMICK

A PLUME BOOK

NEW AMERICAN LIBRARY

A DIVISION OF PENGUIN BOOKS USA INC., NEW YORK
PUBLISHED IN CANADA BY
PENGUIN BOOKS CANADA LIMITED, MARKHAM, ONTARIO

Copyright © 1988 by Mona McCormick

PLUME TRADEMARK REG. U.S. PAT. OFF. AND FOREIGN COUNTRIES
REGISTERED TRADEMARK—MARCA REGISTRADA
HECHO EN BRATTLEBORO, VT., U.S.A.

SIGNET, SIGNET CLASSIC, MENTOR, ONYX, PLUME, MERIDIAN and NAL BOOKS are
published *in the United States* by New American Library, a division of
Penguin Books USA Inc., 1633 Broadway, New York, New York 10019, *in Canada*
by Penguin Books Canada Limited, 2801 John Street, Markham, Ontario L3R 1B4

Library of Congress Cataloging-in-Publication Data

McCormick, Mona.
    The fiction writer's research handbook.
    1. Fiction—Authorship—Research—Handbooks,
manuals, etc.   I. Title
PN3355.M37   1988   808.3'072   88-5168
ISBN 0-452-26444-8

First Printing, September, 1988

2   3   4   5   6   7   8   9   10

PRINTED IN THE UNITED STATES OF AMERICA

Draw your chair up close to the edge of the precipice and I'll tell you a story.

—F. Scott Fitzgerald
Notebooks

Contents

PART III
Creating Fictional Worlds

PART IV
Special Topics

PART V
Other Sources

ACKNOWLEDGMENTS

Many thanks to Pat and Ben, my family, for their continuing support and good humor during this project. Special thanks to Diana Ruth Thatcher and Raymond Soto for their help in so many ways but especially for their computer expertise. I also wish to express my appreciation to the UCLA University Research Library administrators, particularly Ruth Gibbs and Russell Shank, and to the Reference Department head, Ann Hinckley, and acting head, Janet Ziegler, for finding me some time. Thanks to Christine Coleman for research assistance. I am ever grateful to the librarians and staff at UCLA, especially those who have glanced at these pages, making suggestions, and most particularly those in the Reference Department who have helped me find many an elusive title and who have so generously supported this effort.

Introduction

Fiction writers—novelists, screenwriters, dramatists—communicate their artistic vision by creating worlds in which a reader finds truth and pleasure, but only if the reader has been led to *believe* in that world. This guide is intended to help fiction writers find as much information as they need to create believable worlds, even future worlds. It deals with *research methods* and *designs for getting started* so authors can pursue research to fit their needs—a lot or a little—finding facts quickly or delving deeply into all facets of a subject.

Under common topics the arrangement is somewhat hierarchical, with a list of specific titles to find facts fast, a list of possible subject headings to find cataloged books efficiently, appropriate indexes, and for those engaged in more extensive research, bibliographies and guides to in-depth study. That is more or less how each subject area is arranged—depending on the relevance of elements in each field.

Therefore, these are *not* exhaustive lists of all important books in a field, nor is every possible field covered. *The Fiction Writer's Research Handbook* names *sources for finding answers to typical questions that arise for writers, but it also describes research methods and bibliographic guides that enable readers to confidently find answers to more complex questions beyond the scope of this book.* The titles suggested also have bibliographies, leading to more titles and expanding the search to whatever limits writers set.

The procedures and titles listed here are suited to the use of large public libraries and college and university libraries. Because the use of correct subject headings in library catalogs and in indexes is a major stumbling block for most researchers and is a vital key to research, an understanding of subject headings is emphasized here. Some of the headings used in the *Library of Congress Subject Headings* (LCSH) are suggested under various topics. Authors are urged to *look at the full LCSH list of headings for a subject, since only a selection is given in each category*—enough to show the range of available headings and to get started with correct ones. Becoming familiar with Library of Congress headings insures successful searching and builds confidence.

In some sections annotations are given for each individual title; in others, annotations are given in introductory remarks. *Under topics, it is important to read the introductory paragraphs that precede the "Useful Titles" and "Possible LCSH Subject Headings" lists because these discussions annotate the titles and explain headings and their subdivisions.* Subtitles are always included to further describe books. In the bibliographic citations, a date followed by a dash (1945–) means that the entry is still publishing; the date indicates the year it was first published (usually an index or an annual volume and the frequency of publication is also given). There are many cross-references to related chapters and titles, and some titles are repeated—recognizing that a reference work of this kind is not necessarily read from cover to cover but sections referred to as information needs arise.

In addition to research methods, *The Fiction Writer's Research Handbook* offers advice on locating experts, locating special collections, the use of computers in research, creating chronologies, and finding other published fiction dealing with various topics and settings. This guide concludes with a reference bibliography and a bibliography of material on the importance and the use of time and place in fiction, including writing techniques. Throughout the book, writers are urged to consult reference librarians for help and advice with their searches.

In addition to the obvious benefits of finding the information necessary for their particular manuscript, authors often say that the research process has helped them through a period of writer's block and that they have discovered information that they weren't looking for but that greatly augmented their stories and plays. Research can be a way of resting from the writing while continuing to work on the project. Research is discovery and need not be painful—especially if writers are aware of procedures that smooth the way and if they view it as a process that prompts imagination.

> "I might not tell everybody,
> but I will tell you."
>
> —WALT WHITMAN

THE FICTION WRITER'S RESEARCH HANDBOOK

Part I

Research: Why & How

Why Research
for Fiction?

Christopher Isherwood, when he read the book said: "My God, Gore, how could you write about anything without wondering if it was true? I mean you'd be describing a bird in a garden and suddenly there would be that awful question in your mind, did they have birds in the fourth century?" "Vidal to Vidal: On Misusing the Past," *Harper's*, October 1965

Questions do arise for writers, though perhaps not that one. And they arise for the more recent past as well. Sometimes a writer needs just a few facts to establish a time and place, and at other times extensive research (especially the case for a recent evolution, the "nonfiction" novel) is needed to create a believable world and preserve the illusion of reality. The atmosphere of a time and the details of a place can help bring characters and ideas to life. But there are other considerations. If the setting is Paris and an author describes the city with even a small detail that a reader knows to be incorrect, the reader may be lost and refuse to bring the necessary "suspension of disbelief" to the story. It may also be important not to give readers false information (such as medical information) that might be damaging to them. Pure science fiction might be an exception to some rules, but even then, research into current futurist thinking can trigger imagination.

Research in general can be a way of nudging any writer's imagination, and many have found that the research process has ended writer's block and helped them get through troubled times. It is a way of continuing to work on the project in meaningful ways, getting new ideas, giving the creativity of writing a rest, all without actually stopping the work.

Time means many things to the writer—the passage of time in the story or play, the use of time as part of the plot, the pace of the fiction, subjective time (the character's conscious or unconscious mind), the narrator's time, even the time it takes for the performance of a play—there are many interpretations. Though one can feel love or hate for a place, one frequently regards time as something of an enemy. But not here. For the purposes of this guide, *time* refers to the period in which the book, story, or play is set—the 1850s, the 1920s, the 1980s, or any era. *Time* here means researching the details of a historical or present time period.

Place in this guide refers to the total environment in which a story or play takes place and, in that sense, includes the background and the setting of a chapter or scene. The play *Our Town* takes place in the midwestern town of Grovers Corner; what the audience sees (the setting) might be two neighbors' houses or a graveyard. For simplicity, *place* here means all three locations—the town, the houses, the graveyard—and indeed some research might be needed to establish all three convincingly. What did all that look like from 1901 to 1913? So in the discussion of research in this book, the words *setting, scene, background,* and *place* might be used interchangeably, though *place* is the umbrella word covering other meanings.

Research is often necessary to help writers achieve a sense of reality. Eudora Welty comments in her *Place in Fiction* (New York: House of Books, 1957):

> Actuality, it is true, is an even bigger risk to the novel than fancy writing is, being frequently more confusing, irrelevant, diluted, and generally more far-fetched than ill-chosen words can make it. Yet somehow, the world of appearance in the novel has got to *seem* actuality. . . . The moment the place in which the novel happens is accepted as true, through it will begin to glow, in a kind of recognizable glory, the feeling and thought that inhabited the novel in the author's head and animated the whole of his work.

Later in the same work she writes:

Establishing a chink-proof world of appearance is not only the first responsibility of the writer; it is the primary step in the technique of every sort of fiction.

Welty believes that feelings are bound up in place and that one place comprehended can make us understand other places better.

The importance of place in literature has always been recognized, though it comes in and out of fashion in terms of being discussed and taught. It is this importance that makes the research effort necessary; the sense of place is too important to overlook or neglect. Fiction reflects that sense of place found in the real world. Ian Nairn, in *The American Landscape* (New York: Random House, 1965), writes: ". . . it seems a commonplace that almost everyone is born with a need for identification with his surroundings and a relationship to them—with the need to be in a recognizable place. So sense of place is not a fine-art extra, it is something that man cannot afford to do without." Lawrence Durrell has commented on his private notion about the importance of landscape and has been willing to admit that he sees characters almost as functions of a landscape. In the twentieth century, there is concern about a sense of "placelessness," with a constantly moving population, and that too can be conveyed.

There are some splendid opinions, notably from Oscar Wilde ("Life is Art's best, Art's only pupil"), that art is supreme and that life imitates art, not vice versa. If life imitates art, then why must art seem real? Because otherwise it's fantasy; it begins "Once upon a time . . ." and lures us into a different kind of experience. And even then, though the place is fantasized, what could be more important to a fairy tale than a carefully rendered setting, with those wonderful woods and huts, towers and castles? The Emerald City and Alice's Wonderland exist. Certainly there are some places in fiction, real or imagined, that we can almost see more clearly than places we have actually experienced—Wuthering Heights, Mandalay, Joyce's Dublin, Durrell's Alexandria, Dickens's England, Walden Pond, Jane Austen's houses, Damon Runyon's New

York, and Raymond Chandler's Los Angeles. A carefully established reality has seduced us into believing in a time and place unknown to us.

A sense of reality is not the only reason for careful attention to time and place. How characters react to time and place can be a way of revealing who they are. Are they sensitive to what they see, and how do they respond to it? Of course, atmosphere that assists the story can be created by descriptions of places. The key words here are "assists the story," because *the writer selects only what is meaningful to the final purpose of the story.* Time and place are quite functional, supporting the story's goals.

Research, especially extensive study, can be irritating, time-consuming, and absolutely exhausting as the searcher follows the trail from bibliographies, encyclopedias, catalogs, and indexes, to book stacks and periodicals. And frequently the process is unrewarding, as you find, or at least think you find, that some elusive fact has never been recorded. Then you start calling the experts, and fortunately the previous investigation has brought you up on the subject and focused your questions so your conversation with the specialist is intelligent.

ARRANGEMENT OF THIS GUIDE

The process described in this book is meant to help writers cope with fact-finding and take some of the sting out of research. There are chapters discussing various important aspects of research, historical investigation, and the search for more contemporary information. Then there are sources for topics that frequently come up for writers, and under each topic are titles; subject headings to find books; indexes and abstracts to find periodical articles; government documents or other sources where appropriate; and research guides. (Be sure to read the introductory notes before lists of "Useful Titles" and "Possible LCSH Subject Headings," because these discussions annotate the titles and explain subject headings. Only *selected* subject headings are given, so it is best to look at the complete list in the Library of Congress Subject Headings list if you are doing in-depth study.) A research guide is a detailed work on a discipline or field (anthropology, history, or business, for example) that offers advice and bibliographies (reference sources and lists of books and/or articles) on all aspects of the subject. Use of a research guide gets you on the path of serious research. Under the topics listed here the hierarchical arrangement is designed so readers can select the quick way of specific titles or delve into in-depth searching through study guides in specific subject areas. Choose a little or a lot of work; it's your choice to suit your needs. You already know that research is almost always some kind of *work*. But help is here.

Perhaps discipline, not work, is a better word for what is required. Fiction writing itself is a craft that requires discipline, so it's worth practicing. Teachers of research methods hear concerns from authors that the research process, with its often tedious investigations, might stifle creative imagination and put some unwanted limit on freewheeling inventiveness. Almost without exception, when writers begin to successfully search a subject, they find that the research process feeds the creative process, and once they are underway everything they find and read is grist for the mill. Indeed research itself can be conducted creatively—and will be when these guidelines are used.

Note-taking, outlining, and following an intelligent search strategy can give authors a confidence and sense of power that nourish creativity. Kenneth Clark commented in his book *Landscape into Art* (New York: Harper & Row, 1976), "Facts become art through love, which unifies them and lifts them to a higher plane of reality."

Beginning

SEARCH STRATEGIES AND LIBRARIES

What difference does it make if there were no friars in the twelfth century?—Friar Tuck enlivens the story of *Ivanhoe*. The earliest historical novelists did not always distinguish between their stories and fairy tales or thrillers. Since, after all, you are writing fiction, then *perhaps* you can "fudge" a little on pure fact here and there by way of not being rigid and inflexible. But having been cautioned to remain pliant, it is best to remember that today's readers are better informed and expect more accuracy; an author's best stance is probably to omit something rather than to pretend to know what he or she does not know. So determine from the start to tackle the necessary research. The advice of the Tibetan teacher to his meditation student applies here: "How you do it is—you go very, very slowly until you reach fast."

EXPECTATIONS AND PITFALLS

You must develop the searching style best for you, but there are some general guidelines worth following. Many writers do a considerable amount of checking before they begin writing and find, as stated earlier, that it triggers character and story ideas. Others find it suits them to check facts only as required during the writing process, when questions arise. But *at some early point, it is best to do writing and searching in tandem; it is very dangerous to put off all writing until you have completed all research*—that becomes procrastination. Whatever the needs, *do not expect to complete your research all at once, even if you allow a week or a month.* Researching fiction invariably requires many separate forays into the library stacks, or telephone calls to experts, and a more leisurely attitude toward fact-finding will be less frustrating and will facilitate your writing as it progresses. Also, *do not expect to find answers to absolutely everything you want to know*—that's unrealistic. But the good news is that you *can expect to find lots of material you were not looking for but can use* to wonderful advantage. The more relaxed you can be about the investigative process and the more open to what's found, the better. *You should know more than you plan to use* in order to be comfortable with the subject and convincingly dribble factual information into your story. *Beware of ever using the language of the nonfiction source* or you will slip into explaining rather than "storifying" and run the risk of plagiarizing. In other words, *don't strain to use a fact.* When using the library, *ask a reference librarian for help,* making sure you ask for what you really want. For example, don't ask for an encyclopedia of business information when what you really want to know is what happened to a certain stock in January of 1910. People frequently make up a source (usually an encyclopedia of whatever), ask for it, and may get told there is no such thing, when there may be an easy way of finding the information they really want. The idea is to learn how to use the librarian as well as the library. *At some point, stop searching* (see "Knowing When to Stop" in part 4). Remember that though it is always difficult at first to learn about a library and its reference tools, *it will get easier.* That's guaranteed.

NOTE-TAKING

As you write *keep a checklist of everything you need to know* and make a trip to the library when you have *several* things to check. Make careful notes to yourself, because you may think you'll remember what and why your story requires some information, but often you will not, especially if a day or more of writing goes by before you get to the research task. *Make careful notes on your reading, and make a note of the source* (author, title, page number, call number, and if you're using more than one library, the name of the library). Notes can be kept in a notebook or on large file cards that can be "shuffled" or manipulated to put them in a certain order or appropriate sequence for writing. It is best to write on only one side of the notepaper or file cards in order to easily see what's there when you put them in a certain order. Even though you'll be fictionalizing information and will not be citing sources for readers as you would with nonfiction, you may want to return to that source for some reason, and nothing is more irritating than knowing you read something but not being able to find it again.

EVALUATING SOURCES

Not all sources of information are created equal. When conducting research, if something seems too outrageous (or too good to be true in terms of your play or novel), you should check it in more than one source. If you are using standard, reliable reference tools, checking more than one source may not be essential most of the time for the purposes of fiction writing, but it is recommended if you have the slightest doubt about a fact or event. The reliability of a work can be determined by its:

Authority: Who is the publisher and who is the author and what are his or her credentials? (See "Books" [part 3] and "Diaries, Memoirs, and Biographical Tools" [part 2]).

Purpose: What claims does it make (in the Introduction, Preface, etc.), and does it fulfill those goals?

Scope—what is the coverage: does it cover one time period or several, one city or many, etc.?

Audience: Is the work aimed at a juvenile or an adult, an expert or a lay person?

Accuracy and Reliability: Does the work answer typical

questions in its stated field, and does it *document its sources* (have bibliographies; remember, you may want to check the original sources)? You can make some quick comparison of a title with another work on the same subject.

Indexes: Indexes are the keys to accessing information within a work (and a work may need more than one index), so they should be complete and accurate—most readers do not expect to read a reference book from cover to cover, so access through indexes and a Table of Contents is essential.

Bibliographies: Bibliographies (lists of books and/or articles) can lead to other works in the field and are part of the documentation of sources used.

Illustrations: Illustrations may be necessary for clarity, depending on the subject.

Content: All the other qualities support the most important part, the substance of the work—the actual information offered and the completeness of that information.

Ease of use: Are some or all of the above qualities arranged in a reasonable way? (Occasionally a reference book is so complicated that no one can figure it out.)

Reference books can be verified in guides to reference sources (see "Reference Sources," on page 256), and reviews can also help in the evaluation of material—check works such as *Book Review Digest, Book Review Index*, and *American Reference Book Annual (ARBA)* (see "Books" in part 3).

Search Strategies

There are some basic steps in the research process that you can check at the start of your search and then select the methods appropriate for your needs. These steps will be dealt with in more detail throughout this handbook. At any point in this process, *ask a librarian* for help and advice. If a topic is totally unfamiliar to you, consult a librarian first. They can save you time and anxiety by suggesting major reference sources in your field. The search strategy steps are:

OVERVIEW

• Obtain a brief overview of the subject, usually in a general or subject encyclopedia. In many cases an encyclopedia may be all you require, so start there before you make your search more complicated than it needs to be. Encyclopedias will also give you some familiarity with the language and subtopics of a subject. Major general encyclopedias are the *Academic American, Chambers's Encyclopedia, Collier's Encyclopedia, Encyclopedia Americana, The New Encyclopaedia Britannica,* and the *World Book.* In addition there are subject encyclopedias for almost any subject—check the reference bibliography in this guide, especially the *ARBA Guide to Subject Encyclopedias and Dictionaries* and the Kister book, *Best Encyclopedias: A Guide to General and Specialized Encyclopedias.* Subject encyclopedias are also mentioned under topics in this book.

BIBLIOGRAPHIES

• Find bibliographies (lists of books or articles) and research guides on the subject. If you are simply looking for a quick fact, you don't require bibliographies or the next step, research guides. The best reference books offer lists of sources, encyclopedia articles usually have brief bibliographies, and if you're doing a comprehensive search, use *Bibliographic Index*, Besterman's *World Bibliography of Bibliographies,* the *Subject Guide to Books in Print* for current work, and check the library catalog under the topic using the subdivision "bibliography" (e.g. DANCE—BIBLIOGRAPHY). That subject heading subdivision is often, *but not always,* repeated as a possible subject heading under topics discussed in this guide, so remember it as you review the search strategy steps.

RESEARCH GUIDES

• Use research guides to the study of a discipline if extensive research is being conducted. These are also a source of bibliographies and will review the major reference sources in various aspects of a subject.

SUBJECT HEADINGS

• It is very important to determine the appropriate subject headings for locating books (*Library of Congress Subject Headings* [LCSH]—see "Subject Headings" later in this section) or those used in periodical indexes or abstracting services. Under topics in this work, possible Library of Congress subject headings are suggested, but you are urged to look at the full printed list (LCSH) when searching. In indexes and abstracts, the headings used are usually more popular and easier to figure out by trying a few.

LIBRARY CATALOGS

• Using the correct headings, search the library catalogs for books. Look carefully at the card, noticing the date of publication, etc., as described below. Write down the call numbers to locate books.

PERIODICAL INDEXES AND ABSTRACTS

• Use indexes and abstracting services for periodical articles. Then check the library catalog to see if the library owns the magazine or journal and where it is located.

OTHER SOURCES

• Check special sources such as government documents, statistics, and manuscripts. (See various sections on special sources.)

EXPERTS

• Seek the advice of an expert, if appropriate. (See "Locating Experts," in part 5.)

EVALUATION

• Evaluate what you have, as described above, and what you might still need.

Chances are you will not need to use all, or even most, of these steps each time you require information. Use it as a checklist: consider each step and take the ones you need. *The Fiction Writer's Research Handbook* is set up so readers can quickly find titles and the correct subject headings or track down bibliographies and research guides for more thorough searching.

The search strategy is a framework only, but as John Gardener says when discussing the craft of fiction, "Seize the trunk of any science securely, and you have control of its branches." Check the Search Strategy flowchart shown here. Understand these basic concepts, and all research is within your grasp.

Libraries

Samuel Johnson once said: "A man will turn over half a library to make one book." Assume it will be easier than that, but a brief reminder on using libraries might be in order. Though smaller branch libraries are certainly able to answer

SEARCH STRATEGY
FLOWCHART

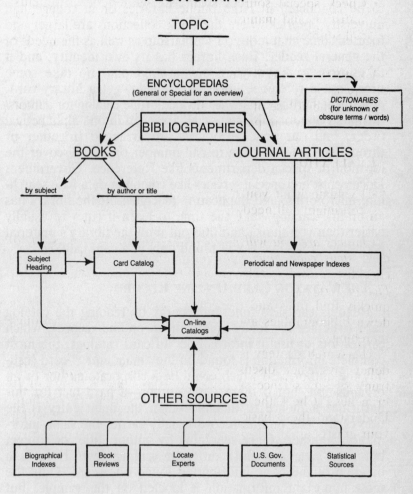

TOPIC

ENCYCLOPEDIAS
(General or Special for an overview)

DICTIONARIES
(for unknown or
obscure terms / words)

BIBLIOGRAPHIES

BOOKS

JOURNAL ARTICLES

by subject

by author or title

Subject
Heading

Card Catalog

Periodical and Newspaper Indexes

On-line
Catalogs

OTHER SOURCES

Biographical
Indexes

Book
Reviews

Locate
Experts

U.S. Gov.
Documents

Statistical
Sources

many questions and will have many of the standard sources mentioned in this guide, the process described here is meant to be conducted in large public libraries or in college and university libraries where the book collections are larger and focused somewhat more on scholarship as well as the needs of the general reader. Each library has its own identity, and it takes time to know your way around one. So take some time—ask a reference librarian for help, get a library card, notice whether the catalog is "divided" (one catalog for authors/ titles and one for subjects) or all arranged in one alphabetical order, find out how periodicals are arranged (together or throughout the collection in call number order), discover the location of special departments like Reference, Government Documents, and special services like computer data-base searching, microforms, and duplicating machines. If the library has an on-line catalog, take the time to learn it (they're usually easier than you think) and find out if all the library's material is on-line or if some is still found only in a card catalog.

THE CATALOG CARD/ON-LINE RECORD

Readers can save time and energy by reading the catalog card (whether it's really a card or an on-line record), which carries lots of useful information. In card catalogs, the most complete information is found on the "main entry" card (usually the author card which could be a corporate author or an organization, but if there is no author—a hard fact for this particular audience to imagine—then the main entry is the title card). The on-line record usually carries the same information whether you're searching by author, title, or subject but may have a slightly different arrangement. Here is a diagram of the basic information found on a card. Only the most important information is labeled on this sample, but often other descriptions of the book are useful—such as the notation on this card that the work has a bibliography and an index.

For many reasons it's often important to *notice the date of publication*; it may matter if some work is, for example,

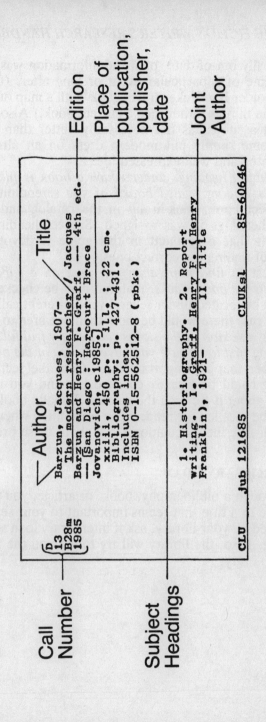

Call
Number

Subject
Headings

Author

Title

Edition

Place of
publication,
publisher,
date

Joint
Author

D
13
B28m
1985

Barzun, Jacques, 1907–
The modern researcher / Jacques
Barzun and Henry F. Graff. — 4th ed.
— [San Diego : Harcourt Brace
Jovanovich, c1985]
xxiii, 450 p. : ill. ; 22 cm.
Bibliography: p. 427–431.
Includes index.
ISBN 0-15-562512-8 (pbk.)

1. Historiography. 2. Report
writing. I. Graff, Henry F. (Henry
Franklin), 1921–   II. Title

CLU   Jub 121685   CLUKsl   85-60646

scientifically out-of-date, or if the information was published at the time of a particular event or long after. (One might need an older Baedecker travel guide with a map of Paris as it was in the thirties rather than a current book.) Also, the latest book on a subject is not necessarily better than an earlier work; some simply put modern dress on an already well-documented and well-expressed idea.

The subject headings under which a book is filed are also useful for finding related books. If you serendipitously find the perfect book, look it up in the catalog and see what subject headings it was assigned. Subject headings are so important that a segment in this guide is devoted to the process of finding the correct ones.

It's best to *find more than one item on a subject before going into the book stacks;* material may be checked out and may also be located under several very different call numbers, in which case there would be more than one area to "browse." *Browsing a section of the stacks can be very fruitful, but check the catalog first to be sure you have an idea of the possibilities.* Remember that an important book from the section you're browsing could be already checked out and you might only find out about it through the catalog. Usually books checked out can be recalled, or readers can be notified when a book is returned. Ask the Circulation Desk about these procedures.

INTERLIBRARY LOAN

If, through a bibliography, book, or article, you've found a reference to a title that seems important to your search but is not owned by your library, ask if interlibrary loan services are available. If so, the library will try to get you the book from another library.

Subject Headings

COKE is a subject heading, but it means the fuel; COCAINE is also a heading. BATTERED WIVES is not a heading, but ABUSED WIVES is (surprisingly, so are ABUSED PARENTS and ABUSED LESBIANS). Some headings are not likely to pop into your head—COLLECTIVE SETTLEMENTS; HIJACKING OF YACHTS; CRYING IN ART; UNICORNS IN LITERATURE; CHASTITY, VOW OF; AMERICAN CHECKERED GIANT RABBITS. If you look up FLYING SAUCERS, you are referred to the heading UNIDENTIFIED FLYING OBJECTS.

What's in a subject heading? Everything. In library research it matters what you name your subject, because library catalogs use strict, uniform words or phrases to bring together material with a common topic. If you look under a heading not chosen by the Library of Congress, you may miss books on your topic. The Library of Congress resists fads and short-lived expressions, using more formal headings listed in the three-volume *Library of Congress Subject Headings* (LCSH), a truly remarkable work that can save researchers time and doubt (about whether or not they've found everything the library owns on their topic). If things were not brought together under "proper" headings, researchers might have to look under many headings and even then worry that they had not covered the territory. These headings are also standard throughout the United States (and cooperatively with some other countries), so searchers in Los Angeles, Chicago, or New York look under the same uniform headings. (If a scholar in Albany was accustomed to finding material under NAPO-

LEON BONAPARTE it would be confusing if, as a visiting scholar in San Francisco, he was able to find the material only by looking under BONAPARTE, NAPOLEON.)

Usually larger libraries use the *Library of Congress Subject Headings* (LCSH); smaller libraries sometimes use *Sears' List of Subject Headings,* which follows the Library of Congress but is abridged and simplified to meet the needs of smaller collections. This chapter will discuss the principles of LCSH (common to academic and large public libraries), and throughout this book suggestions will be made for possible subject headings under specific topics. In the library you're using, ask where the list of headings is kept, so you can refer to it before starting your search.

The Library of Congress list, LCSH, though somewhat formal compared with an index to current magazines that may use more popular headings, is nevertheless not a static list and has been changed and revised over the years, often reflecting our changing social life and customs. For example, a new awareness of women is reflected in the fact that the heading PILGRIM FATHERS is now PILGRIMS (NEW PLYMOUTH COLONY) and headings such as WOMEN AS BANKERS and WOMEN AS PHYSICIANS have become simply WOMEN BANKERS and WOMEN PHYSICIANS, dropping the demeaning "as." WORLD WAR I was originally under EUROPEAN WAR. Though librarians are constantly at work to eliminate discriminatory or antiquated headings, there is still work to be done (MAMMIES is a heading with a cross-reference from MAMMIES, COLORED). In theory though, every attempt is made to keep headings value-free, and sometimes "literary warrant" dictates a certain heading because that is what authors and scholars consistently use in titles and references. Sometimes a necessary revision results in something strange—Buffalo Bill is now found under BILL, BUFFALO. In any case, this wonderful and essential work is always changing and improving. LCSH, as a dynamic list, establishes new headings daily—DESIGNER DRUGS, NIGHT PEOPLE, and PASSIVE SMOKING are some of the newer ones.

Remember that not all libraries have the personnel and money to change their old headings, but if not, the catalog should refer back and forth between old and new headings. The printed list will always refer you to the correct heading. Always keep in mind that these are the headings the library will have used *if the library has books on that subject—just because the subject heading exists does not necessarily mean you will find a book on that subject in your library.*

CHANGES IN LCSH, 11TH EDITION

As part of the changes and improvements mentioned above, for the new eleventh edition, LCSH has changed some of the symbols used in the list. The new form is shown here, along with other changes known at this time, and the old form is given also in case there are previous editions still in use.

General LCSH Guidelines

- *The heading used* (the correct heading) is in **bold print;**
- when (**May Subd Geog.**) appears, it means that a subject may be subdivided geographically—see the example below under Geographic Subdivisions (formerly "Indirect" next to a term meant it could be divided geographically);
- the suggested Library of Congress *class numbers* may appear on a line after the heading; multiple class numbers will appear on separate lines;
- *scope notes* may appear to explain exactly what goes under the heading, especially if there is more than one meaning associated with the heading.
- *Codes used to show the cross-reference structure:*
  USE = Use the heading referred to (formerly *see*)
  UF = Used for (formerly *x*)
  BT = Broader Term (formerly *xx*)
  RT = Related Term (formerly *xx* and *sa*)
  SA = See Also (used to introduce general *see also* references)
  NT = Narrower Term (formerly *sa*)

As you will see in the sample below, these codes lead to correct headings and to related, broader, and narrower terms that might be extremely useful in your search. The codes give you ideas and suggestions for other headings to try.

Subdivisions

To combine several different concepts under a single subject heading, LCSH uses subdivisions—introduced by a long dash without repetition of the main heading. The two volumes of LCSH list only a fraction of all possible headings and subdivision combinations, but basically there are four categories of subdivisions:

1. Topical Subdivisions—Used to limit the concept expressed by the heading (CHILDREN—LANGUAGE).
2. Form Subdivisions—Used to indicate the form in which the material is organized (UNITED STATES—BIOGRAPHY).
3. Chronological Subdivisions—Used to limit a heading to a specific time period (ART, CHINESE—TO 221 B.C.). Dates under countries are usually based on that country's history.
4. Geographic Subdivisions—When the designation (May Subd Geog.) appears after a subject heading or a subdivision, it indicates that a geographic location may be added. LABOR SUPPLY (May Subd Geog.) means, for example, that the cataloger could create a heading such as LABOR SUPPLY—FRANCE, and you could try that heading in the catalog.

Names as Subjects

In most cases, names of persons and names of corporate bodies (jurisdictions, companies, etc.) are omitted from LCSH, which is primarily a listing of topical subject headings. *But* names do appear in library catalogs, so check there for names to discover biographies or the names of societies, associations, and corporations, for example. When appropriate, catalogers simply enter names as subject headings. Some names do appear in LCSH if they require a subdivision or if they are used as patterns (see below), but never assume a name is not in the card catalog as a subject just because it doesn't appear in the printed subject list. Remember the discussion here is about *names as subjects;* names as authors, of course, always appear in the catalog.

Pattern Headings

To avoid repeating all possible subdivisions under all possible subject headings, LCSH has set up "patterns" of possible subdivisions under certain categories. For instance, under Abraham Lincoln you will find the possible subdivisions—the pattern—used for rulers and statesmen. Under Richard Wagner you will find the possible subdivisions for musicians; under William Shakespeare for authors, and so on. The pattern list is printed in the front of volume 1 of LCSH and is reprinted at the end of this segment.

Only the basics are discussed here; this is not a comprehensive review of LCSH, but it is enough to get you started and to stress the importance of subject headings in research. Read the Introduction to LCSH for details if you wish. It is not complicated, as you will discover once you begin to use these volumes and go over the facts below once more, using the sample entries illustrated to actually see how it works. Again, ask a librarian for help with the list if you need it.

Interpretation of LCSH Sample Page

The Subject heading FICTION, used in this sample, is a heading for works *about* fiction, not works of fiction them-

fiction
[PN3311-3503]
UF Metafiction
Novellas (Short novels)
Novels
Stories
BT Literature
Prose literature
SA subdivision fiction under
particular topics for collec-
tions of stories or novels on
those topics, and under his-
torical subjects or characters
for individual works of his-
torical of biographical fiction,
e.g. Children—Fiction: Sta-
lingrad, Battle of, 1942–1943
—Fiction
NT Adventure stories
Allegories
Baseball stories
Bildungsroman
Biographical fiction
Children's stories
Christian fiction
Christmas stories
Code and cipher stories
College stories
Confession stories
Detective and mystery stories
Didactic fiction
Dime novels
Domestic fiction
Epistolary fiction
Erotic stories
Experimental fiction
Fables
Fairy tales
Fantastic fiction
Feuilletons
Fishing stories
Ghost stories
Historical fiction
Horror tales
Humorous stories
Hunting stories
Islamic stories
Legal novels
Legends
Love stories
Martial arts fiction
Musical fiction
Nature stories
Nonfiction novel
Novelists

Novelle
Oral interpretation of fiction
Pastoral fiction
Picaresque literature
Plot-your-own stories
Radio stories
Railroad stories
Religious fiction
Romances
Romanticism
Science fiction
Sea stories
Serialized fiction
Short stories
Sports stories
Spy stories
Tales
Three-decker novels
War stories
Western stories
Young adult fiction
—15th and 16th centuries
—18th century
—19th century
—20th century
——History and criticism
NT Black humor (Literature)
——Stories, plots, etc.
—Authorship
UF Fiction writing
Writing, Fiction
BT Authorship
—Black authors
UF Black fiction
—Collections
[PZ1 (Fiction in English)]
—Dramatic production
USE Chamber theater
—History and criticism
[PN3329-3503]
NT Psychological fiction
—Male authors
USE Fiction—Men authors
—Men authors
UF Fiction—Male authors
—Oral interpretation
USE Oral interpretation of
literature
—Plots
USE Plots (Drama, novel, etc.)
—Religious aspects
——Buddhism, [Christianity, etc.]
—Stories, plots, etc.
—Technique
[PN3355-3383]

selves. Novels and other works of fiction are found in catalogs under the name of the author or the title and not usually given a subject heading. (See segment "Finding Other Fiction by Subject," part 5.)

- If you look at the sample shown under the heading FIC-TION, you will see that a *suggested range of call numbers is given* (PN3311–3503), so you could conceivably browse the stacks in that area, though that may be dangerous—you could miss something that your library has cataloged under a different number, so it is best to start in the card catalog, then browse suggested call number areas.
- Next under FICTION is the symbol UF (Used For), which means that this is the heading used for such subjects as "Metafiction," "Novellas (Short Fiction)," "Novels," and "Stories." If you look in LCSH under any of the headings, you will be told to use the heading FICTION.
- The symbol that follows, BT (Broader Term), refers the reader to two broader headings, LITERATURE, and PROSE LITERATURE.
- SA (See Also) reminds you to see also the "subdivision FICTION under particular topics . . . and under historical subjects or characters . . ." For example: LINCOLN, ABRAHAM, 1809–1865—FICTION.
- NT (Narrower Term) lists more specific headings than FICTION, such as ADVENTURE STORIES, ALLE-GORIES, BASEBALL STORIES, etc., that you can use. Frequently this list will give you other headings to use or a better, more precise heading for your search.
- Following the NT (narrower terms) are *subdivisions that appear in the catalog under FICTION.* In this list, these are preceded by a dash and a second subdivision is preceded by two dashes, indicating how you can build these on to the main heading, FICTION, which is not repeated all the way down the list. So there is a heading FICTION—20TH CENTURY and a further division of that heading, FICTION—20TH CENTURY—HISTORY AND CRIT-ICISM (with a suggested NT [narrower term] under it).

And that is how these headings look in the catalog, all beginning with FICTION and followed by subdivisions.

Dropping down to the subdivision—DRAMATIC PRODUCTION, the list says USE Chamber Theater, telling you that "Fiction—Dramatic Production" is *not* a heading; you are to use CHAMBER THEATER, which is the correct heading.

If you get confused about these symbols, see the front of the LCSH set, ask a librarian for help, or simply look up the heading: if it's in bold print and has notations, etc, it is a legitimate heading; if it says USE (something else) and is not in bold print, it is not a heading and you are to USE the other heading.

Medical Subject Headings

Subject headings for medicine differ from those in LCSH, and the popular name of a disease or scientific subject is probably not used. So when you're searching in a biomedical library catalog or if you're searching *Index Medicus*, the index to biomedical periodicals, consult:

National Library of Medicine. *Medical Subject Headings—Annotated Alphabetic List* (MeSH). Bethesda, MD.: National Library of Medicine, 1963–. Annual.

The acronym MeSH is used to refer to the medical list. An example of the difference between LCSH and MeSH can be seen if you look up "Cancer" in each set. This is the term used in LCSH, but in MeSH you are referred to the term "Neoplasms." An author title, and subject guide to health science books, *Health Science Books 1876–1982* (New York: Bowker, 1982), has a volume with LCSH/MeSH and MeSH/LCSH equivalents that gives clear comparisons and examples of the two systems.

Using subject heading lists will become second nature to you, and after using them for even a short time, you will clearly understand the importance of finding the correct headings and the great boost your research gets from the suggestions and related terms offered by these lists.

Library of Congress Subject Headings
Table of Pattern Headings

Category	*Pattern Heading*
Animals (General)	Fishes
Animals, Domestic	Cattle
Chemicals	Copper
Colonies	Great Britain—Colonies
Diseases	Cancer
	Tuberculosis
Educational institutions	
Individual	Harvard University
Types	Universities and colleges
Indians	Indians of North America
Industries	Construction industry
	Retail trade
Languages and groups of	English language
languages	French language
	Romance languages
Legal topics	Labor laws and legislation
Legislative bodies	United States. Congress.
Literary authors	
Groups of literary authors	Authors, English
Individual literary authors	Shakespeare, William, 1564–1616.
Literary works entered under author	Shakespeare, William, 1564–1616. Hamlet.
Literary works entered under title	Beowulf
Literatures (including individual	
genres)	English literature
Materials	Concrete
	Metals
Military services	United States—Armed Forces
	United States. Air Force.
	United States. Army.

	United States. Marine Corps.
	United States. Navy.
Music compositions	Operas
Musical instruments	Piano
Musicians	Wagner, Richard, 1813–1883.
Newspapers	Newspapers
Organs and regions of the body	Heart
	Foot
Plants and crops	Corn
Religious bodies	
Religious and monastic orders	Jesuits
Religions	Buddhism
Christian denominations	Catholic Church
Rulers, statesmen, etc.	Lincoln, Abraham, 1809–1865.
	Napoleon I, Emperor of the French, 1769–1821.
Sacred works	Bible
Sports	Soccer
Theological topics	Salvation
Vehicles, Land	Automobiles
Wars	World War, 1939–1945
	United States—History—Civil War, 1861–1865

Outlines and Chronologies

Outlining Your Play or Novel

With exceptions, it is probably best to start work on a novel or a play with a plan, no matter how difficult you may think this is. Though there are some authors who do not recommend the process, many writers and teachers of creative writing do suggest formulating an outline of your script or story so you know where it's going and when various events should occur. Outlines help writers remember when characters need to be introduced and what needs to happen at certain points in the fiction. Usually they do not stifle imagination: they only guide. Remember, an outline can be changed at any time (and almost certainly will be) and as often as needed. If you really feel that an outline interferes with the flow of your story, don't make one, *but you will still need to create a chronology of the real-time period you are following.*

An outlined plan for fiction can be as detailed or as skeletal as the author wishes. Usually it begins sketchily and is fleshed out as the work progresses. It can be in any convenient form, from a "treatment" (a brief narrative telling the whole story) to a page or two for each chapter or a storyboard covering a bulletin board or all the walls of the writing room. Doing outlines and revising them sometimes helps writers to understand characters more fully before writing and helps them to see any inevitable progression of the story.

The way authors write is not the subject of this guide, but what applies here is that *an OUTLINE will facilitate research* by assisting in the creation of a CHRONOLOGY of the real-time period, which, in turn, offers story possibilities to augment the outline. But writing styles are personal, so try different approaches, and then do what works for you.

Just as keeping a notebook of ideas, dialogue, and observations can be a sort of incubator for future writing, making an outline prompts not only what comes next but the writing itself, especially if an author has hit a dry period. Hemingway said that he always stopped writing when he knew what was going to happen next so he could be sure of going on the next day. An outline helps you to know what's going to happen next.

Chronologies of Real Events

Time and place can be strong organizing concepts for fiction and make the writing easier. For any research that goes beyond fact-finding, making a chronology is essential. After making an outline of the fictional story, do a time period chronology of major and minor historical or contemporary events, as well as the trivia, so characters are not witnessing or talking about events at the wrong time or performing acts unnatural for that era. The chronology will also give you information with which to thicken the plot.

Watch out for snags in time, too—how long did it take to travel from Chicago to New York or for mail to go from Washington, D.C. to Houston in the era you are working on? (It is tempting to cynically guess that it probably takes longer for mail in 1987 than it did in 1890, but do not guess, find out.) You may think you can remember all of the *Summer of '42*, but check it out. Add any pertinent facts to the chronology itself if necessary, *then match your fictional time to real time.*

Date Books and Historical Outlines

There are some fairly quick and easy ways to develop chronologies. The Kane book, *Famous First Facts* (see "Inventions . . ." part 3), is repeated here because it tells readers when the first refrigerator, advertisement, public school, etc., appeared in America, and it has indexes that arrange the information by years, days of the month, personal names, and geographical locations. Also listed are standard encyclopedias of dates and chronologies.

Useful Titles

Carruth, Gorton, and Associates. *The Encyclopedia of American Facts and Dates*. 8th ed. New York: Harper, 1987.

Collison, Robert L. *Newnes Dictionary of Dates*. 2d rev. ed. London: Newnes, 1966.

Freeman-Grenville, G. S. P. *Chronology of World History; A Calendar of Principal Events from 3000 BC to AD 1976*. 2d ed. London: Collins, 1978.

Gascoigne, Robert Mortimer. *A Chronology of the History of Science, 1450–1900*. New York: Garland, 1987.

Gordon, Lois and Gordon, Alan. *American Chronicle: Six Decades in American Life, 1920–1980*. New York: Atheneum, 1987.

Grun, Bernard. *The Timetables of History: A Horizontal Linkage of People and Events*. New, updated ed. New York: Simon & Schuster, 1979.

Haydn, Joseph T. *Dictionary of Dates and Universal Information Relating to All Ages and Nations by the Late Benjamin Vincent*. Revised and brought up to date by eminent authorities. 25th ed. New York: Putnam, 1911.

Kane, Joseph Nathan. *Famous First Facts: A Record of First Happenings, Discoveries, and Inventions in American History*. 4th ed., expanded and rev. New York: Wilson, 1981.

Langer, William Leonard. *The New Illustrated Encyclopedia of World History*. 2 vols. New York: Abrams, 1975.

Mirkin, Stanford M. *What Happened When: A Noted Researcher's Almanac of Yesterdays.* New York: Ives Washburn, 1966.

Putnam, George Palmer, and Putnam, George Haven. *Dictionary of Events: A Handbook of Universal History.* New York: Grosset, 1936.

Steinberg, Sigfrid Henry. *Historical Tables 58 BC–AD 1985.* 11th ed. London: Macmillan, 1986.

Storey, R. L. *Chronology of the Medieval World, 800 to 1491.* Edited by Neville Williams. London: Barrie & Jenkins, 1973.

Timetables of American History. Edited by Laurence Urdang. New York: Simon & Schuster, 1981.

Williams, Neville. *Chronology of the Expanding World, 1492–1762.* London: Barrie & Rockliff, 1969.

———. *Chronology of the Modern World, 1763–1965.* Rev. ed. Harmondsworth, Eng.: Penguin, 1975.

Other Sources

One can create a chronology using the strategies in this book to include events in music, art, business, politics, etc. Also helpful for this century are ALMANACS, which have a chronology of the previous year in each new volume (libraries have older years, back to 1868), ENCYCLOPEDIA YEAR-BOOKS, and the *Annual Register: A Record of World Events* (London: Longmans), which goes back to 1758.

Calendars

For information on calendars generally and how they are interpreted in various parts of the world in different ages, the following are useful:

The Book of Calendars. Edited by Frank Parise. New York: Facts on File, 1982.

Freeman-Grenville, G. S. P. *The Muslim and Christian Calendars:*

Being Tables for the Conversion of Muslim and Christian Dates from the Hijra to the Year A.D. 2000. London: R. Collings, 1977.

Possible LCSH Subject Headings

ALMANACS
CALENDARS
CHRONOLOGY
CHRONOLOGY, HISTORICAL
CHRONOLOGY, JEWISH (or MEXICAN, ORIENTAL, etc.)

or CHRONOLOGY may be used as a subdivision under a heading, for example:

BIBLE—CHRONOLOGY
STONE AGE—CHRONOLOGY

Part II

Basic Reference Sources

Periodicals

Here, the terms *periodicals, magazines, journals, serials*—all issued periodically—are used somewhat interchangeably, though usually *journal* implies something more scholarly and *magazine* something more popular. Serials cover every conceivable subject and are especially good sources for very current information, which is particularly important in the fields of science and technology and in breaking stories in politics, economics, and business. Periodicals often cover subjects too new or too temporary to have books written about them. Magazines and journals are also valuable for locating contemporary opinions (not just today's but the attitudes of the day in 1930 or any time period during which periodicals were issued). Annual bibliographies in certain fields are also located through journal indexes.

Row upon row of bound indexes can be intimidating, but methodical searches usually go quickly. Methodical means that you check each volume at a time, starting at either end of the set, so that you don't miss any and don't wonder which ones you've checked. Remember, though, that most of the periodical indexes listed here are available as data bases and can be searched by computer if you find the going tough (see segment "On-Line Searching," later in this part). It's usually a good idea to conduct some investigation of the printed sources first so you get an idea of the scope of your search. Computer searching is often a better way if you're searching under more than one subject term.

Indexing and abstracting services *refer* you to the journal or magazine where the complete text can be found; they do not provide the information itself. An index simply gives the full citation (title, author, journal or magazine name, volume, page numbers, date) under the subject; an abstract gives the full citation too but also gives a brief description of what the article contains. (See accompanying examples.)

Readers' Guide to Periodical Literature

Forgery
    See also
    Counterfeits and counterfeiting
    Bogus documents now on sale—$25 and up [immigration docu-
    ments] S. L. Hawkins. il *U S News World Rep* 102:26 Ja 19 '87
Forgetfulness *See* Memory
Forgiveness
    I'll never forgive you! A. Penney. il. *Ladies Home J* 104:42+ Mr
    '87
    When to hold a grudge. M. A. Kellogg. il *Glamour* 85:165+ F '87
Forms, blanks, etc.

INDEX: Only the bibliographic information is given, without a summary. In this *Readers' Guide* example under the subject "Forg-ery," you are first referred to a related heading and then given a citation to one article—title (Bogus Documents Now On Sale . . .), author (S. L. Hawkins), illustrations (il), magazine (*U.S. News & World Report*), and volume, page, and date (102:26 January 19, 1987).

Psychological Abstracts

   9109. **Kaplan, Stanley M.** (Cincinnati Psychoanalysis Inst, OH)
**Narcissistic injury and the occurrence of creativity: Freud's Irma
dream.** *Annual of Psychoanalysis.* 1984–85, Vol 12–13, 367–376.—
Suggests that Freud's (1900) account of the Irma dream may facilitate understanding of the conditions that favor the investigation or
mobilization of creativity. The circumstances surrounding the dream
are examined, and accounts are given of other famous creative
persons who experienced periods of creativity following narcissistic
injury. (11 ref)
   9110. **Kaplan, Steven J. & Schoeneberg, Lynn A.** (U Southern
Florida, Tampa) **An Adlerian understanding of Hillel's maxim.** *Pastoral Psychology,* 1984(Win), Vol 33(2), 93–95.—Interprets the maxim
"If I am not for myself, who will be for me? If I am only for myself,
what am I? And if not now, when?" by the Jewish teacher.

ABSTRACT: A two-step process. Using the Brief Subject Index (or the annual indexes and cumulations), obtain a number and use that to locate the abstract in the volume *covering the same time period as the index*. In this *Psychological Abstracts* example (v. 74, no. 4, April 1987) under "Dream Analysis" in the index you are referred by number to an article in *Annual of Psychoanalysis21, and given the author, author affiliation, title, name of journal or other source, dates, volume numbers, and page numbers, as well as a brief description or summary of the article.*

The front of each bound index volume has instructions on its use and also lists the periodicals covered by that index or abstract. The citation indexes have separate guides to usage.

There are hundreds of indexing and abstracting services on almost any topic. Under subjects in this guide, appropriate ones are listed as sources. Below are listed some of the most common indexes to popular and scholarly journals to give you an idea of the range available, but this is not a comprehensive list. For other subjects, check the bibliographies or ask a reference librarian. Beginning dates are given so you can see how far back in time these indexes go; a dash after the date (1950–) means the index continues to date; otherwise ending dates are given (1886–1974). Poole's, the predecessor to the *Readers' Guide,* covers very early years beginning in 1802, and the *Combined Retrospective . . .* indexes also go back to the eighteen-hundreds.

INDEXES TO POPULAR MAGAZINES

Abstracts of Popular Culture. Bowling Green, Ohio: Bowling Green Univ. Popular Press, 1976–1982. Biannual.

Access: The Supplementary Index to Periodicals. Syracuse, N.Y.: Gaylord, 1975– . Three times a year. (Third issue is the annual cumulation.

Alternative Press Index. Northfield, Minn.: Radical Research Center, 1970– . Quarterly. Irregular.

Magazine Index. Los Altos, Cal.: Information Access, 1976– . Microfilm. Monthly.

Poole's Index to Periodical Literature, 1802–1881. Rev. ed. 2 vols. Boston: Houghton, 1882.

————. Supplements 1882–1907. 5 vols. 1887–1908.

————. *Cumulative Author Index for Poole's Index to Periodical Literature, 1803–1906.* Edited by C. Edward Wall. Ann Arbor, Mich.: Pierian Press, 1971.

Poole's Index Date and Volume Key. By Marion Bell and Jean C. Bacon. Chicago: Assoc. of College and Research Libraries, 1957.

Nineteenth Century Readers' Guide to Periodical Literature, 1890–1899 with Supplementary Indexing 1900–1922. 2 vols. New York: Wilson, 1944.

Readers' Guide to Periodical Literature. New York: Wilson, 1900–   . Various cumulations. Semimonthly, monthly, and annual cumulations.

Popular Periodical Index. Camden, N.J.: Popular Periodical Index, 1973–   . Semiannual.

INDEXES TO GENERAL MAGAZINES AND SCHOLARLY JOURNALS

Air University Library Index to Military Periodicals. Maxwell Air Force Base, Ala.: Air University Library, 1949–   . Quarterly.

Applied Science and Technology Index. New York: Wilson, 1958–   . Monthly.

Art Index. New York: Wilson, 1929–   . Quarterly.

Arts & Humanities Citation Index. Philadelphia: Inst. for Scientific Information, 1976–   . Two softbound issues and annual cumulative hardbound.

Biological and Agricultural Index. New York: Wilson, 1916–   . Earlier title: *Agricultural Index.* Monthly.

Business Periodicals Index. New York: Wilson, 1958–   . Monthly.

Catholic Periodical and Literature Index. Haverford, Pa.: Catholic Library Assoc., 1930–   . Quarterly.

Combined Retrospective Index Set to Journals in History 1878–1974. 11 vols. Wash., D.C.: Carrollton Press, 1977–78.

Combined Retrospective Index Set to Journals in Political Science 1886–1974. 8 vols. Wash., D.C.: Carrollton Press, 1977–1978.

Combined Retrospective Index Set to Journals in Sociology 1895–1974. 6 vols. Wash., D.C.: Carrollton Press, 1978.

Education Index. New York: Wilson, 1929–   . Monthly.

Engineering Index. New York: Engineering Info., 1906–   . Publisher varies. Monthly.

Essay and General Literature Index. New York: Wilson, 1934– Semiannual and annual cumulations.

General Science Index. New York: Wilson, 1978–   . Monthly.

Hispanic American Periodical Index. Los Angeles: UCLA Latin American Center, 1974–   . Annual but frequency varies.

Index Medicus. Wash., D.C.: National Library of Medicine. 1879–   . Early years, publisher and frequency varies. Monthly.

Index to Legal Periodicals. Published for the American Assoc. of Law Libraries. New York: Wilson, 1909–   . Monthly (frequency varies).

Index to Little Magazines. Denver: Alan Swallow, 1949–1970. Frequency and publishers vary.

Index to Periodical Articles By and About Blacks. Boston: G. K. Hall, 1960–   . Title and frequency vary.

MLA International Bibliography of Books and Articles on the Modern Languages and Literature. New York: Modern Language Association of America, 1921–   . Annual.

Music Index. Detroit: Information Service, 1949–   . Monthly.

Philosopher's Index: An International Index to Philosophical Periodicals and Books. Bowling Green, Ohio: Bowling Green Univ., 1967–   . Quarterly.

Public Affairs Information Service Bulletin. New York: Public Affairs Information Service, 1915–   . Semimonthly with various cumulations.

Religion Index One. Chicago: American Theological Library Assoc., 1949–   . Semiannual.

Science Citation Index. Philadelphia: Inst. for Scientific Information, 1961–   . Bimonthly.

Social Sciences and Humanities Index; formerly *International Index.* 1907/15–1974. New York: Wilson, 1916–1974.

Continued by:

Humanities Index. New York: Wilson, 1974–   . Quarterly.

Social Sciences Index. New York: Wilson, 1974–   . Quarterly.

Social Sciences Citation Index. Philadelphia: Inst. for Scientific Information, 1973–   . (Retrospective indexing for 1969–1972.) Three issues per year. Third is annual cumulation.

Subject Index to Periodicals, 1915–1961. London: Library Association, 1954–1961.

British Humanities Index. London: Library Assoc., 1963–   . Quarterly.

British Technology Index. London: Library Assoc., 1963–1980.

Continued by:

Current Technology Index. Phoenix, Ariz.: Oryx Press, 1981–   . Monthly.

SELECTED ABSTRACTING SERVICES

Abstracts in Anthropology. Westport, Conn.: Greenwood Periodicals, 1970–   . Quarterly.

Biological Abstracts. Philadelphia: Bio-Sciences Information Service, 1962–   . Semimonthly.

Chemical Abstracts. Columbus, Ohio: American Chemical Society, 1907–   . Weekly.

Criminal Justice Abstracts. Hackensack, N.J.: National Council on Crime and Deliquency, 1977–   . Quarterly.

Environment Abstracts. New York Environment Information Center, 1971–   . Monthly.

International Political Science Abstracts. Documentation Politique Internationale. Oxford: Blackwell, 1951–   . Quarterly.

Psychological Abstracts. Lancaster, Pa.: American Psychological Assoc., 1927–   . Bimonthly.

Social Work Research and Abstracts. New York: National Assoc. of Social Workers, 1977–   . Supersedes *Abstracts for Social Workers.* Quarterly.

Sociological Abstracts. New York: Sociological Abstracts, 1952–   . Six times per year (frequency varies).

Bibliographies and Directories

The following works, describing and listing periodicals, give basic information (names, addresses, editors, circulation, advertising information, etc.). Remember that the front of each index/abstract volume lists the journals it covers. Ulrich's, and the Chicorel and Marconi books, do the reverse by identifying indexes and abstracts that index a given journal. The Katz book and some others give a magazine's bias (liberal, conservative, etc.). Most are arranged by subject or have a subject index.

Chicorel Index to Indexing and Abstracting Services; Periodicals in Humanities and Social Sciences. 2d. ed. 2 vols. New York: Chicorel Library Pub., 1978.

Gale Directory of Publications: An Annual Guide to Newspapers, Magazines, Journals, and Related Publications. Published since 1880 with various titles (*Ayer Directory of Publications* and *IMS . . . Directory*) and publishers. Detroit: Gale, since 1987. Annual.

Katz, William, and Katz, Linda Sternberg. *Magazines for Libraries*. 5th ed. New York: Bowker, 1986.

Marconi, Joseph. *Indexed Periodicals*. Ann Arbor, Mich.: Pierian Press, 1976.

Standard Periodical Directory. New York: Oxbridge 1964– . Irregular.

Ulrich's International Periodicals Directory: A Classified Guide to Current Periodicals, Foreign and Domestic. New York: Bowker, 1932– . Biennial.

Working Press of the Nation. Burlington, Ia.: National Research Bureau, 1945– . Annual since 1959. Vol. 1, *Newspaper Directory;* vol. 2, *Magazine Directory;* vol. 3, *TV and Radio Directory;* vol. 4. *Feature Writer and Photographer Directory;* vol. 5, *International Publications Directory*.

Locating Periodicals in Libraries

New Serial Titles: A Union List of Serials Commencing Publication

After Dec. 31, 1949. Wash., D.C.: Library of Congress, 1953–   .
Supplements to present.

Union List of Serials in Libraries of the United States and Canada.
3d. ed. 5 vols. Edited by Edna Brown Titus. New York: Wilson,
1965. Covers serials through 1949.

Possible LCSH Subject Headings

The headings listed below will retrieve information in the
catalog *about* periodicals, not articles *in* them. The indexes
are used for finding articles. First, there are two subdivisions
of particular interest when you're looking for information on
periodicals. PERIODICALS and PERIODICALS—INDEXES
may be used as subdivisions under subjects. For example:

ENGINEERING—PERIODICALS
MATHEMATICS—PERIODICALS—INDEXES

Other headings:

AMERICAN PERIODICALS (and GERMAN PERIODI-
    CALS, LATIN AMERICAN PERIODICALS, etc.)
MAGAZINE COVERS
MAGAZINE DESIGN
MAGAZINE ILLUSTRATION
PERIODICALS
PERIODICALS—BIBLIOGRAPHY
PERIODICALS—BIBLIOGRAPHY—UNION LISTS
SCHOLARLY JOURNALS

Newspapers and
News Sources

Obviously newspapers are valuable for our day-to-day information, but they are just as important as records of our past. When there is some distance from an event, accounts of it get sifted, summarized, abbreviated, and even altered (or possibly corrected by hindsight), so it is useful to return to the newspapers of the time for the full details and vivid first impressions surrounding an event. A newspaper eyewitness account is considered a "primary" source in research, along with original manuscripts and documents. This is not to suggest that such articles never stray from the whole truth, but they probably try not to, and they are at least fresh, current responses to occurrences. Sometimes it's important to look at local newspapers for coverage of events in those cities. In addition to the newspaper lists below, try local libraries, which usually have local newspapers (check the *American Library Directory*) and historical societies (check *Directory of Historical Societies and Agencies in the United States and Canada*).

Preservation of newsprint is a problem, but many papers, even for small towns, are now available on microfilm (see *Newspapers in Microfilm* listed below) and can be borrowed on interlibrary loan by your library. Printed indexes for newspapers are expensive to produce and so are not usually available for smaller papers, but if you know the date of an event, that may be enough to locate relevant articles—using an index of dates or the printed index of a major newspaper like the *New York Times* if the story is not just local. Directories of newspapers are listed here so a paper may be contacted directly.

It is best to look at the explanations in the front of newspaper indexes to understand their correct use. *Usually, articles are arranged by subject and, within that, are arranged chronologically.* The current ones usually indicate if a story is short, medium, or long with (S), (M), or (L).

An entry: **Je 6, 1:5** refers you to a story on June 6, page 1, column 5.

GUIDES

Editor and Publisher, Willing's, and *Working Press* . . . give names and addresses of newspapers, editors, and organizations. Some include ethnic papers, weeklies, etc. *Willing's* is British with some international coverage. The *Europa Year Book* is an annual covering the countries of the world with much political information and some description of the status of the press in each country.

Editor and Publisher International Yearbook. New York: Editor and Publisher, 1921– . Annual.

Europa Year Book. London: Europa, 1959– . Annual.

Willing's Press Guide. London: Willing, 1874– . Annual.

Working Press of the Nation. Burlington, Ia.: National Research Bureau, 1945– . Annual. This is a five-volume set with volumes for newspapers, magazines, radio and TV stations, feature writers/photographers, and international publications.

Locating Newspapers

American Newspapers, 1821–1936: A Union List of Files Available in the United States and Canada. Edited by Winifred Gregory. New York: Wilson, 1937.

U.S. Library of Congress. Cataloging Publication Division. *Newspapers in Microfilm: Foreign Countries.* Wash., D.C.: Library of Congress, 1973+

―――. *Newspapers in Microfilm: United States.* Wash., D.C.: Library of Congress, 1973+

The last two titles are kept up-to-date by an annual: *Newspapers in Microfilm* (Wash., D.C.: Library of Congress), which has separate sections for foreign and domestic newspapers.

NEWSPAPER INDEXES

Of available printed indexes, those going far back in time are:

Milner, Anita Cheek. *Newspaper Indexes: A Location and Subject Guide for Researchers*. 3 vols. Metuchen, N.J.: Scarecrow, 1977–1982.

New York Times Index. New York: New York Times, 1913–   . Semimonthly with annual cumulations.

————. "Prior Series" covering 1851–1912. 15 vols. New York: Bowker, 1966–76.

The Times Index. (Title varies) London: Times, 1907–   , Monthly with annual cumulations.

Palmer's Index to the Times Newspaper, 1790–June 1941. London: Palmer, 1868–1943.

There are also indexes to the *Christian Science Monitor,* the *Wall Street Journal,* and the *Washington Post,* among others. Bell & Howell produces several newspaper indexes to major papers—*Chicago Tribune, Denver Post, Los Angeles Times, San Francisco Chronicle,* the *Boston Globe,* are some of them.
Two other index sources are:

National Newspaper Index. Los Altos, Cal.: Information Access Corp. 1979–   . Microfilm. Monthly. This microfilm product indexes five newspapers together—the *New York Times, Wall Street Journal, Christian Science Monitor*, and since 1982, the *Los Angeles Times* and the *Washington Post.*

NewsBank Index. (Title varies) New Canaan, Conn.: NewsBank, 1970–   . Index to microfiche. Monthly with cumulations. This is an index to a microfiche set of *selected* articles (of broad interest) from more than one hundred U.S. newspapers.

GENERAL NEWS SOURCES

The important sources below are *excellent for finding facts and information quickly* and are often the best way to find a date and then proceed to a newspaper index. *Facts on File* is American and began in 1940, and *Keesing's* is British and goes back to 1931. *Keesing's* frequently gives the complete text of a treaty or speech and is a good source of material on World War II. (See "Politics and Government" segment in part 3 for information on *Congressional Quarterly* publications, which are very useful sources for information on the activity of Congress and the government and for the voting records of Congress.)

Facts on File: World News Digest with Index. New York: Facts on File, 1940–   . Weekly with annual bound volumes available.

Keesing's Contemporary Archives: Record of World Events. London: Keesing's, 1931–   . Now monthly.

Possible LCSH Subject Headings

These subject headings locate information about newspapers around the world. Don't forget to look under the name of a specific newspaper (the *New York Times*, the *Washington Post*, etc.) as a heading in the catalog. There are many books on famous newspapers.

AMERICAN NEWSPAPERS (adjectival form used for major languages or areas: ISRAELI NEWSPAPERS, FRENCH NEWSPAPERS, etc.)
AMERICAN NEWSPAPERS—FACSIMILES ("Facsimiles" is also a subdivision used under others such as FRENCH NEWSPAPERS—FACSIMILES, etc.)
JOURNALISM
NEWSPAPER AND PERIODICAL LIBRARIES
NEWSPAPERS
NEWSPAPERS—BIBLIOGRAPHY

NEWSPAPERS—DIRECTORIES
NEWSPAPERS—FACSIMILES
NEWSPAPERS—HEADLINES
NEWSPAPERS—INDEXES (but indexes for individual
  newspapers are listed under the name of the paper with
  the subdivision "Indexes" as in BOSTON GLOBE
  —INDEXES)
PERSONALS
PRESS
REPORTERS AND REPORTING
TABLOID NEWSPAPERS

Looking under a heading like AMERICAN NEWSPAPERS—
FACSIMILES will retrieve a title that permits you to "see"
the news such as:

America's Front Page News 1690–1970. Edited by Michael C. Em-
  ery, et al. Minneapolis: Vis-Com, 1970.

GENERAL INDEXES

Most general indexes include breaking news—the *Readers'
Guide, Public Affairs Information Service,* and the social science and political science indexes (see "Periodicals," above)
and also carry stories *about* newspapers. Two other related
indexes are:

Communications Abstracts. Beverly Hills, Cal.: Sage, 1978–   .
  Quarterly.
Journalism Abstracts. Minneapolis: Assoc. for Education in Journal-
  ism, 1963–   . Annual.

On-Line Searching

Computers are not the "opposite" of books, they are not in competition with books, and they will never, ever replace *your* book, play, poem, short story, or screenplay. Therefore, do not hesitate to enter fully into this end of the twentieth century by taking advantage of computer technology. Though it is not always appropriate to do on-line searching (more on that later), when it is, it's the only way to go. Computers can take some of the drudgery out of work and can be nice, nonjudgmental research companions. Many of the encyclopedias and printed abstracting and indexing sources listed in this guide are available as on-line data bases (the *New Encyclopaedia Britannica, Social Science Citation Index, Historical Abstracts, New York Times Information Bank, Psychological Abstracts,* the *Readers' Guide* and other Wilson indexes, etc.; there are literally hundreds).

Data bases (or *files*) are organized collections of information stored in computers. An *on-line* data base is one that enables you to communicate with it by means of a *modem*, which allows a library or commercial terminal or your microcomputer to "talk" on the phone, extracting information from the on-line data base. Retrieving information this way is called *on-line searching*. Access to data bases is obtained for a fee from commercial *vendors*, or providers. Data bases, often like their printed counterparts, have their own subject headings, and each usually issues a *thesaurus,* a *controlled vocabulary,* or a list of *descriptors* that serves as a subject term guide.

Data bases are either:

1. full text, offering the full text or article—the information itself—or
2. bibliographic, offering a citation, or reference, and sometimes an abstract to the periodical or book where the information can be found.

A researcher chooses on-line searching because:

- It is fast and, when appropriate, can save many hours of manually searching a printed source under several possible headings or synonymous terms.
- It is up-to-date, searches very current and new topics, and though it can search for older topics in sources such as *Historical Abstracts*, it is best for coverage of the last twenty years—at least until older sources have been retrospectively converted to computers. The on-line source is usually more current than the printed source.
- Searching terms can be combined (pollution and smog and Cleveland) and different approaches used (author, topic, keyword).
- Searches can be limited by time periods.
- The printed format can be specified—just titles, citations or abstracts, full text (when available), etc.
- Searching can be done twenty-four hours a day.
- Searching can be more thorough since keywords in titles, adjacent words, and words in abstracts may be searched in addition to the subject terms. In any case, more subject terms are assigned in on-line data bases than in the printed indexes.

When on-line searching would *not* be used:

- If you can't afford it. Though costs will probably go down as these systems are used more and more, at the moment it can get costly since there are fees for the service plus costs per on-line minute. That's one reason too why it's best to plot your on-line course ahead of time—figuring out the correct data bases and terms before you go on-line. It costs more to have the information *printed on-line*, received as you conduct the search, than it does to have it *printed off-line*, results received at a later time, perhaps printed overnight, and sent through the mail from another location. It costs less to search at off-hours or at night than at peak times. It usually costs more for full text or abstracts than it does for citations only.

- If you have an easy, quick, single-term search of just a few years, or
- If you have a complicated, in-depth project requiring lots of reading in full-length books and intricate access to historical material.
- If what you're looking for is not available in a data base.

Basically, it depends on how much and what kind of research you're doing and how much value you put on your time.

ON-LINE SEARCHING SERVICES IN LIBRARIES

Most large public libraries and college and university libraries offer on-line searching for a fee. It is usually conducted by a librarian who is trained to search data bases efficiently and who can offer advice on the feasibility of doing a search on your topic. It usually requires an appointment, and it's a good idea to be present when the search is conducted so you can make changes and modifications as needed. Some libraries offer "ready reference" on-line searching (free short searches at the Reference Desk) and may make some systems available to the public for free use, but so far that is not common. Libraries are now beginning to use "gateway" systems that can search data bases from multiple on-line vendors. (Do not confuse these services with *on-line catalogs*, which are the library's book collection on-line—the card catalog on a computer—not information systems.) There are commercial agencies that do searching also.

ON-LINE SEARCHING AT HOME

If you have a personal computer, you might consider getting a modem and doing data base searches at home. If you only need occasional facts or dates, this is probably not necessary for fiction writing; certainly try a few searches done by someone else first to see how it goes and to discuss which might be the best data bases for you. Popular and reasonable services for home are *Dialog's Knowledge Index, BRS After Dark* and some listed below but check the data base directories to find the ones that are best for you.

BRS Information Technologies/BRS After Dark
1200 Route 7
Latham, New York 12110
800/345-4277

CompuServe, Inc.
5000 Arlington Centre Blvd.
Columbus, Ohio 43220
800/848-8990

Dialog Information Services Inc.
3460 Hillview Avenue
Palo Alto, California 94304
800/334-2564

Mead Data Central
P.O. Box 933
Dayton, Ohio 45401
800/227-4908

MEDLARS
National Library of Medicine
8600 Rockville Pike
Bethesda, Maryland 20894
800/638-8480

Useful Titles

Computer-Readable Databases: A Directory and Data Sourcebook. Edited by Martha F. Williams. Vol. 1, *Science, Technology, Medicine;* vol. 2, *Business, Law, Humanities, Social Sciences.* Chicago: American Library Association, 1985.

Data Base Directory 1984/85. White Plains, N.Y.: Knowledge Industry Pubns. in cooperation with the American Society for Information Science, 1984–   . Annual.

Directory of Online Databases. Santa Monica, Calif.: Cuadra Associates, 1979–   . Quarterly.

Encyclopedia of Information Systems and Services. 7th ed. An international descriptive guide to . . . organizations, systems, and services involved in the production and distribution of information in electronic form. Edited by A. F. Lucas and K. Y. Marcaccio. Vol. 1, *United States Listings;* vol. 2, *International Listings;* vol. 3, *Index.* Detroit: Gale, 1987.

Fenichel, Carol H., and Hogan, Thomas H. *Online Searching: A Primer.* 2d ed. Medford, N.J.: Learned Information, 1984.

Personal Computers

Though it is not within the scope of this guide to advise on whether or not you should own and write on a computer (and there seems to be some disagreement about the issue), don't hesitate to *search* via computer. However, for those interested in personal computers, here are a few relevant titles:

Bowker's Complete Sourcebook of Personal Computing, 1985. New York: Bowker, 1984.

Computer Buying Guide: Rating the Best Computers, Peripherals, & Software. By the editors of *Consumer Guide.* Skokie, Ill.: Publications International, 1984–   . Annual.

Whole Earth Software Catalog for 1986. 2d ed. Edited by Stuart Brand. New York: Doubleday, 1985.

Historical Research

There is a theory that if one goes far back in history, there is less documentation, so a writer can allow artistic imagination full freedom and can do less research. Well, don't count on it. As stated earlier, some basic information is necessary to establish reality for the writer as well as the reader. In the hands of a superior writer, the scarcity of facts goes unnoticed by the reader, but some facts are essential. And in some cases, alas, much research is actually needed or simply mushrooms because what starts out as a search for "background" can become a compulsion to endlessly explore (see segment "Knowing When to Stop," in part 5). Then there is the dreaded possibility that the study of what really happened will turn out to be more interesting than the imagined story. In any case, the world created by the author must be seen as real to that author before it can be made real to readers. To the mind's eye, seeing is believing.

The skeptic's view is that historical fiction has as much relation to actual history as science fiction has to science, but take heart (and take responsible note), because some people read historical fiction *instead* of history. A "historical novel" can mean many things—it can be a novel about real people in history, or it can be about real events but not real people, or it can be historical in the sense that it is merely set in a different era. A historical novel is not necessarily a romance novel. If the study of history is thought to be a means of helping us to understand ourselves better, then historical fiction can contribute to that process with its insights and imagination.

Today, "historical novel" may really mean "anthropological novel." Writing in *Harper's* (March 1974), Stephen Marcus states that our modern historical studies have replaced the old model of historical studies and "what has been substituted for the old required courses in history are assorted projects of study called social studies, or area studies, or cultural studies. . . . There has been a tendency in education to replace history with anthropology. . . . Within recent years a sizable number of historical novels have been published that are essentially or largely anthropological in both subject matter and point of view." No matter how "history" is viewed, it is important for the purpose of research to know if you are looking for a classical view of history or an anthropological view—subject headings and search strategies would change.

Defenders of historical fiction claim that "straight" history is hard to take because it is written with every boring detail included, and so some believe that an imagined story is burdened when it has too many genuine details or too many real figures from the past; the frame must not overpower the painting. Perhaps none of us can take too much reality, or we wouldn't be reading fiction at all.

Many times this work will remind you to check the following sources for historical perspectives:

Art of the time
Literature of the time
Diaries, personal journals, and memoirs
Newspapers and periodicals
Documents

Separate chapters deal in detail with these sources, but an example now of what the literature of the time reveals will give you the idea. *Beowulf*, the Old English heroic poem, deals with events in the early eight century and is believed to have been written sometime between A.D. 700 and 750. Though it contains familiar motifs from folklore, it represents much of the time period as it was. If you look up *Beowulf* in the index to *The New Encyclopaedia Britannica*, you are directed to several articles, among them one which cites it as a source of knowledge on Germanic religion, another citing its view of etiquette at the time, and another mention of it in an article on medieval furniture. Naturally, it would also be useful as an example of the use of language at that time.

The *Cambridge Histories* listed below are outstanding sources. *A History of Private Life* presents everyday life in images searched through murals and mosaics, funerary art, city plans, pottery and weapons, the stones of dwellings, garments and jewelry, and more. It is a brilliant approach to the history of everyday life. There are several books beginning *Everyday Life in . . . [place]*. The *Documentary History of American Life* has mostly political documents, but it also presents a mixture of religious, social, and cultural materials, plus cartoons, giving a broad picture of American life. The *Directory of Historical Societies and Agencies in the United States and Canada* is included because such agencies frequently publish state histories, etc., and because they can be contacted for local history. See also the section in this guide on "Atlases," part 4, for various historical atlases and the "Chronologies" segment, part 1, for world history fact-finding by dates in history.

Useful Titles

Because *history* is such a broad term and its possibilities are so endless, it is more difficult to suggest specific titles here than under specific topics, but there are some general recommendations.

The Arthurian Encyclopedia. Edited by Norris J. Lacy. New York: Garland, 1986.

Brinton, Crane, and others. *A History of Civilization.* 6th ed. 2 vols. Englewood Cliffs, N.J.: Prentice-Hall, 1984.

Cambridge Ancient History. 12 vols. Cambridge: University Press: New York: Macmillan, 1923–39.

Cambridge Ancient History. 2d-3d ed. Vols. 1–3, 7 (in progress) London: Cambridge Univ. Press, 1970–84.

Cambridge Medieval History. 8 vols. Cambridge: University Press; New York: Macmillan, 1911–36.

————. 2d ed. Vol. 4 in 2 vols. 1966–67.

New Cambridge Modern History. 14 vols. Cambridge: University Press, 1957–79.
(There are also Cambridge histories of individual countries— China, India, Iran, Latin America, Poland, etc.)

Directory of Historical Societies and Agencies in the United States and Canada. Madison, Wis.: American Association for State and Local History, 1956–   . Irregular.

Durant, Will and Ariel. *The Story of Civilization.* 11 vols. New York: Simon & Schuster, 1935–1975.

Goldston, Robert C. *The Sword of the Prophet: A History of the Arab World from the Time of Mohammed to the Present Day.* New York: Dial, 1979.

Langer, William. *The New Illustrated Encyclopedia of World History.* 2 vols. New York: Abrams, 1975.

McNeil, William H. *A World History.* 3d ed. New York: Oxford, 1979.

Roberts, John Morris. *History of the World.* New York: Knopf, 1976.

Toynbee, Arnold J. *A Study of History.* 12 vols. New York: Oxford, 1934–1961.

There are various dictionaries and encyclopedias of the history of individual countries such as:

Dictionary of American History. Rev. ed. 8 vols. New York: Scribner's, 1976.

Commager, Henry Steele, ed. *Documents of American History.* 9th ed. New York: Appleton, 1973.

Donald, David, ed. *Documentary History of American Life.* 8 vols. New York: McGraw-Hill, 1966–   .

There are several titles which begin:

Everyday Life in . . .
(Ancient Egypt, Ancient Greece, Ancient Rome, Ancient India, Ottoman Turkey, Renaissance Times, of the Maya, of the Pagan Celts, Anglo Saxon, Viking, and Norman Times, China, Colonial Canada, Classical Athens, and Babylon and Assyria are some.) Also *Life in . . .* ; e.g. *Life in Medieval Barony, Life in a Medieval Castle,* etc.

An especially useful title is:

A History of Private Life. Philippe Aries and Georges Duby, general editors. Edited by Paul Veyne. Translated by Arthur Goldhammer. Vol. 1, *From Pagan Rome to Byzantium.* Cambridge: Harvard Univ. Press, 1987. In progress.

Possible LCSH Subject Headings

Again, the field is so enormous that these are only examples of the kinds of headings available. Both CIVILIZATION and HISTORY are *subdivisions under other headings* for many topics and nations. As always, look under the most specific headings first, then go to broader headings if necessary.

ASTROLOGY—HISTORY
CIVILIZATION, CLASSICAL (and CIVILIZATION, [GRECO-ROMAN, HOMERIC, MEDIEVAL, MODERN, ETC.])
CIVILIZATION—HISTORY
GREECE—CIVILIZATION—TO 146 B.C.
HELLENISM
HISTORY
HISTORY—BIOGRAPHY
HISTORY—ERRORS, INVENTIONS, ETC.
HISTORY—PHILOSOPHY
HISTORY—RESEARCH
HISTORY—SOURCES
HISTORY, ANCIENT
HISTORY, MODERN
LOCAL HISTORY

MATHEMATICS—HISTORY
MIDDLE AGES—HISTORY
NINETEENTH CENTURY
UNITED STATES—HISTORY—CIVIL WAR, 1861–1865
(example; other countries use subdivision HISTORY)

Another useful subdivision under countries is SOCIAL LIFE AND CUSTOMS, though this is fully explored in the segment "Manners and Customs" in part 3. For example: GREAT BRITAIN—SOCIAL LIFE AND CUSTOMS—16TH CENTURY.

As shown in these examples, many headings and subdivisions are followed by specific time periods. Obviously it is an advantage to carefully investigate the *Library of Congress Subject Headings* (LCSH) before beginning a search, and as you can see, you will probably search for books under more than one heading. To illustrate, a title like this one:

Oleson, John Peter. *Bronze Age Greek and Roman Technology: A Select, Annotated Bibliography*. New York: Garland, 1986.

is found under the following headings:

TECHNOLOGY—NEAR EAST—HISTORY—
 BIBLIOGRAPHY
TECHNOLOGY—GREECE—HISTORY—
 BIBLIOGRAPHY
TECHNOLOGY—ROME—HISTORY—
 BIBLIOGRAPHY

Indexes

Many indexes are useful here, depending on how far back in history you're searching (yesterday is history), especially the indexes for social science and political science. Those more specifically useful for history are:

America: History and Life. A Guide to Periodical Literature. 1964– . Santa Barbara, Cal.: ABC-Clio.

C.R.I.S.: the Combined Retrospective Index Set to Journals in History, 1838–1974. 11 vols. Wash., D.C.: Carrollton Press, 1977–1978.

Historical Abstracts. Santa Barbara, Cal.: ABC-Clio with the International Social Science Institute, 1955– .

Writings on American History. 49 vols. Wash., D.C.: American Historical Assoc.; Milwood, N.Y.: Kraus-Thompson, 1904–1978.

————, *1961–73: A Subject Bibliography of Articles.* Edited by James J. Dougherty. 4 vols. Wash., D.C.: American Historical Assoc.; Milwood, N.Y.: KTO Press, 1976.

————, *1973/74–: A Subject Bibliography of Articles.* Edited by James J. Dougherty. Milwood, N.Y.: Kraus-Thompson for American Historical Assoc., 1974– . Annual.

Bibliographies and Research Guides

American Historical Association. *Guide to Historical Literature.* George Frederick Howe, Chairman, Board of Editors. New York: Macmillan, 1961.

Barzun, Jacques, and Graff, Henry. *The Modern Researcher.* 4th ed. San Diego & New York: Harcourt Brace Jovanovich, 1985.

A Bibliography of American County Histories. Compiled by P. William Filby. Baltimore: Genealogical Pub., 1985.

Freidel, Frank, ed. *Harvard Guide to American History.* Rev. ed. 2 vols. Cambridge: Belknap Press of Harvard Univ. Press, 1974.

Henige, David P. *Serial Bibliographies and Abstracts in History: An Annotated Guide.* Westport, Conn.: Greenwood, 1986.

Poulton, Helen J. *The Historian's Handbook: A Descriptive Guide to Reference Works.* Norman: Univ. of Oklahoma Press, 1972.

Shafer, Robert James. *A Guide to Historical Method.* 3d ed. Homewood, Ill.: Dorsey, 1980.

Tracking the
Twentieth Century

There is so much material available on this century that the problem is not locating information but sifting through the mass of data and getting quickly to the specific information needed. There have been spectacular achievements, events, and changes in the twentieth century, most of them well documented. (Naturally there were spectacular events in earlier centuries, but they seemed to take longer—no more hundred years wars, alas.) One does not want time and place overwhelming the human experience in fiction, so authors may need little of what is available. But it had better be accurate, because not only are modern events well documented, there are people who remember or were present at these events.

Another consideration for the depiction of more modern times is what has been called "placelessness." Since distance holds less meaning, modern man is a nomad, easily leaving home and, in America at least, seemingly forever moving—usually west. Theodore Roszak warns that technology and urban sprawl might create "an oppressive urban-industrial uniformity over the earth," leaving almost no place to visit since "almost every place is becoming Anyplace."

In his book, *Place and Placelessness* (London: Pion, 1976), Edward Relph writes:

Placelessness describes both an environment without significant places and the underlying attitude which does not acknowledge significance in places. It reaches back into the deepest levels of place, cutting roots, eroding symbols, replacing diversity with uniformity and experiential order with conceptual order. At its most profound it consists of a pervasive and perhaps irreversible alienation from places as the homes of men.

So contemporary men and women develop "psychological homes," living in inner space, wandering from place to place, and that too must be described. Think of the descriptions of Humbolt and Lolita traveling across the country stopping at gas stations and motels. Joan Didion characters always on the move, in cars. What was playing on the car radio? What movies do characters see, what books do they read, what political speeches do they hear?

Here is Henry Miller discussing America back in 1947 in *Remember to Remember:*

> "America is full of places. Empty places. And all these empty places are crowded. Just jammed with empty souls. All at loose ends, all seeking diversion. As though the chief object of existence were to forget. . . . Finally you get so desperate you decide to go home. To do this one has to be really desperate, because home is the last place on earth to go when you're in despair."
>
> Vol. 2 of *The Air-Conditioned Nightmare.* New York: New Directions, 1947.

Even so, many a modern heroine pines for the loss of the childhood place, a place that formed the character, a place to be described though it is gone. And of course there are still "old-fashioned" places and people with roots, and all that must be described too.

There seems to be a new interest in place as a formal principle in literature, and in recent years the world has had a new interest in endangered places and in the environment generally, which, in turn, are often themes in fiction.

For lists of what happened when look at the segment "Outlines and Chronologies" in part 1 for date books and chronologies, and especially remember *almanacs,* the *Annual Register: A Record of World Events,* and *encyclopedia yearbooks* for quick information on events. As in historical research, a feeling for social life and customs can be seen in areas described elsewhere in this book:

Art of the time
Literature of the time
Diaries, personal journals, and memoirs
Newspapers and periodicals
Film Archives
Documents and oral history collections

But in this century the detail and availability of material found in all of these areas is enormous. There are complete transcripts of congressional hearings and debates, and eyewitness accounts abound and are recorded on film as well as in print. A contemporary newspaper gives much more than the news—book and entertainment reviews, market information, etc. *Advertising is especially revealing of language, life-styles, and the cost of a coat or a house.* Of the titles below, *This Fabulous Century* is very useful, with an illustrated volume for each decade from 1900 to 1970 so far, and a "Prelude" volume covering 1870 to 1900. These are nice overviews of each time period and touch on all aspects of life. The *Annual Register . . .* is a valuable British set that covers the events of each year. *Keesing's . . .* and *Facts on File* are discussed more fully under "Newspapers" because they are primarily news sources, excellent records of the twentieth century. The *New Cambridge Modern History* is a superior, scholarly work with good bibliographies for in-depth searching.

Useful Titles

Annual Register: A Record of World Events, 1758– London: Longmans, 1761–   . Annual.

Atlas of American History. New York: Scribner's, 1978.

Commager, Henry Steele. *Documents of American History.* 9th ed. New York: Appleton, 1973.

Facts on File: World News Digest with Index. New York: Facts on File, 1940–   . Weekly with annual volumes.

Harper Encyclopedia of the Modern World: A Concise Reference History from 1760 to the Present. Edited by Richard B. Morris and Graham W. Irwin. New York: Harper, 1970.

Historic Documents, 1972–. Wash., D.C.: Congressional Quarterly, 1972–   . Annual.

Keesing's Contemporary Archives: Record of World Events. London: Longmans, 1931–   . Weekly to 1983, now monthly.

Morison, Samuel Eliot, Commager, Henry Steele, and Leuchtenburg, William E. *The Growth of the American Republic.* 7th ed. New York: Oxford Univ. Press, 1980.

New Cambridge Modern History. 14 vols. Cambridge University Press, 1957–1979.

New Cambridge Modern History Atlas. Edited by H. C. Darby and Harold Fullard. Cambridge: University Press, 1970.

Pageant of America: A Pictorial History of the United States. Edited by Ralph Henry Gabriel. 15 vols. New Haven: Yale Univ. Press, 1925–29.

Palmer, Alan. *Facts on File Dictionary of 20th Century History 1900–1978.* New York: Facts on File, 1979.

This Fabulous Century. By the editors of Time-Life Books. 8 vols. New York: Time-Life Books, 1969–70.

Bibliographies and Research Guides

(See also guides listed under segment "Historical Research," above.)

Mitterling, Philip. *U.S. Cultural History: A Guide to Information Sources.* Detroit: Gale, 1980.

Roach, John Peter Charles, ed. *A Bibliography of Modern History.* Cambridge: University Press, 1968.

Sources for American Studies. Edited by Jefferson B. Kellog and Robert H. Walker. Westport, Conn.: Greenwood, 1983.

Possible LCSH Subject Headings

(Again, see also suggested headings in "Historical Research" segment, since history headings and the subdivision "History" are used for the twentieth century as well as the more distant past. See the segment "War and Other Disasters" in part 4, which also has headings that apply here, since war has unfortunately dominated this century.)

Many subject headings are divided chronologically [Subject—20TH CENTURY), and countries can be divided by significant time periods or subjects can be modified by the word "modern" (ART, MODERN—19TH CENTURY). Otherwise, of course, just check under contemporary subjects (AIRPLANES or TELEVISION, for example) to find current information. There is a subdivision ENVIRONMENTAL ASPECTS that can be used under subjects and is very relevant in this century. For example: NUCLEAR POWER PLANTS—ENVIRONMENTAL ASPECTS.

AGRICULTURAL CHEMICALS—ENVIRONMENTAL
   ASPECTS (example; see above note)
CIVILIZATION, MODERN—20TH CENTURY
ECOLOGY
ENDANGERED SPECIES
HISTORY, MODERN—20TH CENTURY
HISTORY, MODERN—1945
HUMAN ECOLOGY
MAN—INFLUENCE OF ENVIRONMENT
MAN—INFLUENCE ON NATURE
NINETEEN THIRTY-NINE, A.D.
TWENTIETH CENTURY
TWENTIETH CENTURY—BIOGRAPHY
TWENTIETH CENTURY—FORECASTS
WORLD WAR 1914–1918
WORLD WAR 1939–1945

Indexes

Virtually every possible periodical and newspaper index (see segments "Periodicals" and "Newspapers" earlier in this part) is appropriate for modern times, and most of them cover only the time period in which they are issued.

Diaries, Memoirs, and Biographical Tools

"I never travel without my diary. One should always have something sensational to read on the train," says an Oscar Wilde character. There is the feeling that diaries and memoirs are going to reveal dark secrets and surprises, but even when they don't, they reveal much about the time and place of the writing. The small details of life and especially the language of the time are portrayed as clearly as any shocking gossip. Fortunately, diaries and journals have been kept by the lowly and the mighty for hundreds of years, even before the habit was pronounced to be a psychologically healthy activity. Not only do diaries uncover the time, the diarists themselves can be interesting enough to become the subjects of biographies or the basis for fiction. Sometimes the older the material is the more authentic it seems, but as the quality of such material varies, so does the veracity. After all, memory does not always serve, and frequently the authors knew they were writing for posterity and had no illusions about writing just for themselves. They too were often fiction writers.

Some bibliographies of American and British sources are listed here instead of individual diaries/memoirs or bibliographies for other countries (which can be found by careful use of the variety of subject headings listed below and under the names of people). *Through a Woman's I* leads to autobiographical writings by a variety of women—Emma Goldman, Abigail Adams, and May Sarton, for example—and the work has an "Index of Narratives by Subject Matter," which leads to works on the Black experience and the American Indian experience, on life in prison or in the wilderness, etc. Remember that proper and personal names are not usually listed in LCSH but are used as headings when appropriate, so check the library catalog under names.

Bibliographies

Addis, Patricia K. *Through a Woman's I: An Annotated Bibliography of American Women's Autobiographical Writings 1946–1976.* Metuchen, N.J.: Scarecrow, 1983.

Batts, John Stuart. *British Manuscript Diaries of the Nineteenth Century: An Annotated Listing.* Totowa, N.J.: Rowman and Littlefield, 1976.

Berger, Josef, and Berger, Dorothy, eds. *Diary of America: The intimate story of our nation, told by 100 diarists—public figures and plain citizens, natives and visitors—over the five centuries from Columbus, the Pilgrims, and George Washington to Thomas Edison, Will Rogers, and our own time.* New York: Simon & Schuster, 1957.

Havlice, Patricia. *And So To Bed: A Bibliography of Diaries Published in English.* Metuchen, N.J.: Scarecrow, 1987.

Kaplan, Louis, et al. *A Bibliography of American Autobiographies.* Madison: Univ. of Wisconsin Press, 1961.

Briscoe, Mary Louise, ed. *American Autobiography 1945–1980: A Bibliography.* Madison: Univ. of Wisconsin Press, 1982.

First Person Female American: A Selected and Annotated Bibliography of the Autobiographies of American Women Living After 1950. Edited by Carolyn H. Rhodes. Troy, N.Y.: Whitston, 1980.

Matthews, William. *American Diaries, an Annotated Bibliography of American Diaries Prior to the Year 1861.* 16 vols. Los Angeles: Univ. of California Press, 1945. New ed. in progress; see below.

A revised, expanded edition of the above is:

Arksey, Laura, et al. *American Diaries: An Annotated Bibliography of Published American Diaries and Journals.* Vol. 1– . Detroit: Gale, 1983–   . In progress.

Matthews, William. *American Diaries in Manuscript 1580–1954: A Descriptive Bibliography.* Athens: Univ. of Georgia Press, 1974.

————. *British Diaries: An Annotated Bibliography of British Diaries Written Between 1442 and 1942.* Berkeley: Univ. of California Press, 1950.

Weiss, Harry Bischoff. *American Letter-Writers, 1698–1943.* New York: New York Public Library, 1945.

Possible LCSH Subject Headings

"Memoirs" is not a subject heading—you are referred to AUTOBIOGRAPHY and to BIOGRAPHY and to the subdivision HISTORY—SOURCES under the names of countries (GREAT BRITAIN—HISTORY—SOURCES, for example). Note other subdivisions below using BIOGRAPHY, DIARIES, and PERSONAL NARRATIVES. Once again, names are used as subject headings but do not necessarily appear in the printed LCSH list, so if you have a specific name, try that first.

> AMERICAN DIARIES (and CHINESE DIARIES, ENGLISH DIARIES, etc.)
> AUTOBIOGRAPHIES
> BIOGRAPHY
> BIOGRAPHY—MIDDLE AGES, 500–1500
> BIOGRAPHY—18TH CENTURY (etc.—divided chronologically. Use also subdivision BIOGRAPHY under subjects, classes of persons or names of cities, countries, etc.: ART—BIOGRAPHY; ACTORS—BIOGRAPHY; GERMANY—BIOGRAPHY; etc.)
> DIARIES (Use also subdivision DIARIES under individual literary authors and subdivision PERSONAL NARRATIVES under individual wars and events)
> DIARIES AS CRIMINAL EVIDENCE
> FICTION, AUTOBIOGRAPHIC
> GENEALOGY
> MILITARY BIOGRAPHY
> OBITUARIES
> RELIGIOUS BIOGRAPHY

UNITED STATES—HISTORY—SOURCES (see note above)

GENERAL BIOGRAPHICAL SOURCES

Check the bibliographies below for comprehensive coverage of biographical reference sources and for special directories, lists of scholars, professionals, etc. See also the segment "Locating Experts" in part 5 of this book. The *Dictionary of National Biography* (DNB) and the *Dictionary of American Biography* (DAB) are scholarly works intended to treat biography honestly (as opposed to earlier "glossy" biographies), and the articles usually have bibliographies. *Current Biography* has a wide coverage, from movie and rock stars to political figures and scholars, with photographs of its subjects. The plain *Who's Who* is British. In addition to *Who's Who in America,* there are many *Who's Who in . . .* for subjects (science, history, etc.) as well as countries—check the bibliographies. Under indexes, the obituary indexes from the *New York Times* and the London *Times* are extremely useful sources.

Chamber's Biographical Dictionary. Edited by J. O. Thorne. Rev. ed. New York: St. Martin's, 1977.

Contemporary Authors: A Bio-Bibliographical Guide to Current Authors and Their Works. Detroit: Gale, 1962 to date. Various series. Annual.

Current Biography. New York: H. W. Wilson, 1940– . Monthly except December with annual cumulations.

Dictionary of American Biography. 17 vols. plus suppls. New York: Scribner's, 1926 to date.

Dictionary of National Biography. 22 vols. plus supps. London: Oxford University Press, 1922 to date.

Logan, Rayford, and Winston, Michael R. *Dictionary of American Negro Biography.* New York: Norton, 1982.

New Century Cyclopedia of Names. 3 vols. Edited by Clarence L. Barnhart. New York: Appleton, 1954.

New York Times Biographical Service. New York: New York Times Biographical Edition, 1970 to date.

Notable American Women, 1607–1950: A Biographical Dictionary. 3 vols. Cambridge, Mass.: Belknap Press of Harvard Univ. Press, 1971.

Notable American Women: The Modern Period: A Biographical Dictionary. Cambridge, Mass.: Belknap Press of Harvard Univ. Press, 1980.

The International Dictionary of 20th Century Biography. Shore, Rina and Vernoff, Edward. NAL Books, 1987.

Webster's Biographical Dictionary. Rev. ed. Springfield, Mass.: Merriam, 1983.

Who's Who. London: Black, 1949 to date. Annual.

Who's Who in America. Chicago: Marquis, 1899 to date. Biennial.

Who Was Who in America: A Companion Biographical Reference Work to Who's Who in America. 7 vols. Marquis, 1942–81– . In progress.

Who Was Who in America: Historical Volume 1607–1896. Chicago: Marquis, 1963.

Bibliographies

ARBA Guide to Biographical Dictionaries. Edited by Bohdan Wynar. Littleton, Colo.: Libraries Unlimited, 1986.

Biographical Books, 1876–1949. New York: Bowker, 1983.

Biographical Books, 1950–1980. New York: Bowker, 1980.

Slocum, Robert B. *Biographical Dictionaries and Related Works: An International Bibliography of Approximately 16,000 Collective Biographies.* 2d ed. Detroit: Gale, 1986.

Indexes

Biographical Almanac. Subtitle: A comprehensive reference guide to more than 20,000 famous and infamous newsmakers from

Biblical times to the present as found in over 300 readily available sources. Edited by Anne Brewer. Detroit: Gale, 1981.

Biography and Genealogy Master Index. 2d ed. 8 vols. Supp. 1981–85, 5 vols. Detroit: Gale, 1980.

Biography Index: A Cumulative Index to Biographical Material in Books and Magazines. New York: Wilson, 1947– . Quarterly with annual and three-year cumulations.

The New York Times Obituaries Index, 1858–1968. New York: New York Times, 1970.

The New York Times Obituaries Index, 1969–1978. New York: New York Times, 1980.

Spradling, Mary Mace. *In Black and White: A Guide to Magazine Articles, Newspaper Articles, and Books Concerning More than 15,000 Black Individuals and Groups.* 3d ed. 2 vols. Supp. Detroit: Gale, 1980. Detroit: Gale, 1985.

Language

Thoughts and feelings in fiction, as in real life (or reel life, if you're writing a screenplay), are framed in language, and the way characters talk certainly helps to establish the time and place. *Language,* for the purposes of this research guide, means the speech or dialogue so essential to establishing characters and relationships between characters. Dialogue is a fundamental ingredient of most scenes and can bring a sense of life to fiction. Because, of course, the *way* characters say something is as important as *what* they say, if they are to be believable. Though there are methods for researching the language of various eras, it is also important to follow your instincts about what readers will believe and what might simply "sound" right, whether or not it is literally or completely correct. Mary Renault, in an article, "The Fiction of History," for *London Magazine* (March 1979, 56–57), writes:

> You cannot step twice into the same river, said Herakleitos. People in the past were not just like us, to pretend so is an evasion and betrayal, turning our back on them so as to be easy among familiar. This is why the matter of dialogue is so crucial. No word in our language comes to us sterile and aseptic, free of associations. If it was coined yesterday, it tastes of that, and a single sentence of modern colloquial slang, a turn of phrase which evokes specifically our own society can destroy for me, at any rate, the whole suspension of disbelief. Yet phony archaism merely suggests the nineteenth century instead and actors in ill-fitting tights. . . . Greek is a highly polysyllabic language. Yet when writing dialogue for my Greeks I have found myself, by instinct, avoiding the

polysyllables of the English language, and using, as far as they are still in the living language, the older and shorter words. This is not because the style parallels Greek style, it is entirely a matter of association and ambience. In Greek, polysyllables are old; in English, mostly Latinized and largely modern.

If you are writing a contemporary play or novel, the obvious advice is to *listen* to the world around you; listening is as important for writers as observing. But there are techniques for researching appropriate language for recent time periods as well as the distant past.

The specific titles here are primarily for various types of dictionaries, but remember also to look at:

Literature of the time period (both fiction and nonfiction) for examples of the language—that used by the author and by the characters. (The section on "Books" in part 3 describes literary histories of American and British literature and other literature information.)

Diaries, personal journals, and memoirs for language (see the segment in this guide, "Diaries, Memoirs, and Biographical Tools"), again for any time period.

Newspapers and periodicals, if your setting is in the twentieth century or nineteenth century, offer excellent examples of contemporary usage. Notice the advertising as well as the articles.

Speeches of modern or historical time periods.

DICTIONARIES

Special dictionaries are discussed here. For information on current dictionaries in print for contemporary English, look at:

Kister, Kenneth F. *Dictionary Buying Guide: A Consumer Buying Guide to General English-Language Wordbooks in Print.* New York: Bowker, 1977.

The outstanding and immensely useful dictionary for the English language is the:

Oxford English Dictionary, being a corrected reissue, with an introduction, supplement and bibliography, of *A New English Dictionary* on historical principles; founded mainly on materials collected by the Philological Society and edited by James A. H. Murray [and others]. 12 vols. and supp. Oxford: Clarendon Press, 1933.

————. A supplement to the Oxford English Dictionary. Edited by R. W. Burchfield. 4 vols. Oxford: Clarendon Press, 1972–1986.

This remarkable multivolume set contains hundreds of thousands of words known to have been in use, in speech or literature, since 1150 and before. Based on historical principles, its purpose is to show the history of every word included, from the date of its introduction into the language, giving the differences in meaning, spelling, usage, pronunciation, etc. at different periods. The information is supported by numerous quotations from thousands of authors of all periods, including all writers before the sixteenth century. There is no way to describe how useful this astonishing dictionary really is; one must look at it.

And for precisely American English there are some excellent tools, including the new *Dictionary of American Regional English* (DARE), which covers words and phrases with an emphasis on still-current colloquialisms, and contains much information on folklore, natural history, and children's games.

Craigie, Sir William Alexander, and Hulbert, James R. *A Dictionary of American English Based on Historical Principles.* 4 vols. Chicago: Univ. of Chicago, 1936–44.

Dictionary of American Regional English. Edited by Frederic G. Cassidy. 1 vol. Cambridge, Mass.: Belknap Press of Harvard Univ. Press, 1985–   . In progress. Projected 5 vols.

Mathews, Mitford McLeod. *A Dictionary of Americanisms on Historical Principles.* 2 vols. Chicago: Univ. of Chicago, 1951.

English and American slang dictionaries are valuable tools for current and historical colorful language. Some useful ones are:

Partridge, Eric. *A Dictionary of Slang and Unconventional English, Colloquialisms and Catch Phrases, Fossilized Jokes and Puns, General Nicknames, Vulgarisms and Such Americanisms as Have Become Naturalized.* Edited by Paul Beale. London: Routledge & Kegan Paul, 1984.

Spears, Richard A. *Slang and Euphemism: A Dictionary of Oaths, Curses, Insults, Sexual Slang and Metaphor, Racial Slurs, Drug Talk, Homosexual Lingo, and Related Matters.* Middle Village, N.Y.: David, 1981.

Wentworth, Harold, and Flexner, Stuart Berg. *Dictionary of American Slang.* 2d supp. ed. New York: Crowell, 1975.

Note: a new edition of *Dictionary of American Slang* is now available, edited by Robert Chapman. it is more up-to-date than the 1975 edition but has dropped dates and sources of citations (a serious mistake). Some writers might also find useful the old Berry/Van den Bark, *The American Thesaurus of Slang* (Crowell, 1953, and Landy, *The Underground Dictionary* (Simon & Schuster, 1971); drug slang. For leads to useful dictionaries of preceding centuries, check bibliographies and lists of sources in the above-mentioned texts.

Pictorial Dictionaries

Especially useful for writers are dictionaries in the Oxford-Duden pictorial dictionary series published by Oxford University Press. These dictionaries carry diagrams and pictures which locate and name all the parts of a hotel, a supermarket, a television studio, a farm, a car, etc. An example is the *Oxford-Duden Pictorial English Dictionary* (Oxford: Oxford University Press, 1981) and the series includes pictorial dictionaries in French-English, German-English, Spanish-English, and Japanese-English in case a character's car breaks down in another country. Useful in the same way is *What's What: A Visual Glossary of the Physical World*, edited by Reginald Bragonier and David Fisher (Maplewood, N.J.: Hammond, 1981) which identifies parts of a sink, a disposal, a carpet, a furnace, a tank, and so on.

OTHER APPROPRIATE TITLES

Flexner, Stuart Berg. *Listening to America: An Illustrated History of Words and Phrases from Our Lively and Splendid Past.* New York: Simon & Schuster, 1982. Also by Flexner, *I Hear America Talking.*

Idioms and Phrases Index. Edited by Laurence Urdang. 3 vols. Detroit: Gale, 1983.

Wright, Joseph. *English Dialect Dictionary: Being the Complete Vocabulary of All Dialect Words Still in Use or Known to Have Been in Use During the Last Two Hundred Years; Founded on the Publications of the English Dialect Society.* 6 vols. London: Frowde, 1898–1905.

Possible LCSH Subject Headings

The headings for ENGLISH LANGUAGE are many and worth looking over for all their possibilities. The English Language headings are a "pattern" for use with other languages—so the subdivisions under English Language may be used under any language. DIALECTS and PROVINCIAL-ISM may be used as subdivisions under languages and divided geographically; for example, if you look up "Chicano language" in the LCSH list, you are referred to the possible headings: SPANISH LANGUAGE—DIALECTS—UNITED STATES, and to SPANISH LANGUAGE—PROVINCIAL-ISMS—SOUTHWESTERN STATES.

AMERICANISMS
BLACK ENGLISH (for Afro-American dialects and language)
CONVERSATION
DIALECTS (also used as a subdivision; see note above)
ENGLISH LANGUAGE—DICTIONARIES
ENGLISH LANGUAGE—CONVERSATION AND PHRASE BOOKS (for various groups and with old or new publication dates)

ENGLISH LANGUAGE—DIALECTS (May Subh GEOG)
ENGLISH LANGUAGE—ETYMOLOGY
ENGLISH LANGUAGE—GRAMMAR
ENGLISH LANGUAGE—PARTS OF SPEECH
ENGLISH LANGUAGE—SLANG
ENGLISH LANGUAGE—TERMS AND PHRASES
ENGLISH LANGUAGE—TO 1100
ENGLISH LANGUAGE—MIDDLE ENGLISH (etc., by
  various time periods)
ENGLISH LANGUAGE—USAGE
TABLE TALK (also a subdivision under names of persons;
  for example: SHAW, GEORGE BERNARD—TABLE
  TALK)
URBAN DIALECTS

Indexes

LLBA: Language and Language Behavior Abstracts. New York:
Appleton, 1967–   . Quarterly.

Sutton, Roberta Briggs. *Speech Index: An Index to 259 Collections
of World Famous Orations and Speeches for Various Occasions*.
4th ed. New York: Scarecrow, 1966.

Mitchell, Charity. *Speech Index: An Index to Collections of World
Famous Orations and Speeches for Various Occasions*. A supple-
ment to the title above covering 1966–1980. Metuchen, N.J.:
Scarecrow, 1982.

Bibliographies and Guides

Allen, H. B. *Linguistics and English Linguistics*. 2d ed. Arlington
Heights, Ill.: AHM, 1977.

Baugh, A. C. and Cable, T. A. *A History of the English Language*.
3d ed. Englewood Cliffs, N.J.: Prentice-Hall, 1978.
(Updated by Thomas Cable's *A Companion to Baugh and Cable's
History of the English Language*. Englewood Cliffs, N.J.: Prentice-
Hall, 1983.

McCrum, Robert, et al. *The Story of English.* New York: Viking, 1986.

Mencken, H. L. *The American Language: An Inquiry into the Development of English in the United States.* 4th ed. 2 vols. New York: Knopf, 1936. Supp., 1945–48. Also available in one-volume abridgment by Raven I. McDavid; this also updates Mencken's original, especially with regard to earliest known uses of words.

Part III

Creating Fictional Worlds

Beliefs

When would someone have been influenced by Spinoza, by Freud, by St. Augustine, and exactly what ideas did they hold? Just as there were certain scientific ideas that changed as a result of, say, the discovery that the world was round, there have been times when certain philosophies were popular or presented breakthrough ideas undreamed of by previous generations. Characters in fiction often have strong philosophical or religious beliefs that dictate their behavior and pepper their conversation. What rules do the followers of certain religions live by, and what ceremonies mark important events in their lives?

The works listed here will identify themes and ideas for use in stories and screenplays and give indications of the chronology— when an organization was founded or when certain beliefs flourished. If a philosophy and/or religion is a *major* part of a play or story, use the De George and Tice (for philosophy) and the Gorman (for religion) bibliographies, because the titles here are general. But the various religion encyclopedias are excellent sources, usually with good bibliographies at the end of their articles. The *Harper Encyclopedia of Bible Life* has articles on how the people of the Bible dressed, ate, worked, and has information on their dwellings, medicine, and customs. The *Encyclopedia of Islam* is an important work in English on all Islamic subjects, not just religion. Notice the publication dates on the two Catholic encyclopedias and the two Jewish encyclopedias; the older ones, of course, represent older points of view.

For philosophy, the Macmillan *Encyclopedia of Philosophy*

is important, as is the outstanding *Dictionary of the History of Ideas*. This last work emphasizes interdisciplinary cross-cultural relations, with the aim, according to the Preface, of helping to "establish some sense of unity of human thought and its cultural manifestations in a world of ever-increasing specialization and alienation." Since unbelief has its own beliefs, the Stein title, *Encyclopedia of Unbelief*, is included. It has biographies of people like Charles Darwin and Walt Whitman, and articles on unbelief in ancient times, freethinkers, ethical culture, etc., as well as an article on "Deathbeds of Unbelievers," addressing various deathbed recantation stories.

Useful Titles—Philosophy

Angeles, Peter A. *Dictionary of Philosophy*. New York: Barnes & Noble, 1981.

Dictionary of the History of Ideas: Studies of Selected Pivotal Ideas. Edited by Philip P. Weiner. 4 vols. and index. New York: Scribner's, 1973–74.

Encyclopedia of Philosophy. 8 vols. Edited by Paul Edwards. New York: Macmillan, 1967.

World Philosophy: Essay-Reviews of 225 Major Works. Edited by Frank Magill and Ian P. McGreal. 5 vols. Englewood Cliffs, N.J.: Salem Press, 1982.

Possible LCSH Subject Headings—Philosophy

Remember to look under the specific name of a particular philosophy or philosophical subject (NATURALISM, PRAGMATISM, SOUL, etc.) before using a broader heading. As shown below, some terms, having more than one meaning, have PHILOSOPHY in parentheses to distinguish their application to philosophy. Sometimes the heading ETHICS can be modified: ETHICS, JAPANESE; or the heading may be direct: HINDU ETHICS; FASCIST ETHICS. See the very long list of suggested related headings in LCSH under PHILOSOPHY.

ABSURD (PHILOSOPHY)
AESTHETICS
ALIENATION (PHILOSOPHY)
BANALITY (PHILOSOPHY)
CHRISTIANITY—PHILOSOPHY
COMMUNISM—PHILOSOPHY
CONSCIOUSNESS
ETHICS
ETHICS, ANCIENT
ETHICS, JAPANESE (and Jewish, Chinese, etc.; see note
    above)
ETHICS, MEDIEVAL
ETHICS, MODERN
ETHICS, PRIMITIVE
ETHICS, RENAISSANCE
METAPHYSICS
MYSTICISM
PHILOSOPHY
PHILOSOPHY—HISTORY
PHILOSOPHY, FRENCH (and AMERICAN, HINDU,
    INDIC, etc.)
RATIONALISM
THEISM

Index—Philosophy

The Philosopher's Index: An International Index to Philosophical Periodicals and Books. Bowling Green, Ohio: Bowling Green Univ., 1967– . Quarterly, with annual cumulations.

Bibliographies and Guides—Philosophy

De George, Richard T. *The Philosopher's Guide to Sources, Research Tools, Professional Life and Related Matters.* Lawrence: Regents Press of Kansas, 1980.

Tice, Terrence N., and Slavens, Thomas P. *Research Guide to Philosophy.* Chicago: American Library Assoc., 1983.

Useful Titles—Religion

Abingdon Dictionary of Living Religions. Edited by Keith Crim. Nashville: Abingdon, 1981.

Book of Jewish Books: A Reader's Guide to Judaism. Edited by Ruth S. Frank and William Wollheim. New York: Harper, 1986.

Catholic Encyclopedia: An International Work of Reference on the Constitution, Doctrine, Discipline and History of the Catholic Church. 17 vols. New York: Encyclopedia Press, 1907–1922.

Dictionary of Comparative Religion. S. G. F. Brandon, gen. ed. London: Weidenfeld and Nicolson, 1970.

Encyclopaedia Judaica. 16 vols. Jerusalem: Encyclopaedia Judaica; New York: Macmillan, 1972.

Encyclopaedia of Islam. New ed. Leiden: Brill; London: Luzac, 1954–1983. Index in progress.

Encyclopedia of American Religions. 2d ed. Edited by J. Gordon Melton. Detroit: Gale, 1987.

The Encyclopedia of Religion. Edited by Mircea Eliade. 15 vols. New York: Macmillan, 1987. In progress.

Encyclopedia of Religion and Ethics. Edited by James Hastings. 12 vols. and index. New York: Scribner's, 1908–1927.

Ferguson, John. *An Illustrated Encyclopedia of Mysticism and the Mystery Religions.* London: Thames and Hudson, 1976.

Harper Encyclopedia of Bible Life. 3d rev. ed. New York: Harper & Row, 1978.

Jewish Encyclopedia: A Descriptive Record of the History, Religion, Literature and Customs of the Jewish People from the Earliest Times to the Present Day. Prep. under the direction of Cyrus Adler, et al. 12 vols. New York: Funk & Wagnalls, 1901– 1906.

Malalasekera, G. P., ed. *Encyclopaedia of Buddhism.* 4 vols. Columbo: Govt. Pr., 1961–   . In progress.

Mead, Frank Spencer. *Handbook of Denominations in the United States.* New 8th ed. Revised by Samuel S. Hill. 2 vols. Nashville: Abingdon, 1978.

New Catholic Encyclopedia. Prepared by the staff at the Catholic University of America. 17 vols. New York: McGraw-Hill, 1967–1979.

Shulman, Albert M. *The Religious Heritage of America*. New York: A. S. Barnes, 1981.

Stein, Gordon. *The Encyclopedia of Unbelief*. Buffalo, N.Y.: Prometheus, 1985.

Westminster Dictionary of Christian Ethics. 2d ed. Edited by James Childress and John Macquarrie. Philadelphia: Westminster, 1986.

World Spirituality: An Encyclopedic History of Religious Quest. Edited by Ewert Cousins. 25 vols. New York: Crossroad/ Continuum, 1986–   . In progress.

Possible LCSH Subject Headings—Religion

CATHOLIC CHURCH is used as the "pattern" for Christian denominations, so the subdivisions you see there (CLERGY, HYMNS, LITURGY, etc.) may be used under other denominations but are not repeated each time in the LCSH volumes. BUDDHISM is the pattern for religions. BIBLE is the pattern for sacred works. JESUITS is the pattern for religious and monastic orders. CONDUCT OF LIFE is a heading usually implying ethical or moral behavior. Remember to start by looking directly under the name of the religion or denomination and then to proceed to broader headings if necessary. Only general examples of religion headings are given here.

CHRISTIAN ANTIQUITIES
CHRISTIAN ART AND SYMBOLISM
CHRISTIAN EDUCATION
CHRISTIAN FAMILY
CHRISTIAN LIFE
CHRISTIAN PATRON SAINTS
CONDUCT OF LIFE
CULTS
JUDAISM
JUDAISM—CUSTOMS AND PRACTICES
JUDAISM—HISTORY
JUDAISM—DOCTRINES

RELIGION
RELIGION—CONTROVERSIAL LITERATURE
RELIGION—PSYCHOLOGY
RELIGION—STUDY AND TEACHING
RELIGION, PREHISTORIC
RELIGION, PRIMITIVE
RELIGION AND ETHICS
RELIGION AND POLITICS
RELIGION AND SOCIOLOGY
RELIGION IN LITERATURE
RELIGION IN MOTION PICTURES
RELIGIONS
RELIGIONS—AFRICAN (etc.) INFLUENCES
RELIGIOUS BIOGRAPHY
RELIGIOUS EDUCATION
RELIGIOUS THOUGHT
RELIGIOUS THOUGHT—TO 600
RELIGIOUS THOUGHT—MIDDLE AGES, 600–1500
  (etc., by time period)
RELIGIOUS TOLERANCE
SECTS

Indexes—Religion

Catholic Periodical List: A Cumulative Author and Subject Index to a Selected List of Catholic Periodicals. New York: Catholic Library Assoc., 1939–67. Quarterly with biennial cumulations.

Continued by:

Catholic Periodical and Literature Index. Haverford, Pa.: Catholic Library Assoc., 1968–   . Bimonthly with biennial cumulations.

Index to Jewish Periodicals. Cleveland: Index to Jewish Periodicals, 1963–   . Semiannual.

Religion Index One: Periodicals. Chicago: American Theological Library Assoc., 1953–   . Semiannual with biennial cumulation.

Religion Index Two: Multi-Author Works. Chicago: American Theological Library Assoc., 1978–   . Annual.

Bibliographies and Guides—Religion

Bowman, Mary Ann. *Western Mysticism: A Guide to Basic Works*. Chicago: American Library Assoc., 1978.

Brisman, Shimeon. *A History and Guide to Judaic Bibliography*. Cincinnati: Hebrew Union College Pr.; New York: Ktav, 1977.

Cutter, Charles, and Oppenheim, Micha Falk. *Jewish Reference Sources: A Selective, Annotated Bibliographic Guide*. New York: Garland, 1982.

Ellis, John Tracy, and Trisco, Robert. *A Guide to American Catholic History*. 2d ed. Rev. and enl. Santa Barbara: ABC-Clio, 1982.

Gorman, G. E., and Gorman, Lyn. *Theological and Religious Reference Materials: General Resources and Biblical Studies*. Westport, Conn.: Greenwood, 1984– . In progress. 4 vols. projected.

McCabe, James Patrick. *Critical Guide to Catholic Reference Books*. 2d ed. Littleton, Colo.: Libraries Unlimited, 1980.

Again, these selections are representative—look under specific religions for bibliographies and information on Chinese and Japanese religions, on Buddhism, Hinduism, various Christian denominations, etc.

Mythology

In this century people have scientific answers and theories for questions about why the sun rises and sets, what causes lightning or floods or tornadoes. In earlier times, people explained natural events in terms of myths, stories about gods and goddesses that played an important part of their religious life, so sources of mythology are included in this chapter. Most myths concern divine beings who have supernatural powers. Myths have also been used to explain the unexplainable. Knowledge of mythology can assist in the creation of a certain culture of a certain time, or it can be of use to writers who use language to convey meaning in a concise, immediate fashion.

A reference to Pandora or Janus can bring almost instant understanding of an idea with an economy of words, something that poets have long understood.

Useful Titles—Mythology

Bulfinch, Thomas. *Bulfinch's Mythology: The Age of Fable; The Age of Chivalry; The Legends of Charlemagne.* 2d rev. ed. New York: Crowell, 1970.

Campbell, Joseph. *The Masks of God.* Vol. 1, *Primitive Mythology;* vol. 2, *Oriental Mythology;* vol. 3, *Occidental Mythology;* vol. 4, *Creative Mythology.* New York: Viking, 1959–1968.

Cavendish, Richard, ed. *Mythology: An Illustrated Encyclopedia.* New York: Rizzoli, 1980.

Frazer, James G. *The Illustrated Golden Bough.* New York: Doubleday, 1978.

Graves, Robert. *The Greek Myths.* Ill. ed. Garden City, N.Y.: Doubleday, 1981.

Hamilton, Edith. *Mythology.* Boston: Little, Brown, 1942.

Hart, George. *A Dictionary of Egyptian Gods and Goddesses.* London: Routledge & Kegan Paul, 1986.

Mercatante, Anthony S. *Who's Who in Egyptian Mythology.* New York: C. N. Potter; distr. by Crown, 1978.

———. *Zoo of the Gods: Animals with Myth, Legend, and Fable.* New York: Harper & Row, 1974.

Mythology of All Races. Repr. of 1916–1932 ed. 13 vols. New York: Cooper Square, 1964.

Possible LCSH Subject Headings—Mythology

MYTHOLOGY is a heading and *can be used as a subdivision under subjects.* The subdivision RELIGION AND MYTHOLOGY may be used under INDIANS, INDIANS OF NORTH AMERICA, and under individual Indian tribes.

ANIMALS, MYTHICAL
ART AND MYTHOLOGY
FURIES
GEOGRAPHICAL MYTHS
GODS
HEROES
LEGENDS
MOTHER-GODDESSES
MYTH
MYTH IN THE BIBLE
MYTHOLOGY
MYTHOLOGY—DICTIONARIES
MYTHOLOGY, AFRICAN (or Baltic, British, Buddhist,
   etc.)
MYTHOLOGY, EGYPTIAN
MYTHOLOGY, GREEK
SIRENS
SYMBOLISM

Bibliographies and Guides—Mythology

Diehl, Katharine Smith. *Religions, Mythologies, Folklores: An Annotated Bibliography.* 2d ed. New York: Scarecrow, 1962.

Mythical and Fabulous Creatures: A Source Book and Research Guide. Edited by Malcolm South. Westport, Conn.: Greenwood, 1987.

Smith, Ron, *Mythologies of the World: A Guide to Sources.* Urbana, Ill.: Nat. Council of Teachers of English, 1981.

Behavior

Psychology

They say good behavior is its own reward, but what exactly is good behavior, and who determines it? Hasn't the definition of good behavior, and of bad behavior for that matter, changed over the years? When is it normal to act crazy, as in *Catch-22* and *M*a*s*h*? If you're creating a character for a fictional work, you can certainly invent his behavior as well, but some understanding of psychologically "normal" behavior under different circumstances can add a valuable touch of reality and believability to your work. Investigating psychological and psychiatric literature can also give you ideas about what the possibilities and consequences of certain actions are. This segment on behavior is naturally related to the segment on beliefs, since people act according to what they believe. There are good general sources in psychology and there are bibliographies in some special areas of interest to writers—nonverbal communication, suicide, alienation, stress, group behavior, and so on.

Useful Titles

Comprehensive Handbook of Psychopathology. Edited by Henry E. Adams and Patricia B. Sutker. New York: Plenum, 1984.

Encyclopedia of Psychology. Edited by Raymond J. Corsini. 4 vols. New York: Wiley, 1984.

Encyclopedia of Psychology. Edited by H. J. Eysenck, et al. 3 vols. New York: Herder & Herder, 1972.

Eysenck, Hans J. *Handbook of Abnormal Psychology.* 2d ed. San Diego, Cal.: R. R. Knapp, 1973.

Gordon, Jesse E., ed. *Handbook of Clinical and Experimental Hypnosis.* New York: Macmillan, 1968.

Handbook of Child Psychology. 4th ed. Edited by Paul H. Mussen. 4 vols. New York: Wiley, 1983.

International Encyclopedia of Psychiatry, Psychology, Psychoanalysis, and Neurology. Edited by Benjamin Wolman. 12 vols. New York: Van Nostrand Reinhold for Aesculapius, 1977. Progress volume, 1983.

International Encyclopedia of the Social Sciences. Edited by David L. Sills. 18 vols. New York: Macmillan and the Free Press, 1968–1980.

Wolman, Benjamin B., comp. and ed. *Dictionary of Behavioral Science.* New York: Van Nostrand Reinhold, 1973.

Bibliographies on Special Subjects

Berlin, Irving Norman. *Bibliography of Child Psychiatry and Child Mental Health, with a Selected List of Films.* 2d ed. New York: Human Sciences, 1976.

Davis, Martha. *Understanding Body Movement: An Annotated Bibliography.* New York: Arno, 1972.

———, and Skupien, Janet. *Body Movement and Nonverbal Communication; An Annotated Bibliography, 1971–1981.* Bloomington: Indiana Univ. Press, 1982.

Driver, Edwin D. *The Sociology and Anthropology of Mental Illness: A Reference Guide.* Rev. & enl. ed. Amherst: Univ. of Massachusetts Press, 1972.

Family Therapy and Research: An Annotated Bibliography of Articles, Books, Videotapes and Films Published 1950–1979. 2d ed. Edited by Ira D. Glick, et al. New York: Grune and Stratton, 1982.

Gottsegen, Gloria Behar. *Group Behavior: A Guide to Information Sources.* Detroit: Gale, 1979.

Holmes, Thomas H., and David, Ella M. *Life Change Events Research, 1966–1978; An Annotated Bibliography of the Periodical Literature*. New York: Praeger, 1984.

Lester, David; Sell, Betty H., and Sell, Kenneth D. *Suicide: A Guide to Information Sources*. Detroit: Gale, 1980.

Prentice, Ann E. *Suicide: A Selective Bibliography of over 2,200 Items*. Metuchen, N.J.: Scarecrow, 1974.

Reden, C. W. van; Grondel, A. G.; and Geyer, R. F. *Bibliography, Alienation*. 3d enl. ed. Amsterdam: Stichting Interuniversitair Instituut voor Sociaal-Wetenschappelijk Onderzoek, 1980.

Rigger, T. F. *Stress Burnout: An Annotated Bibliography*. Carbondale and Edwardsville, Ill.: Southern Illinois Univ. Press, 1985.

Rothenberg, Albert, and Greenberg, Bette. *The Index of Scientific Writings on Creativity: General, 1566–1974*. Hamden, Conn.: Archon, 1976.

Possible LCSH Subject Headings

There are as many subject headings for behavior as there are synonyms and psychological meanings for the word. The term *behavior* by itself is *not* a heading. If you look it up you are told to see CONDUCT OF LIFE, which has to do with ethics and morals and is an appropriate heading here, and ETIQUETTE, a heading recommended for locating manners and customs (see that segment later in part 3). HUMAN BEHAVIOR is a heading used for works on *observable patterns of human actions and reactions*. Works on the *general science of and explanation of behavior* are entered under the heading PSYCHOLOGY. Many kinds of behavior can be searched directly under the term (AGGRESSIVENESS, CYNICISM, INFERIORITY COMPLEX, PASSIVITY, etc.). FLIGHT OF IDEAS is also a direct heading (and a name with a certain appeal, making the condition sound desirable). LIFE STYLE is a heading that elicits works on recognizable life-styles such as those of working women, executives, and working-class youth in Belfast. Using the LIFE STYLE heading in a biomedical library will retrieve books about healthy or unhealthy life-styles.

ATTITUDE (PSYCHOLOGY)
BEHAVIOR MODIFICATION
BEHAVIOR THERAPY
BEHAVIORISM (PSYCHOLOGY)
BEHAVIORISM (PSYCHOLOGY)—RELIGIOUS ASPECTS
CHILD PSYCHOLOGY
CONDUCT OF LIFE (also used as a subdivision after classes of persons, e.g. YOUTH—CONDUCT OF LIFE)
CONSCIOUSNESS
CRIMINAL PSYCHOLOGY
HUMAN BEHAVIOR
LIFE STYLE (for works on an individual's distinctive, recognizable way of living and the behavior that expresses it)
MENTAL ILLNESS
NEUROSIS
PSYCHOLOGY (and the subdivisions PSYCHOLOGY and PSYCHOLOGICAL ASPECTS under subjects; e.g. STUDENTS—PSYCHOLOGY, CANCER—PSYCHOLOGICAL ASPECTS)
PSYCHOLOGY, APPLIED (for works on the application of psychology in various fields such as industry, advertising, and military life)
PSYCHOLOGY, PATHOLOGICAL (for works of systematic descriptions of mental disorders. Social aspects are under mental illness. And terms may be searched directly—HYSTERIA, KLEPTOMANIA, PARANOIA, etc.)

Indexes

Child Development Abstracts and Bibliography. Lafayette, Ind.: Purdue Univ., Soc. for Research in Child Development, 1927–   . Issued three times a year.

Psychological Abstracts. Lancaster, Pa.: American Psychological Association, 1927–   . Monthly with cumulations.

Social Sciences Citation Index. Philadelphia: Institute for Scientific Information, 1973–   . Issued three times a year, with cumulations.

Social Sciences Index. New York: Wilson, 1974–   . Quarterly with annual cumulations. (Preceded by *Social Sciences and Humanities Index* and *International Index*—see entries in segment on periodicals.)

Sociological Abstracts. New York: Sociological Abstracts, 1952–   . Issued six times a year with cumulative index issue.

Bibliographies and Guides

Bell, James Edward. *A Guide to Library Research in Psychology.* Dubuque, Ia.: W. C. Brown, 1971.

Greenberg, Bette. *How to Find Out in Psychiatry.* New York: Pergamon, 1978.

Li, Tze-chung. *Social Science Reference Sources: A Practical Guide.* Westport, Conn.: Greenwood, 1980.

McInnis, Raymond G. *Research Guide for Psychology.* Westport, Conn.: Greenwood, 1982.

Reed, Jeffrey G., and Baxter, Pam M. *Library Use: A Handbook for Psychology.* Wash., D.C.: American Psychological Assoc., 1983.

Webb, William H., and Assoc. *Sources of Information in the Social Sciences: A Guide to the Literature.* Chicago: American Library Assoc., 1986.

Anthropology

A discipline for the study of man, anthropology focuses on the naturalistic description and interpretation of the diverse peoples of the world and emphasizes direct observation of human beings and their activities. As such, the material gathered is rich in detail and finds significance in all that concerns human beings. So this is observable behavior, not necessarily a psychological view of behavior. Many of the subject headings overlap with those above, particularly the heading HUMAN BEHAVIOR. There are lots of reference materials available for certain countries, areas, and people, but not a really large number of very general works on anthropology. The *International Bibliography of Social and Cultural Anthropology* is a comprehensive annual and the library catalogs of Harvard's Peabody Museum of Archaeology and Ethnology (now Tozzer Library) are important in the field. The Harvard catalogs are listed below under "indexes" because they include journal articles, contributions to *Festschriften,* and proceedings of congresses. For anyone interested in in-depth searching, the Human Relations Area Files (HRAF) would be a valuable source, but ask a librarian for help with this source and consult the guides to its use. HRAF has collections in hard copy or on microfilm, containing data on approximately 325 primitive, historical, and contemporary cultures. The general subject of anthropology may be divided into cultural anthropology (ETHNOLOGY is the subject heading) and physical anthropology and also into archaeology and linguistics, and then, of course, to narrower names of countries and their tribes and cultures (see list under ETHNOLOGY in the Library of Congress subject headings list).

There is a great deal of material on various ethnic groups, minorities, and women. Only major bibliographies and research guides are listed here, leading to the important works.

Useful Titles

Encyclopedia of Anthropology. Edited by David E. Hunter and Phillip Whitten. New York: Harper & Row, 1976.

Seymour-Smith, Charlotte, *Dictionary of Anthropology.* Boston: G. K. Hall, 1986.

Winick, Charles. *Dictionary of Anthropology.* New York: Philosophical Library, 1956. (Repr. Totowa, N.J.: Roman & Allanheld, 1984.)

Ethnic Groups

Ethnic Information Sources of the United States. Edited by Paul Wasserman. 2 vols. Detroit: Gale, 1983.

Harvard Encyclopedia of American Ethnic Groups. Edited by Stephen Thernstrom. Cambridge, Mass.: Belknap Press of Harvard Univ. Press, 1980.

Miller, Wayne Charles, and others. *Comprehensive Bibliography for the Study of American Minorities*. 2 vols. New York: New York Univ. Press, 1976.

MINORITIES—BIBLIOGRAPHIES

Note: Most sources on Afro-Americans are listed throughout this guide.

Hirschfelder, Arlene B.; Byler, Mary Gloyne; and Dorris, Michael A. *Guide to Research on North American Indians*. Chicago: American Library Assoc., 1983.

Herrera, Diane. *Puerto Ricans and Other Minority Groups in the United States: An Annotated Bibliography*. Detroit: Blaine Eldridge Books, 1979.

Newman, Richard. *Black Access*. Westport, Conn.: Greenwood, 1984.

Prucha, Francis Paul. *A Bibliographical Guide to the History of Indian-White Relations in the United States*. Chicago: Univ. of Chicago Press, 1977.

————. *Indian-White Relations: A Bibliography of Works Published 1975–1980*. Lincoln: Univ. of Nebraska Press, 1982.

Robinson, Barbara J., and Robinson, J. Cordell. *The Mexican-American: A Critical Guide to Research Aids*. Greenwich, Conn.: JAI-Press, 1980.

WOMEN

Ballou, Patricia K. *Women: A Bibliography of Bibliographies*. 2d ed. Boston: G. K. Hall, 1986.

Searing, Susan E. *Introduction to Library Research in Women's Studies*. Boulder, Col.: Westview Press, 1985.

Stineman, Esther F. *Women's Studies: A Recommended Core Bibliography*. Littleton, Col.: Libraries Unlimited, 1979.

Continued by:

Loeb, Catherine R.; Searing, Susan E.; and Stineman, Esther F. *Women's Studies: A Recommended Core Bibliography, 1980–1985*. Littleton, Col.: Libraries Unlimited, 1987.

Possible LCSH Subject Headings

In addition to the headings suggested here, see names of races, tribes, etc. (CAUCASIAN RACE, GUAYAQUI INDIANS) and the subdivision RACE RELATIONS under the names of countries (AFRICA—RACE RELATIONS). And see the list of tribes under the geographic subdivisions for ETHNOLOGY, a list that is literally pages long. Look also at the many possibilities under MINORITIES, which can also be subdivided geographically. Ethnic groups and minorities may be searched by looking under the name directly, e.g. AFRO-AMERICANS.

ACCULTURATION
AFRO-AMERICANS (and ASIAN AMERICANS,
   ITALIAN AMERICANS, etc.)
ANTHROPOLOGY
ARCHAEOLOGY
BLACKS
CIVILIZATION
COLOR OF MAN
ECONOMIC ANTHROPOLOGY
ETHNIC GROUPS
ETHNOLOGY (and the long list of geographic subdivi-
   sions with names of tribes)
FOLKLORE
HEAD-HUNTERS
HUMAN BEHAVIOR
INDIANS OF NORTH AMERICA
MAN

MINORITIES
MINORITIES—HOUSING
MINORITIES—POLITICAL ACTIVITY
NATIVE RACES
PHYSICAL ANTHROPOLOGY
POLITICAL ANTHROPOLOGY
RACE RELATIONS
SOCIALIZATION
URBAN ANTHROPOLOGY
WOMEN (see LCSH for possibilities)

Bibliographies and Guides

Arthur and Elizabeth Schlesinger Library on the History of Women. Radcliffe College. *The Manuscript Inventories and the Catalogs of the Manuscripts, Books and Pictures.* 2d ed., rev. and enl. 10 vols. Boston: G. K. Hall, 1984.

Frantz, Charles. *The Student Anthropologist's Handbook: A Guide to Research, Training and Career.* Cambridge, Mass.: Schenkman, 1972.

Human Relations Area Files. (HRAF) New Haven: Human Relations Area Files, 195–   . (See complete information under "Indexes" below.)

International Bibliography of Social and Cultural Anthropology. 1955–   . Prepared by the International Committee for Social Sciences Documentation in cooperation with the International Congress of Anthropological and Ethnological Sciences. London: Tavistock; Chicago: Aldine, 1958–   . Annual.

Indexes

Abstracts in Anthropology. Westport, Conn: Greenwood Periodicals, 1970–   . Quarterly.

Harvard University. *Peabody Museum of Archaeology and Ethnology. Library. Catalogue: Authors.* 26 vols. Boston: G. K. Hall, 1963.

————. Supps. 1–4. 14 vols. Boston: 1970–1979.

————. *Catalogue: Subjects.* 27 vols. Boston: G. K. Hall, 1963.

————. Supps. 1–4 16 vols. Boston: 1970–1979.

Continued by:

Anthropological Literature: An Index to Periodical Articles and Essays. Compiled by the Tozzer Library, Peabody Museum of Archaeology and Ethnology, Harvard University. Pleasantville, N.Y.: Redgrave Pub., 1979–   . Quarterly.

Human Relations Area Files (HRAF). A collection of data, in hard copy or in microform, on approximately 325 primitive and contemporary cultures. New Haven: HRAF. The key to cultural groups is George Murdock's *Outline of World Cultures* (6th rev. ed. New Haven: HRAF, 1983) and the key to subject categories is the *Outline of Cultural Materials* (5th ed. New Haven: HRAF, 1982). There is a guide by Robert O. Lagace, *Nature and Use of the HRAF Files: A Research and Teaching Guide* (New Haven: HRAF, 1974).

Women's Studies Abstracts. Rush, N.Y.: Women's Studies, 1972–   . Quarterly with Annual Index.

Intellectual Life and Popular Culture

There is some connection here because one person's popular culture can be another person's intellectual life and vice versa—making the boundaries blur. Taking a cue from the Library of Congress, works on art, literature, and music produced for the general public, i.e. for mass consumption, are entered under the subject heading POPULAR CULTURE. Works on traditional, "high" culture are entered under the heading INTELLECTUAL LIFE. KITSCH as a reflection of popular culture is also included as a heading, because it is calculated to have mass appeal though it is sometimes considered a form of "bad" or pretentious art.

This segment will discuss intellectual life and popular culture in very general terms so you can see *examples* of the kind of titles that fall here and so you'll know that some of these interesting subject headings exist. Then the discussion will deal specifically with "Books" and with "Education." Other related material is found under "Arts and Performing Arts" later in this part. Once again the literature, art, and music of each age reflect its tastes and preoccupations, and so looking at these areas is a way of discerning culture at a given time. The *Dictionary of the History of Ideas* (see "Beliefs") is included again because it applies here as well.

Useful Titles

Abel, Lionel. *The Intellectual Follies: A Memoir of the Literary Venture in New York and Paris*. New York: Norton, 1984.

Ain't We Got Fun? Essays, Lyrics, and Stories of the Twenties. Edited by Barbara H. Solomon. New York: New American Library, 1980.

The American Dimension: Cultural Myths and Social Realities. Edited by Susan P. Montague. 2d ed. Sherman Oaks, Cal.: Alfred Pub., 1981.

American Popular Entertainments: Jokes, Monologues, Bits, and Sketches. Edited by Brooks McNamara. New York: Performing Arts Journal Publications, 1983.

American Writers in Paris, 1920–1939. Edited by Karen Lane Rood. Detroit: Gale, 1980.

Brooks, John. *Showing Off in America: From Conspicuous Consumption to Parody Display.* Boston: Little, Brown, 1981.

Brown, Curtis F. *Star-Spangled Kitsch: An Astounding and Tastelessly Illustrated Exposition of the Bawdy, Gaudy, Shoddy Mass-Art Culture in This Grand Land of Ours.* New York: Universe Books, 1975.

Calinescu, Matei. *Faces of Modernity: Avante-Garde, Decadence, Kitsch.* Bloomington, Ind.: Indiana Univ. Press, 1977.

Celebonovic, Aleksa. *Some Call It Kitsch: Masterpieces of Bourgeois Realism.* New York: Abrams, 1974.

Dales, Richard C. *The Intellectual Life of Western Europe in the Middle Ages.* Wash., D.C.: University Press of America, 1980.

Dictionary of the History of Ideas: Studies of Selected Pivotal Ideas. Edited by Philip P. Weiner. 4 vols. New York: Scribner's, 1973–1974.

Dorfles, Gillo. *Kitsch: The World of Bad Taste.* New York: Universe Books, 1969.

5000 Years of Popular Culture: Popular Culture Before Printing. Edited by Fred E. H. Schroeder. Bowling Green, Ohio: Bowling Green Univ. Popular Press, 1980.

Gowans, Alan. *Learning to See: Historical Perspectives on Modern Popular/Commercial Arts.* Bowling Green, Ohio: Bowling Green Univ. Popular Press, 1981.

Handbook of American Popular Culture. Edited by Thomas Inge. 3 vols. Westport, Conn.: Greenwood Press, 1978–1981.

Longley, Marjorie, et al. *America's Taste, 1850–1959.* New York: Simon & Schuster, 1960.

Nisbet, Robert. *History of the Idea of Progress.* New York: Basic Books, 1980.

Perry, Lewis. *Intellectual Life in America: A History.* New York: Watts, 1984.

The Praeger Encyclopedia of Ancient Civilization. By Pierre Devambez, et al. New York: Praeger, 1967.

Seligman, Ben B., comp. *Molders of Modern Thought.* Chicago: Quadrangle Books, 1970.

Suhr, Elmer George. *The Ancient Mind and Its Heritage.* 2 vols. New York: Exposition Press, 1959–1960.

Viorst, Milton. *The Great Documents of Western Civilization.* Philadelphia: Chilton Books, 1965.

Possible LCSH Subject Headings

As noted above, works of art, literature, and music produced for mass consumption are entered under POPULAR CULTURE and works on traditional, "high" culture are entered under INTELLECTUAL LIFE. INTELLECTUAL LIFE may be used as a subdivision under the names of countries, cities, etc. (UNITED STATES—INTELLECTUAL LIFE). INTELLECTUAL LIFE may also be used under the names of ethnic or religious groups (CATHOLICS—INTELLECTUAL LIFE). INTELLECTUAL LIFE can also be divided by time periods. CIVILIZATION is also used as an approach to this subject. TASTE is a heading only when referring to physiology and psychology and if the meaning is aesthetics, you are referred to the heading AESTHETICS.

AESTHETICS
BYZANTINE EMPIRE—INTELLECTUAL LIFE (as example; see note above)
CIVILIZATION
CULTURAL POLICY

CULTURE
CULTURE CONFLICT
GERMANY—INTELLECTUAL LIFE—19TH CENTURY (as example; see note above.)
INTELLECTUAL LIFE (also used as subdivision—see note above)
INTELLECTUAL LIFE—HISTORY
INTELLECTUAL LIFE—19TH CENTURY (20th Century, etc.)
INTELLECTUAL PROPERTY
INTELLECTUALS
INTELLECTUALS IN LITERATURE
KITSCH
LEARNING AND SCHOLARSHIP
MANNERS AND CUSTOMS
MASS MEDIA AND THE ARTS
MASS SOCIETY
POPULAR CULTURE (also used as a subdivision—see note above)
POPULAR CULTURE—ECONOMIC ASPECTS (also a possible subdivision)
POPULAR LITERATURE
STREET LITERATURE
SALONS
SALONS—FRANCE
SALONS—FRANCE—PARIS

Indexes

Most general indexes are useful. See "Periodicals" segment in part 2.

Books

Sometimes convincing fictional conversation or even gossip may center on books or a certain time or place, and books may be a subject in fiction. What would a heroine in 1890 be reading, or what books would a schoolteacher in 1925 be teaching? What were the plots of old best-sellers, and what *were* the best-sellers? What was shocking when first published, and what was banned in Boston? There are reference books that answer these questions, and there are works like the *American Book Trade Directory* that will tell you the names of bookstores in various cities if a character is in need of one. They also describe a bookseller's specialty—foreign language books, science and technology, etc.

For information on locating fiction by subject, see the segment "Finding Other Fiction by Subject," in part 5.

The general sources about books and literature listed here are for the purposes of fiction writing, not usually literary criticism, except for the indexes and book review sources. (Among other uses, the book reviews will tell you how someone like Hemingway was received when he first published.) First listed are books about the book trade and the year in publishing; the *Bowker Annual* covers the library field as well and lists what books sold the best, etc. The titles help to identify famous works, with the Magill titles (formerly *Masterplots*) giving the plots of famous books, and *80 Years of Best Sellers* telling what sold and what shocked for various years and discussing the runners-up. (Until that is updated, the *Bowker Annual* can be used to find the best-sellers for the years from 1975 forward.) The *Annals of American Literature* and the *Annals of English Literature* give the principal publications of each year along with some major events and the births and deaths of famous authors. The bibliographies offer lists of books printed in certain years and, though *Books in Print* for the United States is given here, there are "books in print" for Great Britain, France, Germany, and many other countries as well. Ask a reference librarian if you need to consult the *National Union Catalog* of the Library of Congress (not listed below), a comprehensive list of foreign and English language titles, with a subject index from 1950 to the present. The *Literary History of the United States* and *A Literary History of England* give comprehensive surveys and chronologies of what was published and when, as does the Rogal book, *A Chronological Outline of American Literature*. The Cambridge and Oxford histories will identify and briefly describe well-known works, and though the English and Americans are listed here, there are Oxford companions for various foreign language literatures. The Cassells set has essays on national literatures also.

Book Trade

American Book Trade Directory: Lists of Publishers, Booksellers, Periodicals, Trade Organizations, Wholesalers, etc. New York: Bowker, 1915– . Biennial.

Book Publishing Annual. By the Book Division of R. R. Bowker in collaboration with the staff of Publishers Weekly. (Continues *Publishers Weekly Yearbook.*) New York: Bowker, 1984– . Annual.

The Bowker Annual of Library and Book Trade Information. Sponsored by the Council of National Library Associations. New York: Bowker, 1956– . Annual.

BPR: American Book Publishing Record. New York: Bowker, 1960– . Monthly. Annual cumulations.

International Literary Marketplace. New York: Bowker, 1965– . Biennial.

Literary Market Place: The Business Directory of American Book Publishing. New York: Bowker, 1940– . Annual.

McMurtrie, Douglas C. *The Book: The Story of Printing and Bookmaking.* 3d ed. New York: Oxford Univ. Press, 1943.

Publishers Trade List Annual. A collection of publishers' catalogs. Not all publishers included. New York: Bowker, 1873– . Annual.

U.S. Book Publishing and Directory. White Plains, N.Y.: Knowledge Industry, 1979– . Annual.

Useful Titles

Annuals of American Literature, 1602–1983. Edited by Richard M. Ludwig and Clifford A. Nault, Jr. New York: Oxford, 1986.

Annals of English Literature, 1475–1950: The Principal Publications of Each Year Together with An Alphabetical Index of Authors and Their Works. 2d ed. Oxford: Clarendon, 1961.

Baugh, Albert Croll. *Literary History of England.* 2d ed. 4 vols. London: Routledge & Kegan Paul, 1967.

Benet, William Rose. *Benet's Reader's Encyclopedia.* 3d rev. ed. Harper & Row, 1987.

Cambridge History of American Literature. Edited by William Peterfield Trent et al. 4 vols. New York: Putnam, 1917–1921.

Cambridge History of English Literature. Edited by A. W. Ward and A. W. Waller. 15 vols. Cambridge: Cambridge Univ. Press, 1907–1933.

Cassell's Encyclopedia of World Literature. Rev. and enl. J. Buchannan Brown, gen. ed. 3 vols. London: Cassell, 1973.

Columbia Dictionary of Modern European Literature. 2d ed. Jean-Albert Bede and William B. Edgerton, gen. eds. New York: Columbia Univ. Press, 1980.

Encyclopedia of World Literature in the 20th Century. Rev. ed. Leonard S. Klein, gen. ed. 4 vols. New York: Ungar, 1981–1984.

Great Books of the Western World and the Great Ideas. Editor in Chief, Robert Maynard Hutchins: Associate Editor, Mortimer J. Adler. 54 vols. Chicago: Encyclopaedia Britannica, 1952. Vols. 2–3, entitled *The Great Ideas: Synopticon* (Mortimer J. Adler, Ed. in Chief), are a guide and index to reading.

Hackett, Alice P., and Burke, James H. *80 Years of Best Sellers, 1895–1975.* New York: Bowker, 1977.

Hart, James David. *Oxford Companion to American Literature.* 5th ed. New York: Oxford Univ. Press, 1983.

Literary History of the United States. 4th ed. Edited by Robert E. Spiller, et al. 2 vols. New York: Macmillan, 1974.

Magill, Frank Northen. *Survey of Contemporary Literature.* Rev. ed. 12 vols. Englewood Cliffs, N.J.: Salem Press, 1977. In a sense, continued by the title below.

Magill's Literary Annual. Englewood Cliffs, N.J.: Salem Press, 1978–   . Annual.

Oxford History of English Literature. Edited by Frank Percy Wilson and Bonamy Dobree. Oxford: Clarendon, 1945– (1986–). In progress. To be 12 vols.

Princeton Encyclopedia of Poetry and Poetics. Enl. ed. Edited by Alex Preminger. Princeton, N.J.: Princeton Univ. Press, 1974.

The Reader's Advisor; A Layman's Guide to Literature. 13th ed. 3 vols. New York: Bowker, 1986–   .

Rogal, Samuel. *A Chronological Outline of American Literature.* Westport, Conn.: Greenwood, 1987.

Book Reviews

Book Review Digest. New York: Wilson, 1906–   . Monthly with annual cumulations.

Book Review Index. Detroit: Gale, 1965–   . Bimonthly.

Combined Retrospective Index to Book Reviews in Scholarly Journals, 1896–1974. 15 vols. Arlington, Va.: Carrollton Press, 1979–1982.

The New York Times Book Review Index, 1896–1970. The New York Times and Arno Press, 1973. (And use the *New York Times Index* under "Book Reviews.")

Possible LCSH Subject Headings

BOOKS AND READING is the heading used for works on the significance of reading in people's lives, including their attitudes toward and interest in reading. This is also used as a subdivision under classes of persons, ethnic groups, or names of individuals for works that discuss their reading interests and/or lists of recommended reading for the group, e.g. AFRO-AMERICANS—BOOKS AND READING, COLLEGE STUDENTS—BOOKS AND READING, SHAKESPEARE, WILLIAM, 1564–1616—BOOKS AND READING. For national literature use AMERICAN LITERATURE, MEXI-CAN LITERATURE, etc., and the subdivision LITER-ATURES under the names of countries, cities, etc.

AMERICAN LITERATURE (see note above)
AUTHORS AND READERS
BEST SELLERS
BIBLIOGRAPHY—BEST BOOKS
BOOK BURNING
BOOKS
BOOKS—HISTORY
BOOKS—HISTORY—TO 400 (etc. for other time periods)
BOOKS—PSYCHOLOGY
BOOKS—REVIEWS
BOOKS AND READING (also used as a subdivision; see note above)
CLASSICAL LITERATURE
LITERARY CALENDARS
LITERATURE
LITERATURE—HISTORY AND CRITICISM
LITERATURE—RESEARCH
LITERATURE, ANCIENT
LITERATURE, COMPARATIVE
LITERATURE, IMMORAL
LITERATURE, MEDIEVAL
LITERATURE, MODERN
POLITICS AND LITERATURE
POPULAR LITERATURE
PRINTING—HISTORY
PUBLISHERS AND PUBLISHING

Indexes

Arts & Humanities Citation Index. Philadelphia: Institute for Scientific Information, 1978–   .

British Humanities Index. London: Library Association, 1963–   .

Essay and General Literature Index. New York: Wilson, 1914–

MLA International Bibliography of Books and Articles on the Modern Languages and Literature. Chicago: Modern Language Association, 1921–   .

Bibliographies and Guides

Altick, Richard D., and Wright, Andrew. *Selective Bibliography for the Study of English and American Literature.* 6th ed. New York: Macmillan, 1979.

Books in Print. (BIP) (Authors and Titles) New York: Bowker, 1948–   . Annual.

Subject Guide to Books in Print. New York: Bowker, 1957–   . Annual. There are three volumes for authors, three volumes for titles, and four volumes for subjects. Bowker also publishes *Forthcoming Books,* a bimonthly updating of BIP.

Cumulative Book Index, a World List of Books in the English Language. New York: Wilson, 1933–   . Monthly with cumulations.

Fenster, Valmai Kirkham. *Guide to American Literature.* Littleton, Colo.: Libraries Unlimited, 1983.

New Cambridge Bibliography of English Literature. 5 vols. Cambridge: Cambridge Univ. Press, 1969–77.

Paperbound Books in Print. New York: Bowker, 1955–   . Semiannual.

Education

If your play or story is actually set in a university, it's best to experience the ivy, so to speak, firsthand, but there are lots of times when just the suggestion of a good education or a degree is all that's needed. As usual, if you are in need of details about a college or university, look in the library catalog under the name of the university first, because there are frequently books written about individual institutions. College catalogs are useful, and there is a set on microfiche that many libraries own. For brief descriptions check some of the titles listed below.

One title, the *World of Learning,* merits special attention. It is a Europa Publication arranged by country and lists learned societies and research institutes, libraries, museums, universities, and other institutions of higher education. For most institutions it gives administrators and faculties. Information on UNESCO and international councils and organizations is also provided. *World of Learning* is an annual that began in 1947, so you can go back to those years for historical information on learned societies, universities, etc.

If you give a character a Ph.D. in something from Ohio State, you can make sure if Ohio State offers a Ph.D. in that discipline—in addition to college catalogs. the *College Blue Book* has a volume that lists programs by degrees offered. General information on colleges and universities is in that multivolume set and others including *American Universities and Colleges. Patterson's American Education* lists public and private schools, has an arrangement by state, and covers educational systems and associations. If your characters are into college alternatives, try the Bear book for ideas. For college colors, use H. L. Snyder and for fraternities, the work by Baird.

Useful Titles

American Universities and Colleges. 12th ed. New York: W. de-Gruyter, 1983.

American Community, Technical, and Junior Colleges. New York: American Council on Education/Macmillan, 1984.

Baird's Manual of American College Fraternities. 19th ed. Menasha, Wis.: George Banta, 1977.

Bear, John Bjorn. *The Alternative Guide to College Degrees and Non-Traditional Higher Education.* New York: Stonesong Press, 1980.

College Blue Book. Yonkers, N.Y.: C. E. Burckel, 1923– . Irregular. (19th ed. 1983)

Comparative Guide to American Colleges, for Students, Parents, and Counselors. 11th ed. New York: Harper & Row, 1983.

Encyclopedia of Education. Edited by Lee C. Deighton. New York: Macmillan, 1971.

Handbook of Private Schools. Boston: Sargent, 1915–   . Annual.

The International Encyclopedia of Education: Research and Studies. Oxford and New York: Pergamon, 1985.

Patterson's American Education. Mount Prospect, Ill.: Educ. Directories, 1904–   . Annual.

Peterson's Annual Guide to Independent Secondary Schools. Princeton, N.J.: Peterson's Guides, 1980–   . Annual.

Snyder, Henry L. *Our College Colors.* Kutztown, Pa.: Kutztown Pub., 1949.

Study Abroad. Paris: UNESO, 1948–   . Annual originally, now biennial.

World of Learning. London: Europa, 1947–   . Annual.

Possible LCSH Subject Headings

There are some who believe their lives might have been very different if they had known there was a subject heading EDUCATION OF PRINCESSES. Actually, a fiction writer may be able to use that heading. Another heading to contemplate, but only if you're up to it, is INEFFICIENCY, INTELLECTUAL. Education is, of course, a heading, and it is also a subdivision under the names of denominations, sects, classes of people, social groups, etc.; e.g. JESUITS—EDUCATION; CHILDREN OF MIGRANT LABORERS—EDUCATION. Another subdivision that can be used under special subjects is STUDY AND TEACHING; e.g., SCIENCE—STUDY AND TEACHING. Under EDUCATION there are almost two columns of related headings, so look them over.

BASIC EDUCATION
CLASSICAL EDUCATION
EDUCATION

EDUCATION—AIMS AND OBJECTIVES
EDUCATION—CHINA (etc.—other geographic subdivisions)
EDUCATION—CURRICULA
EDUCATION—EXPERIMENTAL METHODS
EDUCATION—HISTORY
EDUCATION—PHILOSOPHY
EDUCATION—RESEARCH
EDUCATION, BILINGUAL
EDUCATION, COLONIAL
EDUCATION, COMPULSORY
EDUCATION, ELEMENTARY
EDUCATION, GREEK
EDUCATION, HIGHER
EDUCATION, MEDIEVAL
EDUCATION, PRIMITIVE
EDUCATION, RURAL
EDUCATION AND CRIME
EDUCATIONAL INNOVATIONS
EDUCATIONAL PSYCHOLOGY
LEARNING
LEARNING, PSYCHOLOGY OF
LEARNING ABILITY
LEARNING AND SCHOLARSHIP
LEARNING BY DISCOVERY

Indexes

Current Index to Journals in Education. Phoenix, Ariz.: Oryx Press, 1969–   . Monthly, with semiannual cumulations.

Education Index. New York: Wilson, 1932–   . Monthly, with cumulations.

Bibliographies and Guides

Cordasco, Francesco, et al. *The History of American Education; A Guide to Information Sources.* Detroit: Gale, 1979.

Paulston, Rolland G. *Non-Formal Education: An Annotated International Bibliography*. New York: Praeger, 1972.

Woodbury, Marda. *A Guide to Sources of Educational Information*. 2d ed. Arlington, Va.: Information Resources Press, 1982.

Manners and Customs

For those who break the social rules and conventions of society there is no formal trial or sentence. Usually the penalty for a breach of etiquette is the disapproval of the group that has established the norms of behavior, norms simply mandated by custom. The manners and customs of certain groups tell us a lot about those people, and the flaunting of certain customs can have consequences serious enough to start a good story.

As prehistoric people began to interact, they learned to behave in ways that made life easier, and usually early manners began with a practical purpose—it is believed that early humans extended and shook hands to show friendship and to indicate that they were not carrying weapons. "Good manners" is a concept that has existed for some time, with royal courts setting the pace and more and more elaborate rituals designed to create an exclusive society and keep out the unworthy. *Beowulf,* the Old English epic and poem of the early eighth century, describes the queen, "mindful of etiquette," taking the goblet first to the king and then to the courtiers. There was a great flowering of etiquette in the late eighteenth and early nineteenth centuries, still fairly exclusive, but by the middle of the twentieth century, good manners were set forth for ordinary people in everyday life, as recorded by Emily Post and Amy Vanderbilt. Today more flexible guidelines have been suggested by Charlotte Ford for "situations for which there are no longer exact standards of behavior." In her book, chapters for weddings and marriages are followed by "living together," "divorce," and "the single mother." The work by Swartz discusses good manners along with the traditions and customs of various branches of the armed forces, forms of military address, and such matters as flag etiquette.

Useful Titles

Using the subject headings listed below and related headings, you can locate books about manners and etiquette for various historical periods and written guides for different times. Some examples are old but would be useful for various time periods, so notice the publication dates. Under bibliographies the Arthur and Elizabeth Schlesinger Library catalog is given because of the large collection of historical etiquette and cookbooks. See note in segment "Historical Research," part 2, on *A History of Private Life*, which is useful here also.

Aretz, Gertrude Kuntze-Dolton. *The Elegant Woman, from the Rococo Period to Modern Times*. New York: Harcourt, Brace, 1936.

The Babees' Book: Medieval Manners for the Young: Done Into Modern English From Dr. Furnivalls' Texts by Edith Rickert. New York: Duffield, 1923.

Boehn, Max von. *Modes and Manners*. Illustrated with reproductions of contemporary paintings. Translated by Joan Joshua. 4 vols. Philadelphia: Lippincott, 1932–36.

Brash, Rudolph. *How Did It Begin? Customs and Superstitions, and Their Romantic Origins*. New York: D. McKay, 1965.

———. *There's a Reason for Everything: More Customs and Superstitions and How They All Began*. Melbourne, Aust.: Fontana/Collins, 1982.

Brockman, Mary. *What's She Like? A Personality Book for Girls*. New York: Scribner's, 1936.

Brooke, Iris. *Pleasures of the Past: A Lighthearted Commentary on the Enjoyments of Past Generations*. London: Odhams, 1955.

Brosse, Jacques, and others. *100,000 Years of Daily Life: A Visual History*. New York: Golden Press, 1961.

Dowd, Jerome. *Control in Human Societies.* New York: Appleton Century, 1936.

Elias, Norbert. *The Civilizing Process.* Translated by Edmund Jephcott. New York: Citizen Books, 1978–1982.

——. *The Court Society.* Oxford: Blackwell, 1983.

——. *The Quest for Excitement: Sport and Leisure in the Civilizing Process.* Oxford: Blackwell, 1986.

Hirst, David. *Comedy of Manners.* London: Methuen, 1979.

Laver, James. *The Age of Illusion: Manners and Morals, 1750–1848.* London: Weidenfeld & Nicolson, 1972.

Walsh, William Shepard. *Curiosities of Popular Customs and of Rites, Ceremonies, Observances, and Miscellaneous Antiquities.* Philadelphia: Lippincott. 1898. (Rep. Detroit: Gale, 1966.)

Contemporary Guides

Some of the late editions listed here have been publishing for some time (Emily Post and Amy Vanderbilt, for example) so remember that an edition from the 30s or 40s, etc., might be consulted for manners in different eras.

Baldridge, Letitia. *Letitia Baldridge's Complete Guide to Executive Manners.* Edited by Sandi Gelles-Cole. New York: Rawson Associates, 1985.

Ford, Charlotte. *Charlotte Ford's Book of Modern Manners.* New York: Simon & Schuster, 1980.

McCaffree, Mary Jane, and Innis, Pauline B. *Protocol: The Complete Handbook of Diplomatic, Official, and Social Usage.* Englewood Cliffs, N.J.: Prentice-Hall, 1977.

Martin, Judith. *Miss Manners' Guide to Excruciatingly Correct Behavior.* New York: Atheneum, 1982.

Post, Emily. *Emily Post's Etiquette.* 14th ed. Rev. by Elizabeth L. Post. New York: Harper & Row, 1984.

Swartz, Oretha. *Service Etiquette.* 3d ed. Annapolis: Naval Institute Press, 1977.

Vanderbilt, Amy. *The Amy Vanderbilt Complete Book of Etiquette: A Guide to Contemporary Living*. Rev. and expanded by Letitia Baldridge. Garden City, N.Y.: Doubleday, 1978.

Possible LCSH Subject Headings

See the LCSH related headings under MANNERS AND CUSTOMS for suggestions like EXCUSES and FAREWELLS as well as splendid headings like KISSING and HUGGING, which have many customs if not manners. The subdivision in this category under the names of countries, cities, and under the names of ethnic groups is SOCIAL LIFE AND CUSTOMS; e.g. ITALY—SOCIAL LIFE AND CUSTOMS.

ACADEMIC ETIQUETTE
AFRO-AMERICANS—SOCIAL LIFE AND CUSTOMS
   (subdivision under ethnic groups; see note above)
BUSINESS ETIQUETTE
CHURCH ETIQUETTE
DIPLOMATIC ETIQUETTE
ETIQUETTE
ETIQUETTE—AUSTRALIA (BRAZIL, etc.)
ETIQUETTE—BIBLIOGRAPHY
ETIQUETTE—EARLY WORKS TO 1800
ETIQUETTE—HISTORY
ETIQUETTE FOR CHILDREN AND YOUTH
ETIQUETTE FOR MEN
ETIQUETTE FOR WOMEN
ISLAMIC ETIQUETTE
JEWISH ETIQUETTE
LEGAL ETIQUETTE
MANNERS AND CUSTOMS
MANNERS AND CUSTOMS—HISTORY
MANNERS AND CUSTOMS—ORIGINS
MANNERS AND CUSTOMS—PICTORIAL WORKS
MANNERS AND CUSTOMS—PSYCHOLOGICAL
   WORKS

MOURNING ETIQUETTE
UNITED STATES—SOCIAL LIFE AND CUSTOMS (sub-
division under countries and cities; see note above)
WEDDING ETIQUETTE

Indexes

Most general indexes can be used for this subject.

Bibliographies

Arthur and Elizabeth Schlesinger Library on the History of Women
in America. Radcliffe College. *The Manuscript Inventories and
the Catalogs of Manuscripts, Books, and Periodicals.* 2d rev. ed.
Boston: G. K. Hall, 1984.

Bobbitt, Mary Reed. *A Bibliography of Etiquette Books Published
in America Before 1900.* New York: New York Public Library,
1947. (Repr. from the New York Public Library *Bulletin*, Dec.
1947.)

Art and the
Performing Arts

Art here means fine art, and it is combined with the performing arts because they share some common research ground and because much of what is performed is also certainly fine. Art will be discussed first, followed by dance, movies, music, theater, and TV/radio in randomly chosen order, without judgment, without declaring one better than the other. The art of living is best and an artfully lived life must surely include them all. The newer arts have fewer classic research sources, but not for long. "Kitsch"—pretentious art, writing, etc.—though related to art, is treated in this guide as popular culture under the segment "Intellectual Life and Popular Culture."

Art

Art here means the visual arts, including architecture, painting, and sculpture. There are many wonderful books about art, including some classics that preceded the age of the coffee table and are without today's spectacular photography. Of course, as mentioned often, looking at the paintings of a particular time and place can assist writers with their verbal descriptions of that era and location. And it seems that almost every aspect of art has also been covered, including famous forgeries, which frequently make good fiction. Authors can choose to have a character show his good taste and knowledge of art, as James Bond does, and can research a subject that personally interests them so that they may enjoy a mini-education in a subject they may always have wanted to pursue.

An excellent two-volume survey of art covering various times and centuries, as well as type of art, is Gardner's *Art Through the Ages*. Extensive bibliographies for each chapter topic augment the work, which is also well illustrated. The multivolume *Encyclopedia of World Art* is another excellent source covering all ages and styles, well documented with bibliographies and illustrated. The Janson work is a superior history, and the Honour visual arts history has a chronological treatment covering a broad geographical range. The *American Art Directory* provides information on art organizations, schools, museums, and libraries. The Jones guide, *Art Research Methods and Resources: A Guide to Finding Art Information*, is particularly helpful. General and survey books are listed below; books on various kinds of art (abstract, Chinese, Greek, etc.) are not listed here, but careful use of the subject headings described below will retrieve such material. As always, choose the most specific heading first and go to a broader heading if necessary.

Useful Titles—Art

The Britannica Encyclopaedia of American Art. Chicago: Encyclopaedia Britannica Educational Corp., 1973.

Encyclopedia of Painting: Painters and Painting of the World from Prehistoric Times to the Present Day. 4th rev. ed. Edited by Bernard S. Myers, New York: Crown, 1979.

Encyclopedia of World Art. 16 vols. New York: McGraw-Hill, 1959–1983.

Gardner, Helen. *Art Through the Ages.* 7th ed. Revised by Horst de la Croix and Richard Tansey. 2 vols. New York: Harcourt, 1980.

Honour, Hugh, and Fleming, John. *The Visual Arts: A History.* Englewood Cliffs, N.J.: Prentice-Hall, 1982.

Janson, Horst Woldemar, and Janson, Dora Jane. *History of Art: A Survey of the Major Visual Arts from the Dawn of History to the*

Present Day. 3d ed. Revised and expanded by Anthony F. Janson. New York: Abrams, 1986.

McGraw-Hill Dictionary of Art. Edited by Bernard S. Myers. 5 vols. New York: McGraw-Hill, 1969.

Oxford Companion to Twentieth Century Art. Edited by Harold Osborne. Oxford & New York: Oxford Univ. Press, 1981.

Read, Sir Herbert Edward. *A Concise History of Modern Painting.* 3d ed. New York: Praeger, 1975.

DIRECTORIES

American Art Directory. New York: Bowker, 1899–   . Triennial since 1952.

Directory of Museums and Living Displays. 3d ed. Edited by Kenneth Hudson and Ann Nicolls. New York: Stockton Press, 1985.

Museums of the World. 3d rev. ed. New York: Saur, 1981.

The Official Museum Directory. New York: American Association of Museums and Crowell-Collier Educ., 1971–   . Annual.

ARCHITECTURE

Ehresmann, Donald L. *Architecture: A Bibliographic Guide to Basic Reference Works, Histories, and Handbooks.* Littleton, Colo.: Libraries Unlimited, 1984.

Encyclopedia of Architectural Technology. Edited by Pedro Guedes. New York: McGraw-Hill, 1979.

Fletcher, Sir Banister. *Sir Banister Fletcher's A History of Architecture.* 19th ed. Edited by John Musgrove. London: Butterworths, 1987.

Hamlin, Talbot Faulkner. *Architecture Through the Ages.* Rev. ed. New York: Putnam, 1953.

Hunt, William Dudley. *Encyclopedia of American Architecture.* New York: McGraw-Hill, 1980.

SPECIAL ASPECTS

Clapp, Jane. *Art Censorship: A Chronology of Proscribed and Prescribed Art*. Metuchen, N.J.: Scarecrow Press, 1972.

Daniel, Howard. *Encyclopedia of Themes and Subjects in Painting: Mythological, Biblical, Historical, Literary, Allegorical and Topical*. New York: Abrams, 1971.

Hall, James. *Dictionary of Subjects and Symbols in Art*. Rev. ed. London: Murray, 1979.

Mayer, Ralph. *The Artist's Handbook of Materials and Techniques*. Rev. and updated. New York: Viking Press, 1981.

FORGERIES

Arnau, Frank. *The Art of the Faker: Three Thousand Years of Deception*. Boston: Little, Brown, 1961.

The Forger's Art: Forgery and the Philosophy of Art. Edited by Denis Dutton. Berkeley: Univ. of California Press, 1983.

Jeppson, Lawrence. *The Fabulous Frauds: Fascinating Tales of Great Art Forgeries*. New York: Weybright and Talley, 1970.

Reisner, Robert George. *Fakes and Forgeries in the Fine Arts: A Bibliography*. New York: Special Libraries Assoc., 1950.

Possible LCSH Subject Headings—Art

General works on the visual arts (architecture, painting, sculpture, etc.) are entered under ART, singular. Works on the arts in general, including literature, the visual arts, and the performing arts, are entered under ARTS, plural. Both are included briefly here, but the singular ART is most directly related to this section on the visual arts. In the Library of Congress list of subject headings, there are almost two pages of related headings under ART, so look at them. They include headings to specific topics in art, ranging from HAND IN ART and NUDE IN ART to LAUGHTER IN ART and WOMEN IN ART, to specific kinds of art, IMPRESSIONISM

(ART) and EXPRESSIONISM (ART) and CUBISM, for example.

AFRO-AMERICAN ARTISTS
ARCHITECTURE
ARCHITECTURE—DESIGNS AND PLANS
ARCHITECTURE—DETAILS (see also "Domes," "Doors," "Gables," etc.)
ART
ART—BIBLIOGRAPHY
ART—EXTRATERRESTRIAL INFLUENCES
ART—FORGERIES
ART—HISTORY
ART—MUSEUMS
ART—POLITICAL ASPECTS
ART, ABSTRACT
ART, AFRICAN
ART, ANCIENT
ART, GREEK (and ART, AMERICAN; ART, FRENCH; etc.)
ART, MODERN
ART, MODERN—19TH CENTURY—HISTORY
ARTISANS
ARTIST COLONIES
ARTISTS
ARTISTS—RELATIONSHIP WITH WOMEN
ARTISTS, BLACK
ARTISTS, JEWISH
ARTISTS, MEDIEVAL
ARTISTS, NAVAJO
ARTS
ARTS—CENSORSHIP
ARTS—HISTORY
ARTS—SOCIAL ASPECTS
ARTS—THERAPEUTIC
ARTS, AMERICAN (and ARTS, CHINESE; ARTS, FRENCH; etc.)
ARTS, VICTORIAN

ARTS AND CRAFTS MOVEMENT
ETHNIC ARTS
HANDICRAFTS
PAINTING
PAINTING—HISTORY
PAINTING, ABSTRACT
PAINTING, ANCIENT
PAINTING, AMERICAN (and PAINTING, CHINESE;
    PAINTING, FLEMISH; etc.)
PORTRAIT PAINTING
POTTERS
POTTERY
PRINTMAKERS
SCULPTURE

Indexes—Art

Architectural Periodicals Index. London: British Architectural Library, 1974–   . Quarterly.

Art Index. New York: Wilson, 1930–   .

Columbia University. Libraries. Avery Architectural Library. *Avery Index to Architectural Periodicals.* 2d ed. 15 vols. Boston: G. K. Hall, 1973. Supps. 1–4, 1975–1982; other supps. in progress.

(For indexes to reproductions of paintings, see segment "Locating Pictures and Photographs," part 5).

Bibliographies and Guides—Art

Arntzen, Etta Mae, and Rainwater, Robert. *Guide to the Literature of Art History.* Chicago: American Library Assoc., 1980.

Art Books, 1876–1949. New York: Bowker, 1981.

Art Books, 1950–1979. New York: Bowker, 1979.

Arts in America: A Bibliography. Edited by Bernard Karpel. 4 vols. Washington: Smithsonian Institute Press, 1979.

Bell, Doris L. *Contemporary Art Trends, 1960–1980: A Guide to Sources*. Metuchen, N.J.: Scarecrow, 1981.

Jones, Lois Swan. *Art Research Methods and Resources: A Guide to Finding Art Information*. 2d ed. Rev. and enl. Dubuque, Ia.: Kendall/Hunt, 1984.

Dance

Useful Titles—Dance

Beaumont, Cyril William. *Complete Book of Ballets: A Guide to the Principal Ballets of the Nineteenth and Twentieth Centuries*. London: Putnam, 1951. Three supplements through 1955.

Chujoy, Anatole, and Manchester, P. W., comps. *The Dance Encyclopedia*. Rev. and enl. ed. New York: Simon & Schuster, 1967.

DeMille, Agnes. *The Book of the Dance*. New York: Golden Press, 1963.

Dictionary of Modern Ballet. Francis Gaden and Robert Maillard, gen. eds. New York: Tudor, 1959.

Encyclopedia of Dance and Ballet. Edited by Mary Clarke and David Vaughan. New York: Putnam, 1977.

Koegler, Horst. *The Concise Oxford Dictionary of Ballet*. 2d ed. London: Oxford Univ. Press, 1982.

McDonagh, Don. *The Complete Guide to Modern Dance*. Garden City, N.Y.: Doubleday, 1976.

Annuals and Indexes—Dance

Ballet Annual: A Record and Year Book of the Ballet, 1947–63. 18 vols. New York: Macmillan, 1947–1963.

Dance World. New York: Crown, 1966–1979. Annual.

Guide to Dance Periodicals, 1931/35–1961/62. 10 vols. Gainesville: Univ. of Florida Press, 1948–63.

General indexes, especially *Music Index*. See list in "Periodicals" chapter.

Possible LCSH Subject Headings—Dance

BALLERINAS
BALLET (works on scores are under the plural BALLETS.)
BALLET—COSTUME
BALLET—HISTORIOGRAPHY
BALLET—PRODUCTION AND DIRECTION
BALLET—STUDY AND TEACHING
BALLET DANCERS
BALLET DANCING
CHOREOGRAPHY
DANCE COMPANIES
DANCE ORCHESTRAS
DANCE TEACHERS
DANCE THERAPY
DANCERS
DANCING
DANCING—AESTHETICS
DANCING—PHILOSOPHY
DANCING—REVIEWS
DANCING—SOCIAL ASPECTS

And finally, DANCING MICE is really a heading.

Bibliographies—Dance

Magriel, Paul David. *A Bibliography of Dancing: A List of Books and Articles on the Dance and Related Subjects.* New York: Wilson, 1936. 4th cumulated supp. 1941.

New York Public Library, Dance Collection. *Dictionary Catalog of the Dance Collection: A list of authors, titles, and subjects of multi-media materials in the Dance Collection of the Performing Arts Research Center of the New York Public Library.* 10 vols. Boston: G.K. Hall, 1974.

Supplemented by:

———. *Bibliographic Guide to Dance, 1975–* . Boston: G. K. Hall, 1976– . Annual.

Movies

These guides will help you identify what movies were playing when and who starred in them, information useful for setting scenes and establishing time periods. *Halliwell's Film Guide* and the Magill's surveys give plot summaries (and so do some reviews). The Sadoul work gives synopses with descriptions of highlight (usually famous) scenes.

Baer, D. Richard, ed. *The Film Buff's Checklist of Motion Pictures, 1912–1979.* Hollywood: Hollywood Film Archive, 1979.

Bawden, Liz-Anne, ed. *Oxford Companion to Film.* New York: Oxford University Press, 1976.

Halliwell, Leslie. *Halliwell's Film Guide.* 5th ed. New York: Scribner's, 1986.

———. *Halliwell's Filmgoers Companion.* 8th ed. New York: Scribner's, 1984.

International Directory of Films and Filmmakers. Vol. 1, *Films.* Edited by Christopher Lyon. Chicago: St. James Press, 1984.

International Motion Picture Almanac. New York: Quigley, 1929– . Annual.

Magill, Frank N., ed. *Magill's Cinema Annual.* Englewood Cliffs, N.J.: Salem, 1982– . Annual.

———. *Magill's Survey of Cinema: English Language Films.* 1st series 4 vols. 2nd series 6 vols. Englewood Cliffs, N.J.: Salem, 1980, 1981.

———. *Magill's Survey of Cinema: Silent Films.* 3 vols. Englewood Cliffs, N.J.: Salem, 1982.

Maltin, Leonard, ed. *Leonard Maltin's TV Movies and Video Guide.* New York: New American Library, 1987.

New York Times Encyclopedia of Film, 1896–1979. Edited by Gene Brown. New York: Times Books, 1984.

Sadoul, Georges. *Dictionary of Films.* Translated, edited, and updated by Peter Morris. Berkeley: Univ. of California Press, 1972.

Slide, Anthony. *The American Film Industry: A Historical Dictionary.* Westport, Conn.: Greenwood, 1986.

————, and Wagenknecht, Edward. *Fifty Great American Silent Films, 1912–1920: A Pictorial Survey.* New York: Dover, 1980.

Possible LCSH Subject Headings—Movies

Most of these are under MOVING-PICTURES, but look in LCSH to see the long list of related headings, because there are, for example, specific headings for genre, such as HORROR FILMS, and for subjects covered in films, such as DEATH IN MOTION PICTURES, BATHS IN MOTION PICTURES, and many others.

FILM ADAPTATIONS
COMEDY FILMS
CRUELTY IN MOTION PICTURES
DEATH IN MOTION PICTURES
MARRIAGE IN MOTION PICTURES
GANGSTER FILMS
HORROR FILMS
MOVING-PICTURE ACTORS AND ACTRESSES
MOVING-PICTURE AUTHORSHIP
MOVING-PICTURE INDUSTRY
MOVING-PICTURE PLAYS
MOVING-PICTURES
MOVING-PICTURES—BIOGRAPHY
MOVING-PICTURES—CENSORSHIP
MOVING-PICTURES—MORAL AND RELIGIOUS ASPECTS
MOVING-PICTURES—PLOTS, THEMES, ETC.
MOVING-PICTURES, AMERICAN (and FRENCH, etc.)
MOVING-PICTURES, MUSICAL

Indexes—Movies

Most indexing and abstracting services will have articles on film, but there are some specific to film and entertainment. The *Readers' Guide* indexes magazines that carry articles on entertainment and reviews of movies.

Batty, Linda. *Retrospective Index to Film Periodicals, 1930–1971.* New York: Bowker, 1975.

Film Literature Index. Albany, N.Y.: Filmdex, 1974– .

International Index to Film Periodicals. New York: Bowker, 1973– .

MacCann, Richard R., and Perry, Edward S. *The New Film Index: A Bibliography of Magazine Articles in English, 1930–1970.* New York: E. P. Dutton, 1975.

New York Times Directory of the Film. New York: Arno Press, 1971.

Popular Periodical Index. Camden, N.J.: Popular Periodical Index, 1973– .

Readers' Guide to Periodical Literature. New York: Wilson, 1900– .

Reviews—Movies

Alvarez, Max J. *Index to Motion Pictures Reviewed by Variety, 1907–1980.* Metuchen, N.J.: Scarecrow, 1982.

Bowles, Stephen E. *Index to Critical Film Reviews in British and American Film Periodicals.* 3 vols. in 2. New York: Burt Franklin, 1974–75.

Film Review Annual. Englewood, N.J.: Ozer, 1981– .

Film Review Index. Edited by Patricia K. Hanson and Stephen L. Hanson. Phoenix, Ariz.: Oryx, 1986, 1987.

New York Times Film Reviews, 1913–1968. 6 vols. New York: New York Times and Arno Press, 1970.

Selected Film Criticism. Edited by Anthony Slide. Vol. 1, *1896–1911;* vol. 2, *1912–1920;* vol. 3, *1921–1930;* vol. 4, *1931–1940;* vol. 5,

1941–1950; vol. 6, *Foreign Films 1930–1950;* vol. 7, *1951–1960.* Metuchen, N.J.: Scarecrow Press, 1982–1985.

Variety Film Reviews, 1907–1980. 16 vols. New York: Garland, 1983–85.

Bibliographies and Guides—Movies

Academy of Motion Picture Arts & Sciences and the Writers Guild of America, West. *Who Wrote the Movie and What Else Did He Write? An Index of Screen Writers and Their Film Works, 1936–1969.* Los Angeles: The Academy, 1970.

Armour, Robert A. *Film: A Reference Guide.* Westport, Conn.: Greenwood Press, 1980.

Dyment, Alan R. *The Literature of Film: A Bibliographic Guide to Film as Art and Entertainment, 1936–1970.* London: White Lion, 1975.

Enser, A. G. S. *Filmed Books and Plays: A List of Books and Plays from Which Films Have Been Made, 1928–1983.* Brookfield, Vt.: Gower, 1985.

Fisher, Kim N. *On the Screen: A Film, Television, and Video Research Guide.* Littleton, Col.: Libraries Unlimited, 1987.

Rehrauer, George. *The Macmillan Film Bibliography.* 2 vols. New York: Macmillan, 1982.

Sheahan, Eileen. *Moving Pictures: An Annotated Guide to the Selected Film Literature, with Suggestions for the Study of Film.* South Brunswick, N.J.: A. S. Barnes, 1979.

Writers Program, New York. *The Film Index: A Bibliography.* Vol. 1, *The Film as Art.* New York: Museum of Modern Art Film Library and Wilson, 1941; vol. 2, *The Film as Industry*, and vol. 3, *The Film in Society.* New York: Kraus, 1985–   .

Music

Only some basic tools are listed here. Specific subject headings exist and can be searched directly for kinds of music—for

example CHAMBER MUSIC, BIG BANDS, FOLK MU-
SIC, JAZZ MUSIC, OPERA, SONGS, etc. The following
selections will be helpful for finding facts fast, the plots of
operas, identifying people in the field, etc., and some books
here have more scholarly articles. The Duckles research guide
(listed below) is excellent for extensive research, and the
twenty-volume *New Grove Dictionary of Music and Musicians*
will answer many questions and has articles with bibliographies for further research. The work by Grout has a music
chronology, and the Slonimsky has a descriptive chronology
covering 1900–1969. The *New Oxford History of Music* has
volumes that cover ancient and oriental music, medieval music, opera and church music, etc. *The Great American Song
Thesaurus* has a wonderful year-by-year chronology of the top
hits, revivals, and "notables," with a brief review of other
events of the year at the beginning of the lists. It answers, for
example, such questions as: What year was the last Beatles
album issued?

Useful Titles—Music

Gusikoff, Lynne. *Guide to Musical America*. New York: Facts on
File, 1984.

The International Cyclopedia of Music and Musicians. 11th ed. New
York: Dodd, Mead, 1985.

Jablonski, Edward. *The Encyclopedia of American Music*. Garden
City, N.Y.: Doubleday, 1981.

Kennedy, Michael. *The Oxford Dictionary of Music*. Oxford: Oxford Univ. Press, 1985.

The New Grove Dictionary of Music and Musicians. Edited by
Stanley Sadie. 20 vols. London: Macmillan, 1980.

The New Oxford Companion to Music. Denis Arnold, gen. ed. 2
vols. Oxford: Oxford Univ. Press, 1983.

MUSIC HISTORY

Grout, Donald J. *A History of Western Music.* 3d. ed. New York: Norton, 1980.

Hardwick, John M. D. *The Drake Guide to Gilbert & Sullivan.* New York: Drake, 1973.

Oxford History of Music. 2d ed. 8 vols. London: Oxford Univ. Press, 1929–1938.

New Oxford History of Music. London: Oxford Univ. Press, 1954– . In progress; to be 10 vols.

SELECTED TYPES OF MUSIC

Ewen, David, ed. *American Popular Songs from the Revolutionary War to the Present.* New York: Random House, 1966.

Feather, Leonard. *The Encyclopedia of Jazz.* New York: Horizon, 1960. Supplementary yearbooks 1956–1958. Two subsequent books by Feather, *The Encyclopedia of Jazz in the Sixties* and *The Encyclopedia of Jazz in the Seventies* update this title.

Kobbe, Gustav. *The Definitive Kobbe's Complete Book of the Opera.* Edited, revised, and updated by the Earl of Harewood. New York: Putnam, 1987.

Kunst, Jaap. *Ethnomusicology, a Study of Its Nature, Its Problems, Methods and Representative Personalities.* 3d enl. ed. The Hague: Nijhoff, 1959. Repr. with supp. 1974.

Lawless, Ray McKinley. *Folksingers and Folksongs in America: A Handbook of Biography, Bibliography, and Discography.* New rev. ed. with special supp. Westport, Conn.: Greenwood Press, 1981

Lax, Roger, and Smith, Frederick. *The Great Song Thesaurus.* New York: Oxford Univ. Press, 1984.

Nite, Norm N. *Rock On: The Illustrated Encyclopedia of Rock 'n Roll.* 3 vols. New York: Harper & Row, 1978–85.

Simon and Schuster Book of the Opera: A Complete Reference Guide. New York: Simon & Schuster, 1978.

Possible LCSH Subject Headings—Music

Remember that time periods appear under the heading MU-
SIC so you can pinpoint an era (MUSIC—15TH CENTURY)
and that MUSIC is a subdivision under individual ethnic
groups (NAVAJO INDIANS—MUSIC, AFRO-AMERI-
CANS—MUSIC, etc.). Another possible subdivision under
subjects, individuals, and institutions is SONGS AND MU-
SIC (BASEBALL—SONGS AND MUSIC). There are also
headings for different kinds of music, only a few of which are
given here as examples.

BIG BAND MUSIC
BIG BANDS
CHAMBER MUSIC
CHORAL MUSIC
CONCERTS
FOLK MUSIC
FOLK-SONGS
MUSIC
MUSIC—(time period)
MUSIC—BIO-BIBLIOGRAPHY
MUSIC—FIRST PERFORMANCES (also a subdivision
    under headings for music compositions; for example:
    OPERAS—FIRST PERFORMANCES.)
MUSIC—HISTORY AND CRITICISM
MUSIC AND EROTICA
MUSIC AND LITERATURE
MUSIC AND MORALS
MUSIC AND SOCIETY
MUSIC AND WAR
MUSIC APPRECIATION
MUSIC FESTIVALS
MUSIC HALLS (VARIETY-THEATERS, CABARETS,
    ETC.)
MUSIC IN CHURCHES
MUSIC IN SYNAGOGUES
MUSICAL GROUPS

NATIONAL MUSIC
OPERA
SONGS

Indexes—Music

Popular magazine indexes have a great deal on music, especially contemporary music—the *Rolling Stone*, for example, is now indexed in the *Readers' Guide, Popular Periodicals Index*, as well as *Music Index*.

Cushing, Helen Grant. *Children's Song Index: An Index to More than 22,000 Songs in 189 Collections* . . . New York: Wilson, 1936.

International Repertory of Music Literature, RILM Abstracts of Music Literature. Flushing, N.Y.: RILM, 1967– .

Music Index: The Key to Current Music Periodical Literature. Detroit: Information Service, 1950– .

Sears, Minnie Earl. *Song Index*. New York: Wilson, 1926. Supp., 1934.

Bibliographies and Guides—Music

Druesedow, John E. *Library Research Guide to Music: Illustrated Search Strategy and Sources*. Ann Arbor, Mich.: Pierian Press, 1982.

Duckles, Vincent Harris, comp. *Music Reference and Research Materials: An Annotated Bibliography*. 3d ed. New York: Free Press, 1974.

Theater

Comedies, tragedies, music halls, and vaudeville all reflect the world at various times. If your character has a life in the theater or attends or discusses a play or a circus, these books will help set the scene. Responses to a particular play or performance can be as revealing, of course, as the play itself. Reviewing sources divulge what people thought of certain writers and subject matter at the time the plays were produced even though attitudes toward such work may have since changed. The Shipley book listed below discusses first performances and the drama around a given drama such as *Hair* or Marc Connelly's *Green Pastures*.

RESEARCHING INDIVIDUALS AND SPECIFIC PLAYS

Individual playwrights and plays can be searched directly in library catalogs; for an example of the possibilities see SHAKESPEARE, WILLIAM 1564–1616 in the Library of Congress list of subject headings. You will see many, many subdivisions, from BIOGRAPHY and CHARACTERS to DRAMATIC PRODUCTION and STAGE HISTORY. The Library of Congress uses Shakespeare and the subdivisions as a "pattern" for individual literary authors and literary works under authors (SHAKESPEARE, WILLIAM 1564–1616. HAMLET). Plays can be searched in the catalogs under titles as well.

Useful Titles—Theater

Boardman, Gerald. *The Oxford Companion to the American Theatre.* New York: Oxford Univ. Press, 1984.

Bronner, Edwin. *The Encyclopedia of the American Theatre, 1900–1975.* San Diego & New York: A. S. Barnes, 1980.

Crowell's Handbook of Contemporary Drama. By Michael Anderson and others. New York: Crowell, 1971.

The Encyclopedia of World Theater. New York: Scribner's, 1977.

McGraw-Hill Encyclopedia of World Drama: An International Reference Work. 2d ed. Edited by Stanley Hochman. 5 vols. New York: McGraw-Hill, 1984.

Matlaw, Myron. *Modern World Drama: An Encyclopedia.* New York: Dutton, 1972.

Oxford Companion to the Theatre. 4th ed. Edited by Phyllis Hartnoll. Oxford: Oxford Univ. Press, 1983.

Shipley, Joseph Twadell. *The Crown Guide to the World's Great Plays, from Ancient Greece to Modern Times.* Rev. updated ed. New York: Crown, 1984.

Woll, Allen. *Dictionary of the Black Theatre: Broadway, Off-Broadway, and Selected Harlem Theatres.* Westport, Conn.: Greenwood Press, 1983.

Theater History—Selected Titles

Boardman, Gerald Martin. *The American Musical Theatre: A Chronicle.* New York: Oxford Univ. Press, 1978.

Brockett, Oscar Gross. *History of the Theatre.* 4th ed. Boston: Allyn and Bacon, 1982. General history from primitive times to the present.

Howard, Diana. *London Theatres and Music Halls, 1850–1950.* London: London Library Assoc., 1970.

Loney, Glenn Meredith. *20th Century Theatre.* New York: Facts on File, 1983.

Mantzius, Karl. *A History of Theatrical Art in Ancient and Modern Times.* 6 vols. Philadelphia: Lippincott, 1903–1921.

Nagler, Alois Maria. *Sources of Theatrical History.* New York: Theatre Annual, 1952.

Odell, George Clinton Densmore. *Annals of the New York Stage.* 15 vols. New York: Columbia Univ. Press, 1927–1949.

Stevens, David. *English Renaissance Theatre History: A Reference Guide.* Boston: G. K. Hall, 1982.

Wearing, J. P. *The London Stage . . . a Calendar of Plays and Players.* Various volumes covering 1890–1929. Metuchen, N.J.: Scarecrow, 1976, 1981, 1982.

Reviews—Theater

New York Theatre Critics' Reviews. New York: Theatre Critics' Reviews, 1940–   . Annual.

New York Times Theater Reviews, 1870–1982. New York: New York Times, 1971–   . Several volumes, various dates.

Salem, James. *A Guide to Critical Reviews.* 3d ed. Metuchen, N.J.: Scarecrow, 1984–   . In progress.

Samples, Gordon. *How to Locate Reviews of Plays and Films: A Bibliography of Criticism from the Beginnings to the Present.* Metuchen, N.J.: Scarecrow, 1976.

Indexes—Theater

Most popular indexes (see segment "Periodicals" in part 2) and newspapers carry information and reviews for the theater. The titles below index periodicals:

Dramatic Index for 1909–1949, covering articles and illustrations concerning the stage and its players in the periodicals of America and England and including the dramatic books of the year. 41 vols. Boston: Faxon, 1910–1951.

Guide to the Performing Arts, 1957–1968. New York: Scarecrow Press, 1960–1972. Annual.

Because plays are not always published separately but do appear in collections, there are indexes to collected works.

Ottemiller, John Henry. *Ottemiller's Index to Plays in Collections: An Author and Title Index to Plays Appearing in Collections Published Between 1900 and Early 1975.* 6th ed. Revised and enlarged by John M. Connor and Billie M. Connor. Metuchen, N.J.: Scarecrow Press, 1976.

Play Index, 1949–1952, 1953–1960, 1961–1967, 1968–1972, 1973–1977, 1978–1982. 6 vols. New York: Wilson, 1953–83.

Possible LCSH Subject Headings—Theater

Under the headings beginning THEATER, works are entered
that deal with drama as acted upon the stage. Works treating
drama from a literary point of view are under DRAMA,
ENGLISH DRAMA, FRENCH DRAMA, etc. See above
introductory note under "Researching Individuals and Specific Plays" regarding the use of Shakespeare as a "pattern"
for literary authors and works.

ACTORS
ACTRESSES
AFRO-AMERICAN THEATER
AMATEUR THEATER
BLACK THEATER
BURLESQUE (THEATER)
CIRCUS
DRAMA
ENGLISH DRAMA (FRENCH DRAMA, etc.)
ETHNIC THEATER
JEWISH THEATER
MINSTREL SHOWS
MUSIC-HALLS (VARIETY-THEATERS, CABARETS,
    ETC.)
THEATER (see note above)
THEATER—BIBLIOGRAPHY
THEATER—BIOGRAPHY
THEATER—CENSORSHIP
THEATER—FEDERAL AID
THEATER—HISTORY (and then by time period:
    THEATER—HISTORY—MEDIEVAL)
THEATER—POLITICAL ASPECTS
THEATER—PRODUCTION AND DIRECTION
THEATER—RESEARCH
THEATER, YIDDISH
THEATER AND SOCIETY
THEATER OF THE ABSURD
THEATERS (the plural form means architecture, theater
    buildings)

Bibliographies and Guides—Theater

Bailey, Claudia Jean. *A Guide to Reference and Bibliography for Theatre Research.* 2d ed. Columbus: Ohio State Univ. Libraries, 1983.

Whalon, Marion K. *Performing Arts Research: A Guide to Information Sources.* Detroit: Gale, 1976.

TV/Radio

Useful Titles—TV/Radio

Brooks, Tim, and Marsh, Earle. *The Complete Directory to Prime Time Network TV Shows, 1946–present.* 3d ed. New York: Ballantine Books, 1985.

Brown, Les. *Les Brown's Encyclopedia of Television.* New York: Zoetrope, 1982.

Dunning, John. *Tune in Yesterday: The Ultimate Encyclopedia of Old-Time Radio, 1925–1976.* Englewood Cliffs, N.J.: Prentice-Hall, 1976.

Gianakos, Larry James. *Television Drama Series Programming: A Comprehensive Chronicle.* Metuchen, N.J.: Scarecrow, 1978, 1980, 1981, 1983. Four volumes covering years 1947–1982.

Halliwell, Leslie, and Purser, Philip. *Halliwell's Television Guide.* 2d ed. London: Granada, 1982.

International Television Almanac. New York: Quigley, 1956–   .
Annual.

Terrace, Vincent. *The Complete Encyclopedia of Television Programs, 1947–1979.* 2d ed. 2 vols. South Brunswick, N.J.: A. S. Barnes, 1979.

———. *Radio's Golden Years: Encyclopedia of Radio Programs, 1930–1960.* San Diego: A. S. Barnes, 1981.

Indexes—TV/Radio

Again, most popular indexes (see "Periodicals" segment, part 2) cover this subject, and some more scholarly journals deal with the sociological and psychological aspects of TV and radio. There is an index to television periodicals:

International Index to Television Periodicals: An Annotated Guide,
    1979/80– . London: International Federation of Film Archives,
    1983– . Biennial.

Bibliographies and Guides—TV/Radio

McCavitt, William. *Radio and Television: A Selected, Annotated
    Bibliography.* Metuchen, N.J.: Scarecrow, 1978. Supp. 1982.

*NAB Broadcasting Bibliography: A Guide to the Literature of Radio
    & Television.* Compiled by the staff of the NAB Library and
    Information Center, 1984.

Schreibman, Fay C. *Broadcast Television: A Research Guide.* Ed-
    ited by Peter J. Bukalski. Los Angeles: American Film Institute,
    Education Services, 1983.

Possible LCSH Subject Headings—TV/Radio

RADIO (used for technical works)
RADIO BROADCASTING
RADIO BROADCASTING—SOCIAL ASPECTS
RADIO BROADCASTING OF SPORTS
RADIO IN POLITICS
RADIO IN PROPAGANDA
TELEVISION (used for works on the field of TV and
    general technical works)

TELEVISION—LAW AND LEGISLATION
TELEVISION—PSYCHOLOGICAL ASPECTS
TELEVISION ADVERTISING
TELEVISION SERIALS
TELEVISION AND CHILDREN
TELEVISION AND FAMILY
TELEVISION AND HISTORY
TELEVISION AND POLITICS
TELEVISION BROADCASTING (used for works on the
   art and practice of television transmission)
TELEVISION BROADCASTING—BIBLIOGRAPHY
TELEVISION BROADCASTING—MORAL AND RE-
   LIGIOUS ASPECTS
TELEVISION BROADCASTING—NEWS
TELEVISION COMEDY WRITERS
TELEVISION CRITICISM
TELEVISION IN EDUCATION

Politics and Government

The Lindsay and Crouse play, *The State of the Union*, and the novels, *All the King's Men* by Robert Penn Warren, and *The Last Hurrah* by Edwin O'Connor, are examples of wonderful stories with complicated characters using American politics as the theme. They also are grounded in reality, however loosely, and though they are richly imagined works, they are steeped in a realistic atmosphere of political life. At the very least, if a story is set in a certain country at a certain time, the figures in the political landscape can be correct. Though the titles below are primarily reference works, other nonfiction works describing more of the *atmosphere* of the political arena can be located by using the LCSH headings and eyewitness accounts of conventions, elections, etc., to find works like Theodore H. White's *America in Search of Itself: The Making of the President, 1956–1980* (Harper & Row, 1982), his separate *Making of the President* volumes for several presidential elections, and Joe McGinniss's *The Selling of the President* (New York: Trident, 1968).

This discussion is closely related to the segment "Government Publications" in part 5, and many of the titles presented there are also useful for general political background, so see that segment as well.

Of the titles listed below, the *Europa Yearbook* is an outstanding source for an overview of international organizations and the countries of the world, giving a summary of recent history and current information on the country's government, education, religion, press, media, finance, trade, industry, and so on. That is also the general format of the other Europa publications listed below—*Africa South of the Sahara, Middle East and North Africa, Far East and Australasia, South America, Central America, and the Caribbean.* Information on educational and learned societies in the countries of the world is carried by another Europa publication, *World of Learning* (see "Education"). The *Statesman's Year-Book* and the *International Yearbook and Statesmen's Who's Who* are also good for current facts (and they both, like *Europa,* go back some years—*Statesmen's Year-Book* to 1864—so if you want the status of a country in 1951, for example, you can look at that year's volumes). The *Encyclopedia of the Third World* covers several categories for each country including a fact sheet, weather, population, religion, politics, defense, human rights, etc.

In addition to the U.S. Army's *Background Notes,* the department also issues foreign area studies, *U.S. Area Handbooks for [country]*—and now called country studies: *[country name]: A Country Study*—on various countries describing their culture, religion, government, etc. These would probably be found through the Government Documents section of the library.

Useful Titles—Yearbooks, Encyclopedias, etc.

Africa South of the Sahara. London: Europa Publications, 1971– . Annual.

Day, Alan J., and Degenhardt, Henry W. *Political Parties of the World.* 2d ed. Detroit: Gale, 1984.

Encyclopedia of Latin America. Edited by Helen Delpar. New York: McGraw-Hill, 1974.

Europa Year Book. London: Europa Publications, 1959– . Annual. From 1926–1968 various titles and in loose-leaf form.

Far East and Australasia. London: Europa, 1969– . Annual.

Kurian, George Thomas. *Encyclopedia of the Third World.* Rev. ed. 3 vols. New York: Facts on File, 1982.

International Yearbook and Statesmen's Who's Who. London: Burke's Peerage, 1953–   . Annual.

Marxist Governments: A World Survey. Edited by Bogdan Szajkowski. 3 vols. New York: St. Martin's Press, 1981.

Middle East and North Africa. London: Europa Publications, 1948– . Annual (irregular).

Political Handbook of the World. New York: McGraw-Hill, 1975. Biennial.

South America, Central America, and the Caribbean. London: Europa, 1985– . Annual.

Statesmen's Year-Book: Statistical and Historical Annual of the States of the World. London/New York: Macmillan, 1864– .

U.S. Dept. of State. Bureau of Public Affairs. *Background Notes on the Countries of the World.* Wash., D.C.: Government Printing Office. Irregular.

U.S. Area Handbooks for [country]. U.S. Department of Defense. Army Dept. Wash., D.C.: Government Printing Office. Irregular. (Also called "Country Studies.")

World Encyclopedia of Political Systems and Parties. 2d ed. Edited by George E. Delury. 2 vols. New York: Facts on File, 1987.

Worldmark Encyclopedia of the Nations. 6th ed. 5 vols. New York: Worldmark, 1984.

Bibliographies and Guides

Harmon, Robert Bartlett. *Political Science: A Bibliographic Guide to the Literature.* New York: Scarecrow, 1965. Supps. 3 vols. Metuchen, N.J.: Scarecrow, 1968–1974.

Holler, Frederick L. *Information Sources of Political Science.* 4th ed. Santa Barbara, Cal.: ABC-Clio, 1986.

Information Sources in Political Science: A Survey Worldwide. Edited by Dermot Englefield and Gavin Drewry. London: Butterworths, 1984.

LaBar, Dorothy F., and Singer, Joel David. *The Study of International Politics: A Guide to the Sources for the Student, Teacher and Researcher.* Santa Barbara, Cal.: ABC-Clio, 1976.

UNITED STATES

See titles listed in the segment "Government Publications," part 5, such as the *Congressional Directory* and the *U.S. Government Organizational Manual*. The Watergate bibliography is an example of the availability of material on specific political events. The *Congressional Quarterly* (CQ) publications listed below are invaluable sources for American politics and government, and the weekly can be used as a sort of index to the week in Congress. The CQ weekly and annual volumes give information on bills and legislation, appointments, hearings, voting records of individual members of Congress, election statistics, summaries of activity in certain areas like education, environment, etc. During the Iran/Contra hearings, for example, you may have wished to go back and see who said what and who supported the Boland amendment; this is the kind of source that would help you do that search. Congressional Quarterly also publishes other related works.

Austin, Eric W. *Political Facts of the United States since 1789*. New York: Columbia University Press, 1986.

Congressional Quarterly Almanac. Wash., D.C.: Congressional Quarterly, 1945– . Annual.

Congressional Quarterly Weekly Report. Wash., D.C.: Congressional Quarterly, 1946– . Weekly.

Congress and the Nation: A Review of Government and the Nation in the Postwar Years, 1945/64– . Wash., D.C.: Congressional Quarterly Service, 1965– . Now quadrennial.

Encyclopedia of American Political History: Studies of the Principal Movements and Ideas. Edited by Jack P. Greene. 3 vols. New York: Scribner's, 1984.

Findling, John E. *Dictionary of American Diplomatic History*. Westport, Conn.: Greenwood, 1980

Plano, Jack C., and Greenberg, Milton. *The American Political Dictionary*. 7th ed. New York: Holt, Rinehart & Winston, 1985.

Scammon, Richard M., ed. *America Votes: A Handbook of Contemporary American Elections Statistics*. Vols. 1–2, New York: Macmillan, 1956, 1958. Vols. 3–6, Pittsburgh: Univ. of Pittsburgh

Press, 1959–1966. Vols. 7– , Wash., D.C.: Congressional Quarterly, 1968– . Biennial.

Whisker, James B. *A Dictionary of Concepts on American Politics*. New York: Wiley, 1980.

BIBLIOGRAPHIES AND GUIDES—UNITED STATES

Brooks, Alexander D. *Civil Rights and Liberties in the United States: An Annotated Bibliography*. New York: Civil Liberties Educ. Foundation, 1962.

Guide to American Foreign Relations Since 1700. Edited by Richard D. Burns. Santa Barbara, Cal.: ABC-Clio, 1983.

Mauer, David J. *U.S. Politics and Elections: A Guide to Information Sources*. Detroit: Gale, 1978.

Plischke, Elmer. *U.S. Foreign Relations; A Guide to Information Sources*. Detroit: Gale, 1980.

Smith, Myron J. *Watergate: An Annotated Bibliography of Sources in English, 1972–1982*. Metuchen, N.J.: Scarecrow, 1983.

Unity in Diversity: An Index to the Publications of Conservative and Libertarian Institutions. The New American Foundation. Edited by Carol L. Birch. Metuchen, N.J.: Scarecrow. 1983.

Vose, Clement E. *A Guide to Library Sources in Political Science: American Government*. Wash., D.C.: American Political Science Assoc., 1975.

Possible LCSH Subject Headings

"Politics" alone is not a heading; you are referred to POLITICAL SCIENCE as the heading and, since the subject is so large, directed to take a look at the related headings under POLITICAL SCIENCE. Individual, well-documented incidents have their own headings; e.g. WATERGATE AFFAIR, 1972–1974, and TEAPOT DOME SCANDAL, 1921–1924. So, as always, use the most specific or narrow heading first, and then if you need to, use broader headings like POLITICAL PARTIES. A useful subdivision is POLITICAL AC-

TIVITY, used under the names of groups such as the aged, youth, etc.; e.g. CLERGY—POLITICAL ACTIVITY. Also the names of well-known parties throughout the world and throughout history may be searched as subject headings.

For countries use the name of the country and the sub-division POLITICS AND GOVERNMENT; e.g. FRANCE—POLITICS AND GOVERNMENT, or the subdivision FOR-EIGN RELATIONS; e.g. BRAZIL—FOREIGN RELA-TIONS. Remember that the subdivisions used by the Library of Congress under the names of countries are given in LCSH under UNITED STATES, which is a "pattern" for the possi-ble subdivisions that may be used under any country—these subdivisions are not necessarily repeated in the printed sub-ject headings list under each country but may be used.

CAMPAIGN FUNDS
CAMPAIGN MANAGEMENT
CAUCUS
CORRUPTION (IN POLITICS)
DEMOCRATIC PARTY
ELECTIONS
GOVERNMENTS IN EXILE
INTERNATIONAL ORGANIZATION
INTERNATIONAL RELATIONS
POLITICAL CONVENTIONS
POLITICAL CRIMES AND OFFENSES
POLITICAL FICTION
POLITICAL ORATORY
POLITICAL PARTIES
POLITICAL PARTIES—UNITED STATES
POLITICAL PLAYS
POLITICAL RIGHTS
POLITICAL SCIENCE
POLITICAL SCIENCE—HISTORY
POLITICS, PRACTICAL
RIGHT AND LEFT (POLITICAL)
SOCIALIST PARTIES
SOVIET UNION—FOREIGN RELATIONS (see note above)

UNITED STATES—POLITICS AND GOVERNMENT
(see note above)
VOTING
YOUTH—POLITICAL ACTIVITY (see note above)

Indexes

See the general indexes listed in the segment "Periodicals," part 2, because most indexes cover the subject of politics in one way or another, including the *Readers' Guide, Public Affairs Information Service,* and the history indexes like *Historical Abstracts* and *American History and Life.* Other useful sources for political science are:

International Bibliography of Political Science. Bibliographic Internationale des Sciences Sociales. London: Tavistock; Chicago: Aldine, 1953–   . Annual.

International Political Science Abstracts. Documentation Politique Internationale. Oxford: Blackwell, 1951–   . Quarterly.

South American Handbook: A Yearbook and Guide to the Countries and Resources of South and Central America, Mexico, and the West Indies. London: Trade and Travel Publications, 1924–   . Annual.

Invention, Scientific Discovery, and Exploration

For purposes of a good story you may need to know that there were no wheels before about 3000 B.C., no thermometers before 1593, no safety matches before 1844, no safety pins before 1849, no typewriters before 1867, no liquid-fuel rockets before 1926, and so on. You get the idea—you can't have a character zipping up her dress before 1893, when zippers were invented. The same principle applies to exploration and discovery—you can't have a character sailing for America too soon. Sometimes a story or play centers on the effects of an important invention or discovery of the lives of people at the time, or again, it simply helps to establish a time and place. Discovery occurs when something that exists in nature is recognized for the first time; invention is the creation of something that never existed before. It is possible to explore both those things already in nature and the ideas that lead to inventions.

The tool for the quickest check of "firsts" is Kane's *Famous First Facts*, which aims to establish the earliest date of achievements and inventions in America (first printed play, dynamite, flag, jeans, kidnapping, advertisement, alarm clock). It gives descriptions and a few reference sources and has some very useful indexes—by year, by day of the month, by geographical location, and by personal name. The encyclopedia, *The Discoverers*, has world-wide coverage, with biographical, geographical, and topical articles, most with bibliographies. The Hodges book is an example of the availability of sources for specific time periods. The surveys and encyclopedia titles give overviews and usually some indication of society's reasons for exploring and inventing.

Useful Titles

Clark, Ronald W. *The Scientific Breakthrough: The Impact of Modern Invention.* New York: Putnam, 1974.

Day, Alan Edwin. *Discovery and Exploration: A Reference Handbook.* Vol. 1, *The Old World*; vol. 2, *The New World* (in progress). Munchen: Saur; London: Clive Bingley, 1980–   .

Daumas, Maurice, ed. *A History of Technology and Invention: Progress Through the Ages.* 3 vols. New York: Crown, 1969–1979.

DeBono, Edward. *Eureka! An Illustrated History of Inventions from the Wheel to the Computer.* New York: Holt, 1974.

The Discoverers: An Encyclopedia of Explorers and Exploration. Edited by Helen Delpar. New York: McGraw-Hill, 1980.

Encyclopedia of Modern Technology. Ed. by David Blackburn and David Holister. Boston: G.K. Hall, 1987.

Jones, Stacy V. *Inventions Necessity Is Not the Mother of: Patents Ridiculous and Sublime.* New York: Times Books, 1973.

Hodges, Henry. *Technology in the Ancient World.* New York: Knopf, 1970.

Humble, Richard. *The Explorers.* New York: Time, Inc., 1978.

Kane, Joseph Nathan. *Famous First Facts: A Record of First Facts: A Record of First Happenings, Discoveries, and Inventions in American History.* 4th ed. New York: Wilson, 1981.

Lacey, Peter, ed. *Great Adventures That Changed Our World: The World's Great Explorers, Their Triumphs and Tragedies.* New York: Norton, 1978.

Lewis, Richard S. *From Vinland to Mars: A Thousand Years of Exploration.* New York: Times Books, 1976.

Obregon, Mauricio. *Argonauts to Astronauts.* New York: Harper, 1980.

Parker, John. *Discovery: Developing Views of the Earth from Ancient Times to the Voyages of Captain Cook.* New York: Scribner's, 1972.

Strandh, Sigvard. *A History of the Machine.* New York: A & W Publishers, 1979.

Possible LCSH Subject Headings

The subject heading is DISCOVERIES (IN GEOGRAPHY). If you look up "Discoveries (in science)" you are referred to the related headings of INDUSTRIAL ARTS, INVENTIONS, PATENTS, SCIENCE. There are some important subdivisions under the names of countries: DISCOVERY AND EXPLORATION, DESCRIPTION AND TRAVEL, EXPLORING EXPEDITIONS. The GEOGRAPHY headings followed by the centuries (see below) are for the Age of Reason and the Industrial Revolution, times of great discovery.

ADVENTURE AND ADVENTURERS
CREATIVE ABILITY IN TECHNOLOGY
DISCOVERIES (IN GEOGRAPHY)
EXPLORERS
EXPLORERS, WOMEN
GEOGRAPHY—15TH–16TH CENTURIES
GEOGRAPHY—17TH–18TH CENTURIES
INDUSTRIAL ARTS
INDUSTRIAL ARTS—HISTORY
INVENTIONS
INVENTIONS, EMPLOYEES'
INVENTORS
OUTER SPACE—EXPLORATION
PATENTS
PROSPECTING
SCIENTIFIC EXPEDITIONS
TECHNOLOGICAL INNOVATIONS
VOYAGES AND TRAVELS
UNDERWATER EXPLORATION

Indexes

Most general indexes apply, but especially *Historical Abstracts, America: History and Life,* and *Applied Science and Technology Index.* See Segment "Periodicals," part 2, for complete list.

Bibliographies

Ferguson, John. *Bibliographical Notes on Histories of Inventions and Books of Secrets.* London: Holland Press, 1959.

Goodman, Edward J. *The Exploration of South America: An Annotated Bibliography.* New York: Garland, 1983.

Kaempffert, Waldemar. *Invention and Society.* Chicago: American Library Assoc., 1930.

Wagner, Henry R. *The Plains and the Rockies: A Bibliography of Original Narratives of Travel and Adventure, 1800–1860.* San Francisco: J. Howell, 1921.

Outer Space

Part of exploring the unknown is the exploration of the "last frontier," outer space. The space age began in 1957 when Russia launched *Sputnik I,* the first artificial satellite to circle the earth. In the years that followed there have been many developments and some tragedies, all carefully documented in books, periodicals, and newspapers. Several works below are histories of the space program, reviews of the first years in space, and the works by Grey and Moore discuss the future in space. *Jane's Spaceflight Directory* describes space programs by nation, as well as vehicles and payloads, and satellite orbit information. It also has articles on military uses of space, space launchers, space centers, etc.

Useful Titles—Outer Space

Asimov, Isaac. *Exploring the Earth and the Cosmos: The Growth and Future of Human Knowledge.* New York: Crown, 1982.

The First 25 Years in Space: A Symposium. Edited by Alan A. Needell. Wash., D.C.: Smithsonian Institute, 1983.

Furniss, Tim. *Manned Spaceflight Log.* London: Jane's, 1983.

Grey, Jerry. *Beachheads in Space: A Blueprint for the Future.* New York: Macmillan, 1983.

Hartman, William K., et al. *Out of the Cradle: Exploring the Frontier Beyond Earth.* New York: Workman Pub., 1984.

A Meeting with the Universe: Science Discoveries from the Space Program. Edited by Bevan M. French and Stephen P. Maran. Wash., D.C.: NASA, 1981.

Moore, Patrick. *The Next Fifty Years in Space.* New York: Taplinger Pub., 1978.

Newell, Homer E. *Beyond the Atmosphere: Early Years of Space Science.* Wash., D.C.: Scientific and Information Branch, NASA, 1980.

Turnill, Reginald, *Jane's Spaceflight Directory.* London: Jane's, 1984.

U.S. National Commission on Space. *Pioneering the Space Frontier: Report of the National Commission on Space.* New York: Bantam Books; Wash., D.C.: National Commission on Space, 1986.

Von Braun, Wernher and Frederick I. Ordway, 3rd. *History of Rocketry & Space Travel.* New York: Crowell, 1975.

Voght, Gregory. *A Twenty-Fifth Anniversary Album of NASA.* New York: Watts, 1983.

Weber, Ronald. *Seeing Earth: Literary Responses to Space Exploration.* Athens, Ohio: Ohio Univ. Press, 1985.

The World in Space: A Survey of Space Activities and Issues. Prepared for UNISPACE '82; United Nations. Edited by Ralph Chipman. Englewood Cliffs, N.J.: Prentice-Hall, 1982.

Yenne, Bill. *The Encyclopedia of U.S. Spacecraft.* New York: Exeter Books, 1985.

SPACE COLONIES AND SPACE STATIONS

Adelman, Saul J., and Adelman, Benjamin. *Bound for the Stars.* Englewood Cliffs, N.J.: Prentice-Hall, 1981.

Oberg, Alcestis R. *Spacefarers of the '80s and '90s: The Next Thousand People in Space.* New York: Columbia Univ. Press, 1981.

Space Settlements: A Design Study. Edited by Richard D. Johnson and Charles Holbrow. Wash., D.C.: Scientific and Technical Information Office, NASA, 1977.

The Space Station: An Idea Whose Time Has Come. Edited by Theodore R. Simpson. New York: IEEE Press, 1985.

Space Station Program: Description, Applications,, and Opportunities. By Space Station Task Force, NASA. Park Ridge, N.J.: Noves Pub., 1985.

SPACE WEAPONS

Manno, Jack. *Arming the Heavens: The Hidden Military Agenda for Space, 1945–1995.* New York: Dodd, Mead, 1984.

Weapons in Space. Edited by Franklin Long, et al. New York: Norton, 1986.

UFOs

Eberhart, George M. *UFOs and the Extraterrestial Contact Movement: A Bibliography.* Metuchen, N.J.: Scarecrow, 1986. 2 vols.

Fitzgerald, Randall. *The Complete Book of Extraterrestrial Encounters: The Ideas of Carl Sagan, Erich Von Daniken, Billy Graham, Carl Jung, John C. Lilly, John G. Fuller, and Many Others.* New York: Macmillan, 1979.

Hendry, Allan. *The UFO Handbook: A Guide to Investigating, Evaluating and Reporting UFO Sightings.* New York: Doubleday, 1979.

Story, Ronald D. *The Encyclopedia of UFOs.* New York: Doubleday, 1980.

Possible LCSH Subject Headings—Outer Space

SPACE SCIENCES is the heading used for astronautical undertakings; general works on the universe are entered under ASTRONOMY. Works on the physics and technical details of flight beyond the earth's atmosphere are entered under

SPACE FLIGHT; general works and imaginary accounts on travel to the planets or to the stars are entered under INTER-PLANETARY VOYAGES or INTERSTELLAR TRAVEL. Look at the Library of Congress list for other distinctions between more technical headings.

ASTRONAUTS
ASTRONAUTS—UNITED STATES (etc.; other geographical subdivisions)
INTERPLANETARY VOYAGES
INTERSTELLAR TRAVEL
OUTER SPACE
OUTER SPACE—EXPLORATION
OUTER SPACE—EXPLORATION—BIBLIOGRAPHY
SPACE
SPACE COLONIES
SPACE DEBRIS
SPACE ENVIRONMENT
SPACE FLIGHT
SPACE FLIGHT—PSYCHOLOGICAL ASPECTS
SPACE FLIGHT TO JUPITER (and TO MARS, TO MERCURY, TO THE MOON, etc.)
SPACE MEDICINE
SPACE SUITS
SPACE STATIONS
SPACE VEHICLES
SPACE WARFARE
SPACE WEAPONS

Indexes—Outer Space

All of the general science indexes and abstracting services (see below under "General Science") as well as:

International Aerospace Abstracts. Phillipsburg, N.J.: Technical Information Service, American Inst. of Aeronautics and Astronautics, 1961–   . Semimonthly.

U.S. National Aeronautics and Space Administration. *Scientific and Technical Aerospace Reports: A Semimonthly Abstract Journal with Indexes.* Wash., D.C.: NASA, 1963– .

Bibliographies and Guides—Outer Space

Catoe, Lynn E. *UFOs and Related Subjects: An Annotated Bibliography.* Prepared by the Library of Congress Science and Technology for the Air Force Office of Scientific Research, Office of Aerospace Research, USAF; supplemented by *Unidentified Flying Objects*, by Kay Rodgers. Detroit: Gale, 1978.

Ordway, Frederick I. *Annotated Bibliography of Space Science and Technology, with an Astronomical Supplement.* A history of astronomical book literature—1931 through 1961. 3d ed. Wash., D.C.: Arfor Pub., 1962.

Outer Space: A Selective Bibliography. L'Espace Extra-Atmospherique: Bibliographie Selective. New York: United Nations, 1982.

General Science

By now, readers of this guide are aware of the importance of looking for material on special topics using subject headings that are as specific as possible. This is true of the hundreds of topics within the many fields of science, so if you need a theory in physics or information on a particular botanical matter, look under the subjects and names in library catalogs and indexes. There are some general sources for quick scientific information and some excellent indexes and guides.

Encyclopedias—General Science

Diagram Group. *Comparisons of Distance, Size, Area, Volume, Mass, Weight, Density, Energy, Temperature, Time, Speed, and Number Throughout the Universe.* New York: St. Martin's Press, 1980.

McGraw-Hill Encyclopedia of Science and Technology. 6th ed. 20 vols. New York: McGraw-Hill, 1987.

Powell, Russell H., ed. *Handbooks and Tables in Science and Technology.* 2d ed. Phoenix, Ariz,: Oryx Press, 1983.

Van Nostrand's Scientific Encyclopedia. 6th ed. New York: Van Nostrand Reinhold, 1983.

The Way Things Work: An Illustrated Encyclopedia of Modern Technology. 2 vols. New York: Simon & Schuster, 1967–1971.

Indexes—General Science

Applied Science and Technology Index. New York: Wilson, 1913– . Monthly with annual cumulations.

Biological & Agricultural Index: A Cumulative Subject Index to Periodicals in the Fields of Biology and Agriculture, and Related Sciences. New York: Wilson, 1964– . Monthly with annual cumulations.

Biological Abstracts. Philadelphia: BioSciences Information Service, 1926– . Semimonthly.

Chemical Abstracts. Columbus, Ohio: American Chemical Society, 1907– . Weekly.

General Science Index. New York: Wilson, 1978– . Monthly with annual cumulations.

Science Abstracts. London: Inst. of Electrical Engineers, 1898– . Semimonthly.

Science Citation Index. Philadelphia: Institute for Scientific Information, 1961– . Bimonthly with annual cumulations.

Guides—General Science

Chen, Chung-cheh. *Scientific and Technical Information Sources.* 2d ed. Cambridge, Mass.: MIT Press, 1987.

Herner, Saul. *A Brief Guide to Sources of Scientific and Technical Information.* 2d ed. Arlington, Va.: Information Resources Press, 1980.

Malinowsky, Harold R., and Richardson, Jeanne M. *Science and Engineering Literature: A Guide to Reference Sources.* 3d ed. Littleton, Colo.: Libraries Unlimited, 1980.

Primack, Alice Lefler. *Finding Answers in Science and Technology.* New York: Van Nostrand Reinhold, 1984.

Part IV

Special Topics

Crime and Criminals

"Murder, though it have no tongue, will speak
With most miraculous organ."

So said Shakespeare in *Hamlet*. Certainly Shakespeare used murder in many plots, and it remains, along with other crimes, a favorite of fiction writers. Several special bibliographies are listed here to give you an idea of the range of subjects within the broader subject of crime. Some biographical sources are included, describing the beginnings and some terrible endings of criminals. The *Almanac of World Crime* and the *Encyclopedia of American Crime* also have biographies. The Suvak *Memoirs* . . . has three sections: (1) civil prisoners, both criminal and prisoners of conscience; (2) voluntary prisoners committed for the purpose of studying and reporting on the institutions; (3) military prisoners, from the Revolutionary War to World War II internment camps. The Elsevier dictionary gives criminal science terms in eight languages in case your character travels to or comes up against a law enforcer from another country. Several special bibliographies are included as a sampling of what's available, including one by Trott on the Mafia. (For related material on criminal investigation see Forensic Medicine in the section "Medicine" and for material on firearms see Arms and Armor in the section "War.")

Useful Titles

Encyclopedia of Crime and Justice. Edited by Sanford H. Kadish. 4 vols. New York: Free Press, 1983.

Nash, Jay Robert. *Almanac of World Crime.* New York: Anchor/ Doubleday, 1981.

Sifakis, Carl. *The Encyclopedia of American Crime.* New York: Facts on File, 1982.

DICTIONARIES

DeSola, Ralph. *Crime Dictionary.* New York: Facts on File, 1982.

Elsevier's Dictionary of Criminal Science, in Eight Languages: English/ American, French, Italian, Spanish, Portuguese, Dutch, Swedish, and German. Compiled by Johann Anton Adler. Amsterdam: Elsevier, 1960.

Language of the Underworld. Edited by David W. Maurer. Lexington: Univ. of Kentucky Press, 1981.

BIOGRAPHIES

Gaute, J. H. H. and Odell, Robin. *The Murderers' Who's Who: Outstanding International Cases from the Literature of Murder in the Last 150 Years.* New York: Methuen, 1979.

Nash, Jay Robert. *Bloodletters and Badmen: A Narrative Encyclopedia of American Criminals from the Pilgrims to the Present.* New York: M. Evans, 1973.

Suvak, Daniel. *Memoirs of American Prisons: An Annotated Bibliography.* Metuchen, N. J.: Scarecrow, 1979.

POLICE

Hewitt, William H. *A Bibliography of Police Administration, Public Safety, and Criminology to July 1, 1965.* Springfield, Ill.: Thomas, 1967.

Simpson. Antony E., and Duchaine, Nina. *The Literature of Police Corruption.* 2 vols. New York: John Jay Press, 1977–79.

Whitehouse, Jack E. *A Police Bibliography*. New York: AMS Press, 1980.

MURDER

Jerath, Bal K., et al. *Homicide: A Bibliography of Over 4,500 Items*. Augusta, Ga.: Pine Tree Pubns., 1982.

McDade, Thomas M. *The Annals of Murder: A Bibliography of Books and Pamphlets on American Murders from Colonial Times to 1900*. Norman: Univ. of Oklahoma Press, 1961.

SPECIAL BIBLIOGRAPHIES

Cabot, Phillippe Sidney de Q. *Juvenile Delinquency: A Critical, Annotated Bibliography*. Westport, Conn.: Greenwood, 1946, 1971.

Christianson, Scott. *Index to Minorities and Criminal Justice: An Index to Periodicals and Books Relating to Minorities and Criminal Justice in the United States*. 1981 cumulative ed. Albany, N.Y.: Center on Minorities and Criminal Justice, School of Criminal Justice, State Univ. of New York, Albany, 1981.

Cordasco, Francesco, and Alloway, David N. *Crime in America: Historical Patterns and Contemporary Realities: An Annotated Bibliography*. New York: Garland, 1985.

Felkenes, George T., and Becker, Harold K. *Law Enforcement: A Selected Bibliography*. 2d ed. New York: Scarecrow, 1977.

Hopkins, Isabella, et al. *Organized Crime: A Selected Bibliography*. Austin: Univ. of Texas School of Law, 1973.

Prostano, Emanuel T., and Piccirillo, Martin L. *Law Enforcement: A Selective Bibliography*. Littleton, Colo.: Libraries Unlimited, 1974.

Trott, Lloyd. *Mafia: A Select Annotated Bibliography*. Cambridge, Eng.: Institute of Criminology, Cambridge Univ. 1977.

STATISTICS

*Sourcebook of Criminal Justice Statistics, 1973–   *. Wash., D.C.:

National Criminal Justice Information and Statistics Service; Government Printing Office, 1974–   . Annual.

U.S. Federal Bureau of Investigation. *Uniform Crime Reports for the United States and Its Possessions.* Wash., D.C.: Government Printing Office, 1930–   . Annual.

Possible LCSH Subject Headings

Two categories are listed here, those headings generally used for POLICE and related terms and those used for CRIME AND CRIMINALS. As always, check the most specific terms first—headings for individual crimes (ROBBERY, MURDER, etc.). There are subject headings, by the way, for finding fiction: DETECTIVE AND MYSTERY PLAYS, DETECTIVE AND MYSTERY TELEVISION PROGRAMS, DETECTIVE AND MYSTERY STORIES, CRIME AND CRIMINALS—FICTION.

Headings for POLICE:

    AGENTS PROVOCATEURS
    ARREST (POLICE METHODS)
    BORDER PATROL
    CONSTABLES
    DETECTIVES
    HARBOR POLICE
    NARCOTICS, CONTROL OF
    POLICE
    POLICE—ADMINISTRATION
    POLICE—ASSAULTS AGAINST
    POLICE—ATTITUDES
    POLICE—AUTHORSHIP
    POLICE—BRUTALITY COMPLAINTS
    POLICE—JOB STRESS
    POLICE—POLITICAL ACTIVITY
    POLICE—PSYCHOLOGICAL ASPECTS
    POLICE—SPECIAL OPERATIONS UNITS

POLICE—SPECIAL WEAPONS AND TACTICS
POLICE MURDERS
POLICE POWER
POLICE QUESTIONING
POLICE SOCIAL WORK
SECRET SERVICE
UNDERCOVER OPERATIONS

Headings for CRIME AND CRIMINALS:

ALCHOLISM AND CRIME
ASSASSINATION
BRIGANDS AND ROBBERS
COMPUTER CRIMES
CONSPIRACIES
CRIME AND CRIMINALS
CRIME AND CRIMINALS—CROSS-CULTURAL
  STUDIES
CRIME AND CRIMINALS—IDENTIFICATION
CRIME AND SUPERSTITION
CRIME AND THE PRESS
CRIME AND THE WEATHER
CRIME PASSIONNEL
CRIME PREVENTION
CRIME SCENE SEARCHES
CRIMES WITHOUT VICTIMS
CRIMINAL STATISTICS
DRUG ABUSE AND CRIME
GANGS
HOMICIDE
MAFIA
NARCOTICS AND CRIME
ORGANIZED CRIME
PRISONS
VICTIMS OF CRIMES
VIOLENT CRIMES
WAR AND CRIME
WHITE COLLAR CRIMES

Indexes

Criminal Justice Abstracts. Hackensack, N.J.: National Council on Crime and Delinquency, 1977–   . Quarterly.

Criminal Justice Periodical Abstracts. Ann Arbor: Indexing Services, University Microfilms, 1975–   . Three issues per year.

Criminology and Penology Abstracts. Amsterdam: Kugler Pubns., 1961–   . Bimonthly.

Index to Legal Periodicals. Publ. for the American Assoc. of Law Libraries. New York: Wilson, 1909–   . Monthly (frequency varies).

And most general indexes (see "Periodicals" segment, part 2 as well as newspaper indexes.

Research Guide

Wright, Martin. *Use of Criminology Literature.* Hamden, Conn.: Archon Books, 1974.

SPIES

There are many personal accounts by real spies, former members of the CIA and the KGB, etc., which can be found under the subject heading SPIES in library catalogs. A few general titles are listed here.

Useful Titles

Blum, Richard H. *Deceivers and the Deceived: Observations on Confidence Men and Their Victims, Informants and Their Quarry, Political and Industrial Spies and Ordinary Citizens.* Springfield, Ill.: Thomas, 1972.

Buranelli, Vincent, and Buranelli, Nan. *Spy/Counterspy: An Encyclopedia of Espionage.* New York: McGraw-Hill, 1982.

Dobson, Christopher, and Payne, Ronald. *Who's Who in Espionage.* New York: St. Martin's, 1985.

Jeffreys-Jones, Rhodri. *American Espionage: From Secret Service to C.I.A.* New York: Free Press, 1977.

Joesten, Joachim. *They Call It Intelligence: Spies and Spy Techniques Since World War II.* New York: Abelard-Schuman, 1963.

Knightley, Philip. *The Second Oldest Profession: The Spy as Bureaucrat, Patriot, Fantasist and Whore.* New York: Norton, 1987.

Maclean, Fitzroy. *Take Nine Spies.* New York: Atheneum, 1978.

McGarvey, Robert, and Caitlin, Elise. *The Complete Spy.* New York: Putnam, 1983.

Seth, Ronald. *Anatomy of Spying.* New York: Dutton, 1963.

Singer, Kurt D. *Spies and Traitors of World War II.* New York: Prentice-Hall, 1945.

Stern, Philip V. *Secret Missions of the Civil War.* Westport, Conn.: Greenwood, 1975. Reprint of 1959 ed.

Possible LCSH Subject Headings

AGENTS PROVOCATEURS
DETECTIVES
ESPIONAGE
HOUSE DETECTIVES
SECRET SERVICE
SPIES
SUBVERSIVE ACTIVITIES
WOMEN SPIES

Bibliographies—Spies

Blackstock, Paul W., and Schaf, Frank L. *Intelligence, Counterespionage, Covert Operations: A Guide to Information Sources.* Detroit: Gale, 1978.

Constantinides, George C. *Intelligence and Espionage: An Analytical Bibliography.* Boulder, Col.: Westview, 1983.

Scholar's Guide to Intelligence Literature: Bibliography of the Russell J. Bowen Collection in the Joseph Mark Lauinger Memorial Library. Frederick, Md.: University Pubns. of America, 1983.

CODES

There are few current books on this subject unless you turn to children's books—perhaps because children admit to an interest in secrets.

Barker, Wayne G. *The History of Codes and Ciphers in the United States During World War I.* Laguna Hills, Cal.: Aegean Park Press, 1979.

—— *History of Codes and Ciphers in the United States Prior to World War I.* Laguna Hills, Cal.: Aegean Park Press, 1978.

Bosworth, Bruce. *Codes, Ciphers & Computers: An Introduction to Information Security.* Hasbrouck Heights, N.J.: Hayden, 1982.

Bryan, William G. *Cryptographic ABCs.* 2 vols. Sorrento, Fla.: American Cryptogram Society, 1967.

Gaines, Helen F. *Cryptanalysis: A Study of Ciphers and Their Solution.* New York: Dover, 1956.

Gardner, Martin. *Codes, Ciphers & Secret Writing.* New York: Dover, 1984.

Kahn, David. *Kahn on Codes: Secrets of the New Cryptology.* New York: Macmillan, 1983.

Laffin, John. *Codes and Ciphers: Secret Writing Through the Ages.* New York: Abelard-Schuman, 1964.

Pratt, Fletcher. *Secret and Urgent: The Story of Codes and Ciphers.* Norwood, Pa.: Telegraph Books, 1981. Reprint of 1942 ed.

Smith, Laurence D. *Cryptography: The Science of Secret Writing.* New York: Dover, 1971. Reprint of 1943 ed.

Ruffner, Frederick G. *Code Names Dictionary: A Guide to Code Names, Slang, Nicknames, Journalese and Similar Terms: Aviation, Rockets and Missiles, Military, Aerospace, Meteorology, Atomic Energy, Communications and Others.* Detroit: Gale, 1963.

Possible LCSH Subject Headings

"Codes" is not a subject heading. You are referred to the correct heading CIPHERS.

CIPHER AND TELEGRAPH CODES
CIPHERS
CODE NAMES
CRYPTOGRAPHY

Dress

———————◆———————

Cave paintings in Spain show Paleolithic women wearing fur skirts in about 8000 B.C., when probably the only endangered species was mankind. In a cave of Cro-Magnon time in France, a hairpin was found in a position near a body that left no doubt of its use. There are ways of finding out what people in different centuries and cultures wore and perhaps even why they wore certain things. Paintings from different periods show what people wore, and diaries, literature and poetry discuss the subject. Don't forget to look at the magazines and newspapers of the day for the last hundred years or so; the advertising as well as the fashion or news photographs. Fashion today might be the most challenging to figure out a century from now.

Most of the titles listed below are well illustrated. The Monro index and the Davenport *Book of Costume* are standard works for the past, as are the history titles, and the Houck *Fashion Encyclopedia* discusses contemporary designers and fashion.

Useful Titles

Cunningham, C. W. *The History of Underclothing*. London: Faber & Faber, 1982.

Cunningham, Phyllis Emily, and Lucas, Catherine. *Occupational Costume in England, from the Eleventh Century to 1914*. London: Black, 1967.

Davenport, Millia. *The Book of Costume.* 2 vols. New York: Crown, 1948.

Glynn, Prudence. *In Fashion: Dress in the Twentieth Century.* New York: Oxford Univ. Press, 1978.

Gorsline, Douglas W. *What People Wore: A Visual History of Dress from Ancient Times to Twentieth Century America.* New York: Crown, 1952.

Harrold, Robert. *Folk Costumes of the World in Colour.* Poole, Eng.: Blandford Press, 1978.

Hill, Margot Hamilton, and Bucknell, Peter A. *The Evolution of Fashion: Pattern and Cut from 1066 to 1930.* London: Batsford, 1967.

Houck, Catherine. *The Fashion Encyclopedia: An Essential Guide to Everything You Need to Know About Clothes.* New York: St. Martin's, 1982.

Laver, James. *Costume and Fashion: A Concise History.* London: Thames and Hudson, 1982.

Lister, Margot. *Costume: An Illustrated Survey from Ancient Times to the Twentieth Century.* London: Jenkins, 1967.

———. *Costumes of Everyday Life: An Illustrated History of Working Clothes.* London: Plays, 1972.

McClellan, Elizabeth. *History of American Costume, 1607–1870.* New York: Tudor, 1937. (Repr. Tudor, 1969.)

Payne, Blanche, *History of Costume, from the Ancient Egyptians to the Twentieth Century.* New York: Harper, 1965.

Sichel, Marion. *Costume Reference.* 10 vols. Boston: Plays, 1977–1979.

Tilke, Max. *National Costumes from East Europe, Africa, and Asia.* New York: Hastings House, 1978.

Truman, Nevil. *Historic Costuming.* 2d ed. London: Pitman, 1966.

Yarwood, Doreen. *Costume of the Western World: Pictorial Guide and Glossary.* New York: St. Martin's Press, 1980.

———. *Encyclopedia of World Costume.* New York: Scribner's, 1978.

Possible LCSH Subject Headings

Works on the clothing of particular places or periods as well as costumes for the theater are under the heading COSTUME in the Library of Congress list of headings. Dress from the standpoint of utility as covering for the body, and works on the art of dress are under the heading CLOTHING AND DRESS. (The word *costume* in a title may not make these distinctions.) You can use these and other *more specific* headings (FASHIONS, JEWELRY, HATS, HAIRDRESSING, JEANS, OVERALLS, SHOES, etc.). FADS is also sometimes an appropriate heading for fashion.

ARMS AND ARMOR
CLERGY—COSTUME
CLOTHING AND DRESS
CLOTHING AND DRESS, PRIMITIVE
COSTUME
COSTUME—HISTORY (and then by time periods; for example: COSTUME—HISTORY—15TH CENTURY)
COSTUME—CHINA (and FRANCE, UNITED STATES, etc.)
COSTUME, ARAB (and JEWISH, ORIENTAL, SLAVIC, etc.)
COSTUME DESIGN
COSTUME DESIGNERS
MONASTICISM AND RELIGIOUS ORDERS—HABIT
UNIFORMS, MILITARY

Indexes

Monro, Isabel Stevenson, and Cook, Dorothy E. *Costume Index: A Subject Guide to Plates and to Illustrated Texts*. New York: Wilson, 1937. Supp. 1957.

And most general indexes. See "Periodicals" in Section 2.

Bibliography

Hiler, Hilaire, and Hiler, Meyer. *Bibliography of Costume: A Dictionary Catalog of About Eight Thousand Books and Periodicals* . . . Edited by Helen Grant Cushing. New York: Wilson, 1939.

Travel

Yes, go there if you can and get a tan if you're lucky, but if you can't go to Hawaii or Yugoslavia in order to write a few pages on a character's vacation or search for a mysterious art treasure, there are always ways to describe places you haven't visited.

You can write to the Tourist Bureau or Chamber of Commerce in most cities. They usually respond with colorful brochures, maps, and miscellaneous information. The *Hotel and Motel Red Book,* which also covers resorts in the United States and some other countries, usually gives 800 numbers so you can quickly obtain material.

Hotels and Chambers of Commerce

Financial Times Ltd. *Financial Times World Hotel Directory.* London: Financial Times, 1975–   . Annual.

Hotel and Motel Red Book. New York: American Hotel Assoc. Directory Corp., 1886–   . Annual.

World Wide Chamber of Commerce Directory. Loveland, Col.: Johnson Publishing, 1986–   . Annual.

Guidebooks

There are thousands of travel guides to almost everywhere. Some of the best have been publishing for a long time, making them valuable sources for older city maps, etc., so remember that you might sometimes want an edition that is not current. The best-known authentic and complete guides for the serious traveler are the *Baedeker* series, *Muirhead's Blue Guides*, and *Nagel's Travel Guides*. These have in-depth information on the history of cities, the sights and lore, and contain detailed plans and maps. Other popular guides are *Fodor's, Mobil, Shell, Frommer's, and Fielding's* guides.

Federal and state governments also publish information on travel. See the "Government Publications" segment in part 5 of this guide for the full citations for the Sears and Moody *Using Government Publications* and the Parish *State Government Reference Publications*, both of which have chapters on travel publications. A good bibliography is:

Heise, Jon O. *The Travel Book: Guide to the Travel Guides.* New York: Bowker, 1981.

An especially useful older series on U.S. cities and states, filled with interesting detail and very well written, is:

American Guide Series. Compiled by the Federal Writers' Project (later called Writers' Program). (Various publishers), 1937–49. Volumes for states, major cities, regions, and some special subjects.

Other Useful Titles

Boyer, Richard, and Savageau, David. *Places Rated Almanac: Your Guide to Finding the Best Places to Live in America.* 2d ed. New York: Rand McNally, 1985.

Cities of the World: A Compilation of Current Information on Cultural, Geographical, and Political Conditions in the Countries and Cities of Six Continents, Based on the Department of State's "Post Reports." 2d ed. 4 vols. and supp. Detroit: Gale, 1985.

Cole, Garold. *Travels in America from the Voyages of Discovery to the Present: An Annotated Bibliography of Travel Articles in Periodicals, 1955–1980.* Norman: Univ. of Oklahoma, 1984.

Cure, Karen. *The Travel Catalogue.* New York: Holt, Rinehart & Winston, 1978.

Encyclopedia of Geographic Information Sources. 4th ed. Edited by Jennifer Mossman. U.S. Volume. Detroit: Gale, 1987.

Marlin, John T., and Avery, James S. *The Book of American City Rankings.* New York: Facts on File, 1983.

The New Book of American Rankings. FYI Information Services. New York: Facts on File, 1984.

Shakman, Robert A. *Where You Live May Be Hazardous to Your Health: A Health Index to over 200 American Communities.* New York: Stein & Day, 1979.

Traveler's Reading Guides: Background Books, Novels, Travel Literature, and Articles. Edited by Maggy Simony. Bayport, N.Y.: Freelance Publications, 1982.

Possible LCSH Subject Headings

TRAVEL is a subject heading, but it retrieves information about travel itself, not information about places. But it is worth looking at the list of "see also" headings suggested under that heading in LCSH. Some are: CUSTOMS ADMINISTRATION AND TOURISTS, OCEAN TRAVEL, PASSPORTS, SAFARIS, YOUTH TRAVEL, etc. There are other interesting headings referring to travel itself such as:

JET LAG
TRAVEL, ANCIENT
TRAVEL, MEDIEVAL

For guidebooks and information on places themselves, use the subdivisions (under the names of countries, etc.) DESCRIPTION AND TRAVEL—GUIDE-BOOKS or (under names of cities) DESCRIPTION—GUIDE-BOOKS. For example:

FRANCE—DESCRIPTION AND TRAVEL—GUIDE-BOOKS
PARIS—DESCRIPTION—GUIDE-BOOKS

Indexes

Most, if not all, periodical and newspaper indexes may be searched for articles on cities, countries, and places in general. See list in "Periodicals" in Section 2.

Atlases, Gazetteers, and Maps

These sources are filled with miscellaneous and very useful information and offer visual impressions that help "set" a place in memory. Historical atlases will show you the way the world was then, and an atlas like the *Rand McNally Commercial Atlas and Marketing Guide* gives much more encyclopedic information than just a road map—statistical tables of population, business and manufacturers, agriculture, and other commercial features. Watch for publication dates on these materials. Some of the older ones are still very good sources but may be out-of-date in terms of any statistical information offered. Again, you may want a historical view, but remember that even the names of countries may have changed, as well as factual data. One of the newest, *Earthbook*, has encyclopedic information and uses space-age technology and satellite photography.

Useful Titles

Atlas of American History. Rev. ed. Edited by Kenneth T. Jackson. Original edited by James Truslow Adams. New York: Scribner's, 1978.

Columbia Lippincott Gazetteer of the World. Edited by Leon E. Seltzer with the Geographical Research Staff of Columbia Univ. Press and with the cooperation of the American Geographical Society, with 1961 supp. New York: Columbia Univ., 1962.

Earthbook World Atlas. Tallahassee, Fla.: Graphic Learning, 1987.

Goode, John Paul. *Goode's World Atlas.* 16th ed. Edited by Edward B. Espenshade, Jr. Chicago: Rand McNally, 1983.

Heyden, A. A. M. van der, and Scullard, Howard H. *Atlas of the Classical World.* London: Nelson, 1959.

Muir, Ramsay. *Muir's Historical Atlas: Ancient, Medieval, and Modern.* 10th ed. Edited by R. F. Treharne and Harold Fullard. New York: Barnes & Noble, 1964.

New York Times Atlas of the World. Rev. ed. New York: Times Books, 1980.

Paullin, Charles Oscar. *Atlas of the Historical Geography of the United States.* Edited by John K. Wright. Westport, Conn.: Greenwood Press, 1975. Reprint of 1932 ed.

Rand McNally Commercial Atlas and Marketing Guide. New York: Rand McNally, 1876– . Annual.

Shepherd, William Robert. *Historical Atlas.* 9th ed. New York: Barnes & Noble, 1964.

Times, London. *Index-Gazetteer of the World.* London: Times Pub., 1965.

Webster's New Geographical Dictionary. Springfield, Mass.: Merriam-Webster, 1984.

Possible LCSH Subject Headings— Atlases and Maps

Though there are headings ATLASES, MAPS, and GAZET-TEERS, these are general headings. For such material in relation to places, you must use those terms as subdivisions under the names of cities, countries, deserts, mountains, etc. For example:

AFRICA—MAPS
CANADA—MAPS, TOURIST
FRANCE—ATLASES
FRANCE—HISTORY—ATLASES
UNITED STATES—GAZETTEERS

and you can use various headings under GEOGRAPHY, which can be divided chronologically and by subject such as "ancient." For example:

GEOGRAPHY—15TH–16TH CENTURIES
GEOGRAPHY—ANCIENT
GEOGRAPHY—MEDIEVAL
GEOGRAPHY—POLITICAL

Index—Geography

Geo Abstracts. Norwich, Eng.: Univ. of East Anglia, 1972– . Formerly *Geographical Abstracts* 1966–71. Published six times a year with annual indexes.

Research Guides—Geography

Brewer, James Gordon. *The Literature of Geography: A Guide to Its Organization and Use*. 2d ed. London: Bingley, 1978.

Dunbar, Gary S. *The History of Modern Geography: An Annotated Bibliography of Selected Works*. New York: Garland, 1985.

Encyclopedia of Geographic Information Sources, U.S. Volume. 4th ed. Detroit: Gale, 1985.

Encyclopedia of Geographic Information Sources, International Volume: A Bibliographic Guide to Approximately 12,000 Citations for Publications and Organizations of Interest to Business Personnel, Covering More than 160 Cities, Countries and Regions. 4th ed. Edited by Jennifer Mossman. Detroit: Gale, 1988.

Harris, Chauncy Dennison. *Bibliography of Geography*. Chicago: Univ. of Chicago Dept. of Geography Research Papers. 1976–1984. In progress.

IMAGINARY PLACES

Or you can forget all this and just invent the places your characters inhabit. But be careful; that might be even harder. There are examples in:

Manguel, Alberto, and Guadalupi, Gianni. *The Dictionary of Imaginary Places*. New York: Macmillan, 1980.

This is a "gazetteer" to more than 1000 imaginary places of literature and includes maps. And to find more, there is a subject heading GEOGRAPHICAL MYTHS. The Library of Congress has covered everything!

Weather

Sunny, balmy days, hot days, droughts, rain, sleet, snow, storms at sea—all kinds of weather can augment or cause an event in a story, and the way characters respond to weather can reveal something about them. But if you're using a real and specific date in the near or not-to-distant past, be careful about inventing weather. Readers have vivid memories about the weather on specific dates—such as their wedding day, the day they buried Mom, VJ day, or the day of a New York City blackout. Either be vague about the actual date or get the weather right.

Diaries, memoirs, and personal journals frequently mention weather. Two of the best sources of recent times are the *daily newspaper* and *almanacs*. The daily newspapers give each day's forecast and will frequently mention the previous day's weather in a story if there was a significant heat wave or storm. *Historical Statistics of the U.S.* (see "Statistics" segment, part 5) has a summary chapter on "Climate." The Sears and Moody *Using Government Publications* (see segment "Government Publications," part 5) has a section on "Climate" as searched in government documents. The Ludlum book, *The Weather Factor*, has interesting accounts of how weather has affected events in American history—battles, elections, aviation, the Kentucky Derby, famous football games, and other sports events.

Useful Titles

The Climates of the States: National Oceanic and Atmospheric Administration Narrative Summaries, Tables, and Maps for Each State, with an Overview of State Climatologist Programs. 3d ed. New material by James A. Ruffner. Detroit: Gale, 1985.

The Encyclopedia of Climatology. Ed. by John E. Oliver and Rhodes W. Falbridge. Van Nostrand Reinhold, 1987.

Ludlum, David. *Early American Winters I 1604–1820; Early American Winters II 1821–1870; Early American Hurricanes 1492– 1870; Early American Tornadoes 1586–1870.* Boston: American Meteorological Society, 1963, 1966, 1968, 1970.

———. *The Weather Factor.* Boston: Houghton Mifflin, 1984.

Ruffner, James A., and Bair, Frank B. *Weather Almanac.* 5th ed. Detroit: Gale, 1987.

U.S. Environmental Data Service. *Climatological Data . . .* Various daily, weekly, monthly, and annual publications from 1914–   . Wash., D.C./Asheville, N.C.: Weather Bureau and various U.S. agency sponsorship.

Visher, Stephen Sargent. *Climatic Atlas of the United States.* Cambridge: Harvard Univ. Press, 1954. Repr. 1966.

World Weather Records. Edited by H. Helm Clayton. Wash., D.C.: Smithsonian Institute, 1927.

World Weather Records. 1921–30, 1931–40. 2 vols. Wash., D.C.: Smithsonian Institute, 1934–37.

Continued by:

U.S. Weather Bureau. *World Weather Records.* 1941–50. Washington, 1959.

———. *World Weather Records.* 1951–60. Wash., D.C.: Government Printing Office, 1965–68.

Continued by:

World Weather Records. 1961–70. 2 vols. Asheville, N.C.: Dept. of Commerce, National Oceanic and Atmospheric Admin., Environmental Data and Information Service, National Climatic Center, 1979.

Possible LCSH Subject Headings

Any kind of weather you can name is probably a subject heading. The subdivision CLIMATE can be used under the names of countries, cities, etc. (COLORADO—CLIMATE).

CLIMATOLOGY
CRIME AND WEATHER
GREAT BRITAIN—CLIMATE (example; see note above)
HUMIDITY
HURRICANES
METEOROLOGY
RAIN AND RAINFALL
SEASONS
SNOW
STORMS
TORNADOES
TYPHOONS
WEATHER
WEATHER—PSYCHOLOGICAL EFFECTS
WEATHER—RESEARCH
WEATHER IN ART
WEATHER IN LITERATURE
WINDS

Indexes

In addition to checking the daily newspapers for forecasts, the subject "weather" can be searched in the *New York Times Index* (going back to 1851), the London *Times* indexes (going back to 1790), and in the *Readers' Guide* (back to 1900) and its predecessors, *Poole's Index to Periodical Literature, 1802–1906* and *Nineteenth Century Readers' Guide to Periodical Literature 1890–1899.* "Weather" can also be searched in indexes in any subject field, revealing its aspect or influence—*Business Periodicals Index, Psychological Abstracts,* etc.

Food

————————

Food, or lack of it, and the details of cooking it can be as important in fiction as in life. And if we are what we eat, then a warrior character won't eat like a grandmother character. There are books to tell you perhaps more than you want to know about food—many of you know that a sandwich was named after the Earl of Sandwich, but did you know that pretzels were first made by monks in southern Europe as a reward for students who learned their prayers? The pretzel's crossed ends represent praying hands. Of the titles below, *The World Encyclopedia of Food* gives description and discussions of where and how an item was eaten or drunk and what it tastes like, and the Simon work offers notes on "the production, taxation, distribution and consumption of food and drink, their use and abuse in all times and among all peoples." The Axford and Lowenstein are bibliographies of early cookbooks (which would show not only what kind of food was being eaten but also how it was prepared). The Bitting covers works from the fifteenth to the twentieth centuries and includes American cookbooks produced by societies, lodges, and churches. The *Larousse Gastronomique* is, of course, translated from the French, who seem to know a thing or two about cooking. Ethnic cooking and national cooking can be searched through appropriate subject headings as suggested below. Lichine's encyclopedia discusses the history, making, and serving of wine.

Don't forget that you can get ideas from the literature, fine art, diaries, newspapers, and periodicals of different time periods.

Useful Titles

Axford, Lavonne B. *English Language Cookbooks, 1600–1973*. Detroit: Gale, 1976.

Coyle, L. Patrick. *The World Encyclopedia of Food*. New York: Facts on File, 1982.

Driver, Christopher, and Berriedale-Johnson, Michelle. *Pepys at Table: Seventeenth Century Recipes for the Modern Cook*. Berkeley: Univ. of California Press, 1984.

Food and Food Production Encyclopedia. Edited by Douglas M. Considine. Van Nostrand Reinhold, 1982.

Gelb, Barbara L. *The Dictionary of Food and What's in It for You*. New York: Paddington Press, 1978.

Lichine, Alexis. *New Encyclopedia of Wines and Spirits*. 4th ed. In collaboration with William Fifield. New York: Knopf, 1985.

Lowenstein, Eleanor. *Bibliography of American Cookery Books, 1742–1860*. Wooster, Mass.: American Antiquarian Society, 1972.

Montagne, Prosper. *Larousse Gastronomique: The Encyclopedia of Food, Wine and Cookery*. New York: Crown, 1961.

Ritchie, Carson I. A. *Food in Civilization: How History Has Been Affected by Human Tastes*. New York: Beaufort Books, 1981.

Simon, Andre Louis. *Biblioteca Gastronomica, a Catalog of Books and Documents on Gastronomy*. London: Wine and Food Society, 1953.

U.S. Dept. of Agriculture. *Will There Be Enough Food? The 1981 Yearbook of Agriculture*. Wash., D.C.: Government Printing Office, 1981.

Possible LCSH Subject Headings

FOOD may be used as a subdivision under subjects (INDIANS—FOOD, BIRDS—FOOD). Cookery of nations or certain styles of cooking are entered as COOKERY, AMERICAN and COOKERY, CHINESE, etc. Works for specific localities are entered as COOKERY—GEORGIA—SAVANNAH. FOOD HABITS is an especially important heading; notice the possible subdivisions under it. The heading for wine is actually WINE AND WINE MAKING, but wine may be used with certain subdivisions such as WINE—RELIGIOUS ASPECTS. As usual, before going to a broad heading like FOOD, try the most specific heading you might need first, because there are headings like TEMPURA and TORTI-LLAS and even a heading ACORNS AS FOOD. Sometimes the heading MANNERS AND CUSTOMS will bring up related titles like this one: *Convivial Dickens: The Drinks of Dickens and His Times*, by Edward Hewett (Ohio Univ. Press, 1983).

BEVERAGES
BREAD
COFFEE
COOKERY
COOKERY, AFRICAN (see long list of possibilities in
    LCSH)
DIET
FAMINES (also a subdivision under names of regions or
    countries)
FOOD
FOOD HABITS
FOOD HABITS—HISTORY
FOOD HABITS—FRANCE—HISTORY (and other coun-
    tries and cities, e.g. FOOD HABITS—ITALY—NA-
    PLES—HISTORY, as well as certain time periods, e.g.
    FOOD HABITS—ENGLAND—HISTORY—17TH CEN-
    TURY)
FOOD—PRESERVATION
FOOD—RELIGIOUS ASPECTS
FOOD—SENSORY EVALUATION
FOOD CONTAMINATION
FOOD HABITS
FOOD IN THE BIBLE
FOOD POISONING
FOOD SUPPLY
MEAT

NUTRITION
TABLE
TABLE ETIQUETTE
VEGETARIANISM
WINE—RELIGIOUS ASPECTS
WINE AND WINE MAKING

Indexes

Most general indexes have information on food from various points of view—diet and nutrition, political, historical, and psychological aspects, famine, poverty. See list in "Periodicals" segment, part 2.

Holidays

What and why we celebrate also reveals us. Most of the titles here have an American or British emphasis but indicate other origins, and some are universal (a good one being Gregory's *Anniversaries and Holidays*). The *Chase's* events calendar is a paperback (so might be kept in the library's pamphlet files and not catalogued) and is contemporary—giving dates for Secretary's Day and National Library Week, Dance Day, etc. Perhaps enough mysterious, fictional encounters between lovers have taken place during Mardi Gras, but there are lots of other exotic feasts from which to choose—maybe the Garlic Festival in Gilroy, California, or a romantic Ohio Frog Jumping Contest.

Useful Titles

Chambers, Robert. *Books of Days: A Miscellany of Popular Antiquities in Connection with the Calendar, Including Anecdote, Biography, and History, Curiosities of Literature, and Oddities of Human Life and Character*. 2 vols. Philadelphia: Lippincott, 1899.

Chase, William D., and Chase, Helen M. *Chase's Annual Events*. Chicago, Ill.: Contemporary Books. Annual.

Festivals Sourcebook. 2d ed. Edited by Paul Wasserman. Detroit: Gale, 1984. Subtitle: A reference guide to fairs, festivals and celebrations in agriculture, antiques, the arts, theater and drama, arts and crafts, community, dance, ethnic events, film, folk, food and drink, history, Indians, marine, music, seasons and wildlife.

Frewin, Anthony. *The Book of Days*. London: Collins, 1979.

Gaster, Theodor Herzl. *Festivals of the Jewish Year: A Modern Interpretation and Guide.* New York: Sloane, 1953. Repr. William Morrow, 1978.

Gregory, Ruth W. *Anniversaries and Holidays.* 4th ed. Chicago: American Library Assoc., 1983.

Harper, Howard V. *Days and Customs of All Faiths.* New York: Fleet, 1957.

Samuelson, Sue. *Christmas: An Annotated Bibliography.* New York: Garland, 1982.

Shemanski, Frances. *A Guide to Fairs and Festivals in the United States.* Westport, Conn.: Greenwood, 1984.

Spicer, Dorothy Gladys. *Festivals of Western Europe.* New York: Wilson, 1958.

Weiser, Francis Xavier. *Handbook of Christian Feasts and Customs: The Year of the Lord in Liturgy and Folklore.* New York: Harcourt, 1958. Abr. ed. Paulist Press, 1963.

Possible LCSH Subject Headings

Many holidays and festivals are entered under their own name or type of festival (CHRISTMAS or HANUKKAH or GION FESTIVAL or DANCE FESTIVALS or DRAMA FESTIVALS or HOLY INNOCENTS, FEAST OF). And see the geographic subdivisions under HOLIDAYS and under FESTIVALS.

ANNIVERSARIES
BIRTHDAYS
CHURCH YEAR
DAYS
FASTS AND FEASTS
FESTIVALS
FESTIVALS—INDIA (JAPAN, etc., see note above.)
FESTIVALS—JEWS
HOLIDAYS
HOLIDAYS—JEWS

HOLIDAYS—MEXICO (example; see note above)
HOLIDAYS—PSYCHOLOGICAL ASPECTS
HOLIDAYS—SONGS AND MUSIC (and see subdivision
   under specific days, e.g. FOURTH OF JULY—SONGS
   AND MUSIC)

Indexes

There is no specific index to holidays, but most general and
social science indexes refer to holidays and festivals, often
seasonally. See list in "Periodicals" segment, part 2.

War and
Other Disasters

The Library of Congress has a subject heading IMAGINARY WARS AND BATTLES; it would be wonderful if all the literature on the subject qualified for that heading. There has been much published on the subject of real wars, both in fact and in fiction, and a lot is available on the history of war. This is also an area where memoirs and journals are helpful, and for recent wars, newspaper eyewitness accounts are valuable. Historically, it is interesting to find accounts of the events at the time of, say, the American Civil War and then read current, hindsight views and opinions of what happened and why. There is not a specific section here on peace (reflecting society?) but a few titles are offered for a tiny balance.

The works listed are representative, with mostly American and general international titles; there is so much published on all wars it is impossible here to be more than selective. Wars are searchable directly under their names and also under the names of countries followed by HISTORY, MILITARY (see below). The *Jane's* titles are arranged by country and give the numbers and kinds of aircraft and fighting ships and the specifications as well as other related information. The Keegan title *Zones of Conflict* has a disturbing subtitle: *An Atlas of Future Wars*. Nash's *Darkest Hours* describes disasters from ancient times to the present. Under "Bibliographies" below, there are two titles on the holocaust.

Useful Titles

Banks, Arthur. *A Military Atlas of the First World War.* With commentary by Alan Palmer. New York: Taplinger, 1975.

————. *A World Atlas of Military History.* 4 vols. In progress. New York: Hippocrene books, 1973–1984.

Blackey, Robert. *Revolutions and Revolutionists; A Comprehensive Guide to the Literature.* Santa Barbara, Cal.: ABC-Clio, 1982.

Boatner, Mark M. *The Civil War Dictionary.* New York: McKay, 1959.

————. *Encyclopedia of the American Revolution.* Bicentennial ed. Rev. and exp. New York: McKay, 1974.

Dupuy, Richard E., and Dupuy, Trevor N. *The Encyclopedia of Military History from 3500 B.C. to the Present.* Rev. ed. New York: Harper & Row, 1977.

Dupuy, Trevor Nevitt, and Hammerman, Gay M. *People and Events of the American Revolution.* New York: Bowker, 1974.

Goralski, Robert. *World War II Almanac, 1931–45: A Political and Military Record.* New York: Putnam, 1981.

Harbottle, Thomas B. *Dictionary of Battles.* 3d rev. ed. Edited by George Bruce. New York: Van Nostrand, 1981.

Israel, Fred L. *Major Peace Treaties of Modern History: 1648–1967.* 4 vols. New York: Chelsea House and McGraw-Hill, 1967.

————, ed. *Major Peace Treaties of Modern History, 1967–1979: The Continuing Search for Peace; Major Treaties, Agreements, Resolutions, and Multilateral Accords.* New York: Chelsea House, 1980.

Jane's All the World's Aircraft. London: S. Low, 1909– . Annual.

Jane's Fighting Ships. London: S. Low, 1898– . Annual.

Janke, Peter. *Guerrilla and Terrorist Organizations: A World Directory and Bibliography.* Brighton, Eng.: Harvester, 1983.

Keegan, John, and Wheatcroft, Andrew. *Zones of Conflict: An Atlas of Future Wars.* London: Cape, 1986.

Kidron, Michael, and Smith, Dan. *The War Atlas: Armed Conflict— Armed Peace.* New York: Simon & Schuster, 1983.

Middleton, Harry J. *The Compact History of the Korean War.* Cambridge, Mass.: Hawthorn, 1965.

The Military Balance. London: International Inst. for Strategic Studies, 1959– . Annual.

Sanderson, Michael W. B. *Sea Battles: A Reference Guide.* Middletown, Conn.: Wesleyan Univ. Press, 1975.

The Simon and Schuster Encyclopedia of World War II. Edited by Thomas Parish. New York: Simon & Schuster, 1978.

10 Eventful Years: A Record of Events of the Years Preceding, Including, and Following World War II, 1937 Through 1946. Edited by Walter Yust. 4 vols. Chicago: Encyclopaedia Britannica, 1947.

UNESCO Yearbook on Peace and Conflict Studies. Westport, Conn.: Greenwood, 1981– . Annual.

United Nations Disarmament Yearbook. New York: United Nations, 1977– . Annual.

The Vietnam War: An Almanac. Edited by John S. Bowman. New York: World Almanac Pubs., 1985.

Warry, John. *Warfare in the Classical World: An illustrated Encyclopedia of Weapons, Warriors, and Warfare in the Ancient Civilizations of Greece and Rome.* New York: St. Martin's, 1981.

World Armaments and Disarmament: SIPRI Yearbook. New York: Humanities Press, 1970– . Annual.

Disasters

Cornell, James. *The Great International Disaster Book.* 3d ed. New York: Scribner's, 1982.

Nash, Jay Robert. *Darkest Hours: A Narrative Encyclopedia of Worldwide Disasters from Ancient Times to the Present.* Chicago: Nelson-Hall, 1976.

Terrorism

Lakos, Amos. *International Terrorism: A Bibliography.* Boulder, Col.: Westview Press, 1986.

Mickolus, Edward F. *The Literature of Terrorism: A Selectively Annotated Bibliography.* Westport, Conn.: Greenwood Press, 1980.

Schmid, Alex Peter. *Political Terrorism: A Research Guide to Concepts, Theories, Data Bases, and Literature.* Amsterdam: North Holland; New Brunswick (USA): Transaction Books distributor, 1983.

Possible LCSH Subject Headings

This is an area where you can be creative and construct your own best headings, depending on how thorough you need to be and if you want to go beyond the obvious first choice, the name of the battle or war. When you look under "Wars" (plural) in the list of subject headings, you are referred to MILITARY HISTORY, NAVAL HISTORY, and WAR (singular) and also directed to look directly under the specific names of wars, battles, sieges, etc. Under MILITARY HISTORY, it is suggested that you also look under the names of countries followed by the subdivision HISTORY, MILITARY, and it is further suggested that you look under names of countries, then the branch of the military and history, e.g. UNITED STATES. ARMY—HISTORY. If you look under WAR (singular), there are many, many suggestions; some appear in the list below.

ARMISTICES
CRIMES AGAINST PEACE
DISARMAMENT
HOLOCAUST, JEWISH (1939–1945)
MILITARY HISTORY
(name of country)—HISTORY, MILITARY
NAVAL HISTORY
PEACE
PEACE TREATIES
REVOLUTIONS
TERRORISM
WAR—CASUALTIES

WAR—MORAL AND ETHICAL ASPECTS
WAR (ROMAN LAW)
WAR CRIMES
WAR FILMS
WAR GAMES
WORLD WAR, 1914–1918
WORLD WAR, 1939–1945

Some headings for disasters are:

ACCIDENTS
CATASTROPHICAL, THE
DISASTERS
DISASTERS—PSYCHOLOGICAL
MURPHY'S LAW
NATURAL DISASTERS

Indexes

Most indexes cover this subject, including *Historical Abstracts* and the newspaper indexes; a few others that are particularly useful are:

International Political Science Abstracts. Oxford: Blackwell, 1951–1972; Paris: International Political Science Assn.: 1973– . Bimonthly.

Public Affairs Information Service Bulletin. New York: PAIS, 1915– . Semimonthly.

Peace Research Abstracts Journal. Dundas, Ont.: Peace Research Institute, 1964– . Monthly.

Bibliographies and Research Guides

Aimone, Alan C. *The Official Records of the American Civil War: A Researcher's Guide.* 2d ed. West Point, N.Y.: U.S. Military Academy, 1978.

Bayliss, Gwyn M. *Bibliographic Guide to the Two World Wars: An Annotated Survey of English-Language Reference Materials.* London and New York: Bowker, 1977.

Blanco, Richard L. *The War of the American Revolution: A Selected Annotated Bibliography of Published Sources.* New York: Garland, 1984.

Boulding, Elise, et al. *Bibliography on World Conflict and Peace.* 2d ed. Boulder, Col.: Westview Press, 1979.

Burns, Richard Dean, and Leitenberg, Milton. *The Wars in Vietnam, Cambodia and Laos, 1945–1982: A Bibliographic Guide.* Santa Barbara, Cal.: ABC-Clio, 1984.

Carroll, Berenice A., et al. *Peace and War; A Guide to Bibliographies.* Santa Barbara, Cal.: ABC-Clio, 1983.

Divale, William T. *Warfare in Primitive Societies: A Bibliography.* Santa Barbara, Cal.: ABC-Clio, 1973.

Edelheit, Abraham, and Edelheit, Hershel. *Bibliography on Holocaust Literature.* Boulder, Col.: Westview Press, 1986.

Floyd, Dale E. *The World Bibliography of Armed Land Conflict from Waterloo to World War I: Wars, Campaigns, Battles, Revolutions, Revolts, Coups d'Etat, Insurrections, Riots, Armed Confrontations.* 2 vols. Wilmington, Del.: Michael Glazier, 1979.

Guide to the Sources of United States Military History. Edited by Robin Higham. Hamden, Conn.: Archon Books, 1975. Supp. 1981. Supp. II 1985.

The Holocaust: An Annotated Bibliography and Resource Guide. Edited by David M. Szonyi. Hoboken, N.J.: Ktav Pub. House for the National Jewish Resource Center, New York, 1985.

Lewis, John R. *Uncertain Judgment: A Bibliography of War Crimes Trials.* Santa Barbara, Cal.: ABC-Clio, 1979.

Stanford University. Hoover Institution on War, Revolution and Peace. *The Library Catalogs of the Hoover Institution . . . Catalog of the Western Language Collections.* 63 vols. Boston: G. K. Hall, 1969. Supps. 1972–1977.

Ziegler, Janet. *World War II: Books in English, 1945–65.* Stanford, Cal.: Hoover Institution Press, 1971.

ARMS AND ARMOR

Useful Titles

Beckett, Brian. *Weapons of Tomorrow*. New York: Plenum Press, 1983.

Canby, Courtlandt. *A History of Weaponry*. New York: Hawthorn Books, 1963.

The Complete Encyclopedia of Arms and Weapons. Subtitle: The most comprehensive reference ever published on arms and armor from prehistoric times to the present—with over 1,250 illustrations. Ed. by Leonard Tarassuk and Claude Blair. New York: Simon and Schuster, 1982.

Diagram Group. *Weapons: An International Encyclopedia from 5000 BC to 2000 AD*. New York: St. Martin's Press, 1980.

Dupuy, Trevor N. *The Evolution of Weapons and Warfare*. London: Jane's, 1982.

Ezell, Edward Clinton. *Small Arms of the World*. Harrisburg, Pa.: Stackpole Books, 1977.

Garavaglia, Louis A. and Worman, Charles G. *Firearms of the American West*. 2 vols. Albuquerque: Univ. of New Mexico Press, 1984–85.

Oakeshott, R. Ewart. *The Archaeology of Weapons: Arms and Armor from Prehistory to the Age of Chivalry*. London: Butterworth Press, 1960.

———. *A Knight and His Armour*. London: Butterworth Press, 1961.

Peterson, Harold L. *Arms and Armor in Colonial America, 1526–1783*. New York: Bramhall House, 1956.

Wilkinson-Latham, Robert. *Phaidon Guide to Antique Arms and Armour*. Oxford: Phaidon, 1981.

Wise, Terence. *Saxon, Viking and Norman*. London: Osprey, 1979.

Possible LCSH Subject Headings—Arms

There is a heading WEAPONS SYSTEMS, but if you look for a single heading "weapons" you are referred to ARMS AND ARMOUR and FIREARMS. Types of weapons can be searched directly under the name—BAYONETS, BLOW-GUNS, BOOMERANGS, BOW AND ARROW, DAGGERS, MACHINE-GUNS, PISTOLS, RIFLES, SPEARS, SWORDS, etc. The heading ARMS AND ARMOR can be divided geographically (ARMS AND ARMOR—GREECE—CRETE, etc.)

ANTITANK WEAPONS
ARMS AND ARMOR
ARMS AND ARMOR—HISTORY
ARMS AND ARMOR—HISTORY—19TH CENTURY
  (and other time periods)
ARMS AND ARMOR—INDIA (Example, see note above.)
ARMS AND ARMOR, ANCIENT
ARMS AND ARMOR, ISLAMIC
ARMS AND ARMOR, MYCENAEAN
ARMS AND ARMOR, PRIMITIVE
BINARY WEAPONS
COSTUME
DIRECTED-ENERGY WEAPONS
FIREARMS
FIREARMS—ACCIDENTS
FIREARMS—DESIGN AND CONSTRUCTION
FIREARMS—IDENTIFICATION
FIREARMS—LAW AND LEGISLATION
FIREARMS—MARKINGS
FIREARMS THEFT
MARTIAL ARTS WEAPONS
MILITARY PARAPHERNALIA
NEUTRON WEAPONS
NUCLEAR WEAPONS
SPACE WEAPONS
TOURNAMENTS

Bibliography—Arms

Riling, Raymond L. *Guns and Shooting.* A selected, chronological bibliography prepared for the use of the arms collector, ballistician, gunsmith, handloader, technician, student, and author, as well as for all who are interested in the history and development of firearms and their use in war and peace, in the field and at target. New York: Greenberg, 1951.

Medicine

This can be risky. A responsible author would not want to give out misinformation that might alarm or hurt readers, and unless an illness and symptoms are entirely fabricated, authors want to use accurate details when writing about diseases that readers may recognize or even have. If you do a really good research job, it is not uncommon for you to begin to think you have the complaint . . . but that would probably be just another procrastination ploy. Six months in a TB sanatorium is not a viable alternative to writing. Medicine is a field where talking to an expert or at least having an expert react to the writing is a good idea (see segment "Locating Experts," in part 5).

On the other hand, researching in this subject area can give you lots of plot ideas as you investigate symptoms, therapies, and the side effects or contraindications of various drugs. That's a good reason to do this kind of research ahead of the writing if a medical problem is to dominate a story or play.

If your interest is in the ETHICS OF SOCIOLOGY OF MEDICINE, look at these titles:

Encyclopedia of Bioethics. Edited by Warren T. Reich. 4 vols. New York: Free Press, 1978.

Pearsall, Marion. *Medical Behavioral Science: A Selected Bibliography of Cultural Anthropology, Social Psychology, and Sociology in Medicine.* Lexington: Univ. of Kentucky Press, 1963.

For books on a wide range of HOLISTIC HEALTH AND HEALING see:

Inglis, Brian, and West, Ruth. *The Alternative Health Guide*. New York: Knopf, 1983.

Popenoe, Cris. *Wellness*. Wash., D.C.: Yes! Inc., 1977. A bibliography.

Some of the titles listed below, such as the *PDR* and the *Merck Manual*, are found at most reference desks; others, like *Harrison's Principles* and *Goodman and Gillman's*, the favorites of medical students, are found in medical libraries. In this field it may be necessary to use a specialized medical library.

Useful Titles—Anatomy

Gray, Henry. *Anatomy of the Human Body*. 30th American ed. Edited by Carmuine D. Clemente. Philadelphia: Lea & Febiger, 1985.

The Way Things Work Book of the Body. Edited by C. Van Amerongen. New York: Simon & Schuster, 1979.

Useful Titles—Medicine

American Hospital Association. *The AHA Guide to the Health Care Field*. Chicago: American Hospital Association, 1972–   . Annual. Information on hospitals and health care institutions.

American Medical Association Family Medical Guide. Edited by Jeffrey R. M. Kunz. New York: Random House, 1982.

Complete Home Medical Guide. Columbia University College of Physicians and Surgeons. New York: Crown, 1985.

Dorland's Illustrated Medical Dictionary. 26th ed. Philadelphia: Saunders, 1981.

Harrison's Principles of Internal Medicine. 11th ed. New York: McGraw-Hill, 1987.

Health Science Books 1876–1982. New York: Bowker, 1982.

Magalini, Sergio I., and Scarascia, Euclide. *Directory of Medical Syndromes*. 2d ed. Philadelphia: Lippincott, 1981.

Merck Manual of Diagnosis and Therapy. Rahway, N.J.: Merck, 1899– . Irregular.

Miller, Sigmund S. *Symptoms: The Complete Home Medical Encyclopedia.* New York: Crowell, 1978.

Stedman, Thomas L. *Illustrated Stedman's Medical Dictionary.* 24th ed. Baltimore: Williams & Wilkins, 1982.

Useful Titles—Forensic Medicine

These titles are of help with stories involving detection of the cause of death and medical descriptions of the scene of the crime. For example, a book like *The Essentials of Forensic Medicine* describes the identification of certain injuries, thermal and electrical injuries, hanging, strangulation, drowning, suffocation, etc. It even has a section on how the pathologist must behave at the scene of the crime—advising that a pathologist should notice the temperature of the scene, the clothing, blood stains, the posture of the body, drag marks, hairs, dents in the floor, etc. The *Medical Subject Headings* (MeSH) described below have some headings especially useful for forensic medicine. Some examples are:

CRIMINAL INVESTIGATION
CRIMINAL INVESTIGATION—CASE STUDIES
CRIMINAL INVESTIGATION—LABORATORY MANUALS
CRIMINAL PSYCHOLOGY
FORENSIC MEDICINE
WOUNDS AND INJURIES
WOUNDS, GUNSHOT
WOUNDS, NONPENETRATING
WOUNDS, PENETRATING

Curry, Alan S. *Poison Detection in Human Organs.* 3d ed. Springfield,. Ill.: Thomas, 1976.

DiMaio, Vincent J. M. *Gunshot Wounds: Practical Aspects of Firearms, Ballistics and Forensic Techniques.* New York: Elsevier, 1985.

The Essentials of Forensic Medicine. 4th ed. Edited by C. J. Polson, et al. New York: Pergamon Press, 1985.

Forensic Medicine. 9th ed. Edited by Keith Simpson with Bernard Knight. London: Edward Arnold, 1985.

Forensic Osteology: Advances in the Identification of Human Remains. Edited by Kathleen J. Reichs. Springfield, Ill.: Thomas, 1986.

Human Identification: Case Studies in Forensic Anthropology. Edited by Ted A. Rathbun and Jane E. Buikatra. Springfield, Ill.: Thomas, 1984.

The Human Skeleton in Forensic Medicine. 2d ed. Edited by Wilton Krogman and Hehmet Yasar Iscar. Springfield, Ill.: Thomas, 1986.

Jaffe, Frederick A. *A Guide to Pathological Evidence.* Toronto: Carswell, 1976.

Useful Titles—Drugs

Goodman and Gilman's The Pharmacological Basis of Therapeutics. 7th ed. New York: Macmillan, 1985.

Graedon, Joe. *Joe Graedon's The New People's Pharmacy: Drug Breakthroughs for the '80s.* New York: Bantam/Graedon Enterprises, 1985.

Morgan, Brian L. *Food and Drug Interaction Guide.* New York: Simon & Schuster, 1986.

Physician's Desk Reference: PDR. Rutherford, N.J.: Medical Economics, 1946–   . Annual.

Physician's Desk Reference for Nonprescription Drugs. Oradell, N.J.: Medical Economics, 1980–   . Annual.

United States Pharmacopeia Dispensing Information: USP DI. Vol. 1, *Drug Information for the Health Care Provider;* vol. 2, *Advice for the Patient.* Rockville, Md.: U.S. Pharmacopoeial Convention, 1983.

Research Guides

Information Sources in the Medical Sciences. 3d ed. Edited by L. T. Morton and S. Godbolt. London: Butterworths, 1984.

Roper, Fred, and Boorkman, Jo Anne. *Introduction to Reference Sources in the Health Sciences.* 2d ed. Chicago: Medical Library Assoc., 1984.

Physicians

ABMS Compendium of Certified Medical Specialists. 7 vols. Evanston, Ill.: American Board of Medical Specialists, 1986.

American Medical Directory. 30th ed. Chicago: American Medical Association, 1986. Biennial. In four volumes, including a geographical index.

Directory of Medical Specialists. 22d ed. 1985–86. 3 vols. Chicago: Publ. for the American Board of Medical Specialists by Marquis Who's Who, 1985. Biennial.

Possible Subject Headings

As discussed in the chapter on Subject Headings, if you're in a medical library, you should be using the National Library of Medicine's *Medical Subject Headings* (MeSH), but medical subjects can be searched in the *Library of Congress Subject Headings* (LCSH) for sociological, anthropological, or more popular interpretations of the subjects. One volume of the work above, *Health Science Books 1876–1982*, has an informative guide to LCSH/MeSH and MeSH/LCSH equivalents, showing the differences in headings from both lists on the same subjects. An example that illustrates the difference is that CANCER is a heading in LCSH with many subdivisions; in MeSH, under "Cancer," you are told to "see NEOPLASMS." There are, of course, many headings in LCSH such as DISEASES and SYMPTOMATOLOGY, and headings for individual medical problems such as DIABETES and HEART—

DISEASES. So check the appropriate lists, as always using the most specific term and going to broader terms if necessary (the lists will usually give you a "see" or "use" reference to the correct heading).

Indexes

Medical subjects can be searched in almost all periodical indexes depending on your need—*Readers' Guide* for popular information, *Social Science Index* and *Psychological Abstracts* for more scientific approaches, and so on. The primary index for medicine is:

Index Medicus. Wash., D.C.: National Library of Medicine. 1960– . Monthly with cumulations. Published since 1879 with various publishers and titles.

This most comprehensive index to the world's medical literature has, since 1966, been compiled by mechanized means and represents a partial printout of the MEDLARS (Medical Literature Analysis and Retrieval System), computer-based file.

It can be searched by computer on MEDLINE and is well worth a paid search, which can limit your search by language (this is an international index) and date and save much time if you have an in-depth investigation. *Index Medicus* uses the MeSH headings.

Money:
Economics and Business

What do gold, silver, paper, shells, beads, whales' teeth, cattle, feathers, and tobacco have in common? They are a few of the forms used for money throughout history, having been assigned a value agreed upon by one or more societies. That agreed-upon value is what separates money from run-of-the-mill paper, shells, etc. As long people think something has a certain worth and social convention supports that view, that item has a value beyond its "face." Once again it is the abundance or lack of money that makes a story, as well as characters' responses to money.

There are ways to find the historical forms of money, the given value of money, and the evolution of money. This is the kind of subject where an overview given in an encyclopedia article might save time by giving you appropriate terms to try in the card catalog—for your time period and society should you be looking under COINS, ANCIENT or under WAM-PUM. The Einzig book on primitive money is a dazzling account of almost all forms of money, from leather and fur to tusks, beeswax, and cocoa beans.

Useful Titles

Burns, Arthur R. *Money and Monetary Policy in Early Times*. A. M. Kelley, Bookseller, 1965.

Burr, Susan. *Money Grows Up in America*. Wash., D.C.: Service Center for Teachers of History, 1962.

Ederer, Rupert. *The Evolution of Money*. Wash., D.C.: Public Affairs Press, 1964.

Einzig, Paul. *Primitive Money in Its Ethnological, Historical, and Economic Aspects*. 2d rev. ed. New York: Pergamon Press, 1966.

Krause, Chester L., and Lemke, R. F. *Standard Catalog U.S. Paper Money*. New York: Krause, 1981.

McCusker, John J. *Money and Exchange in Europe and America, 1600–1775: A Handbook*. Chapel Hill, N.C.: Published for the Institute of Early American History and Culture, Williamsburg, Va., by the Univ. of North Carolina Press, 1978.

Spufford, Peter. *Handbook of Medieval Exchange*. London: Boydell and Brewer, 1986.

Sterns, Robert E. C. *Ethno-conchology: A Study of Primitive Money*. Wash., D.C.: Government Printing Office, 1889.

Woodward, Arthur. *The Denominators of the Fur Trade: An Anthology of Material on the Fur Trade*. 2d. print. rev. Pasadena, Cal.: Westernlore Press, 1979.

Possible LCSH Subject Headings

Works on the study of coins, medals, tokens, etc. are entered under the heading NUMISMATICS, and works on the study of coins only are under COINS and such headings as COINS, AMERICAN (or FRENCH, ITALIAN, etc.). MONEY can be divided geographically and then by time period; see below.

COINS
DEMAND FOR MONEY
DOLLAR
DOLLAR, AMERICAN
HEARTH MONEY
HOARDING OF MONEY
INDIANS OF NORTH AMERICA—MONEY (example of type of heading)
LEGAL TENDER
MONEY

MONEY—[Place]—HISTORY (and then divided by time period; e.g. MONEY—UNITED STATES—HISTORY—COLONIAL PERIOD)
MONEY, PRIMITIVE
NUMISMATICS
PIECES OF EIGHT

ECONOMICS

Some basic, general tools in this broader area are listed below. consult the Library of Congress list of subject headings for all of the related headings and the bibliographies to pinpoint specific aspects of the subject. (See also "Statistics" in part 5 of this guide.)

Chandler, Lester V. *America's Greatest Depression, 1929–1941.* New York: Harper, 1970.

Directory of Business and Financial Services. 8th ed. Edited by Mary McNierney Grant and Riva Berleant-Schiller. New York: Special Libraries Association, 1984.

Encyclopedia of American Economic History: Studies of the Principal Movements and Ideas. New York: Scribner's, 1980.

Encyclopedia of Economics. Edited by Douglas Greenwald. New York: McGraw-Hill, 1982.

Kindleberger, Charles P. *Manias, Panics, and Crashes: A History of Financial Crisis.* New York: Basic Books, 1978.

Moffitt, Michael. *The World's Money: International Banking from Bretton Woods to the Brink of Insolvency.* New York: Simon & Schuster, 1983.

The Money Encyclopedia. Edited by Harvey Rachlin. New York: Harper & Row, 1984.

Sterling, John G. *Great Depressions: 1837–1844, 1893–1898, 1929–1939.* New York: Scott, Foresman, 1966.

Possible LCSH Subject Headings

ECONOMICS is a heading and is used as a subdivision under
countries with the form ECONOMIC CONDITIONS; e. g.
PERU—ECONOMIC CONDITIONS. ECONOMICS—HIS-
TORY can be subdivided chronologically, and DEPRESSIONS
can be subdivided by date and place (see below).

DEPRESSIONS (may be subdivided by date and country;
   e.g. DEPRESSIONS—1929—UNITED STATES)
ECONOMIC DEVELOPMENT
ECONOMIC HISTORY
ECONOMIC INDICATORS
ECONOMIC HISTORY
ECONOMIC POLICY
ECONOMICS (under names of countries use subdivision
   [place]—ECONOMIC CONDITIONS)
ECONOMICS—BIBLIOGRAPHY
ECONOMICS—HISTORY (can be divided chronologically;
   e.g. ECONOMICS—HISTORY—19TH CENTURY)
ECONOMICS—PSYCHOLOGICAL ASPECTS
ECONOMICS—RELIGIOUS ASPECTS

Indexes

Business Periodicals Index. New York: Wilson, 1958–   . Monthly
with annual cumulations.

Index of Economic Articles in Journals and Collective Volumes.
1886/1924–   . Homewood, Ill.: R. D. Irwin, 1961–   . Annual, but frequency varies.

Predicasts F&S Index. Cleveland: Predicasts, 1968–   . Monthly
with cumulations.

Wall Street Journal Index. New York: Dow Jones, 1958–   . Monthly
annual cumulations.

Bibliographies and Guides

Amstutz, Mark R. *Economics and Foreign Policy: A Guide to Information Sources*. Detroit: Gale, 1977.

Brownstone, David M., and Carruth, Gorton. *Where to Find Business Information: A Worldwide Guide for Everyone Who Needs the Answers to Business Questions*. 2d ed. New York: Wiley, 1982.

Daniells, Lorna M. *Business Information Sources*. 2d rev. ed. Berkeley, Cal.: Univ. of California Press, 1985.

Encyclopedia of Business Information Sources. 5th ed. Edited by Paul Wasserman, et al. Detroit: Gale, 1983.

Information Sources in Economics. 2d ed. Edited by John Fletcher. London: Butterworths, 1984.

Lavin, Michael R. *Business Information: How to Find It, How to Use It*. Phoenix, Ariz.: Oryx Press, 1987.

Parapsychology and Occult Sciences

Mysterious events happen in the real world as well as in the fictional world, and there is certainly a lot to feed the writer's imagination. One of the all-time great subject headings appears in this field: MARVELOUS, THE.

Useful Titles

Encyclopedia of Occultism and Parapsychology. 2d ed. Edited by Leslie Shepard. 3 vols. Detroit: Gale, 1984. Based on substantially revised material from the work by Spense, listed below.

Bletzer, June G. *The Donning International Encyclopedic Psychic Dictionary.* Norfolk, Va.: Donning, 1986.

Handbook of Parapsychology. Edited by Benjamin B. Wolman. New York: Van Nostrand Reinhold, 1977.

Robbins, Rossell Hope. *The Encyclopedia of Witchcraft and Demonology.* New York: Crown, 1959.

Spense, Lewis. *Encyclopedia of Occultism: A Compendium of Information on the Occult Sciences, Occult Personalities, Psychic Science, Magic, Demonology, Spiritism and Mysticism.* London: Routledge, 1920.

Thorndike, Lynn. *History of Magic and Experimental Science.* 8 vols. New York: Macmillan, 1923; Columbia Univ. Press, 1943–58.

Possible LCSH Subject Headings

"Occultism" by itself is not a heading (use OCCULT SCI-

ENCES), and "Parapsychology" by itself is not a heading (use PSYCHICAL RESEARCH). There are lots of possibilities in this subject area. A few are:

ALCHEMY
ASTRAL PROJECTION
ASTROLOGY
CLAIRVOYANCE
CONJURING
CRYSTAL-GAZING
DEMONOLOGY
DIVINATION
FORTUNE-TELLING
GHOSTS
MAGIC
MARVELOUS, THE
MEDIUM
MIND-READING
OCCULT SCIENCES
OCCULT SCIENCES AND CRIMINAL INVESTIGA-
TION
PARAPSYCHOLOGY AND ANIMALS
PARAPSYCHOLOGY AND ANTHROPOLOGY
PARAPSYCHOLOGY AND CRIME
PARAPSYCHOLOGY AND CRIMINAL INVESTIGA-
TION
PSYCHIC GAMES
PSYCHICAL RESEARCH
PSYCHICAL RESEARCH—MILITARY ASPECTS
PROPHESIES (OCCULT SCIENCES)
SATANISM
SPIRITUALISM
SUPERSTITION
WITCHCRAFT

Bibliographies and Guides

Claire, Thomas C. *Occult Bibliography: An Annotated List of Books Published in English, 1971 Through 1975*. Metuchen, N.J.: Scarecrow, 1978.

——— *Occult/Paranormal Bibliography: An Annotated Bibliography of Books Published in English, 1976 Through 1981*. Metuchen, N.J.: Scarecrow, 1984.

Eberhardt, George M. *A Geo-Bibliography of Anomalies: Primary Access to Observations of UFOs, Ghosts, and Other Mysterious Phenomena*. Westport & London: Greenwood, 1980.

Melton, J. Gordon. *Magic, Witchcraft, and Paganism in America: A Bibliography*. New York: Garland, 1982.

White, Rhea A., and Dale, Laura A. *Parapsychology: Sources of Information*. Metuchen, N.J.: Scarecrow, 1973.

Indexes

Parapsychology Abstracts International. Dix Hills, N.Y.: Parapsychology Sources of Information Center, 1983–   . Semiannual.

And general indexes listed in segment "Periodicals," part 2, especially *Psychological Abstracts*.

The Future
and Science Fiction

When George Orwell wrote *1984*, he got quite a lot of things right about that year for at least some of the world even though the book was published in 1949. The "future" here is meant in that sense—an imagined world set in the future. Science fiction titles and headings are included here also for those involved in the fantastic or even weird sciences. This kind of writing does require a lot of imagination, but there are books to look at and read that will prompt imagination because there are a lot of interested futurists predicting possible new worlds. Often just a projected number for the future (as in population) will set a story line in action—or looking at some of the works listed above on stations in space. Note the subject headings discussion below, cautioning on the various meanings of *futures, futurism, futurists*. It's worth noting that Lamantine said: "History teaches everything, even the future."

There are organizations that focus on the future and publish material on the subject. The *Encyclopedia of Associations* (see segment "Locating Experts," in part 5) describes them, including two that have been in existence since the late sixties, the Institute for the Future, in Menlo Park, California, and the World Future Society, in Bethesda, Maryland. The World Future Society publishes, among other things, the *Futurist: A Journal of Forecasts, Trends, and Ideas About the Future*, which is well worth browsing. It carries articles on new technology and "tomorrow in brief," and interesting cover stories—for example, one on Paolo Soleri's city in the Arizona desert, Arcosanti, based on the principles of "Arcology," a term coined to describe the marriage of architecture

216

and ecology. Institutions like the World Future society can be searched in the catalogs by name, as can the Global 2000 Study and the Commission on the Year 2000 of the American Academy of Arts and Sciences named below. *Future Shock* (included along with newer titles by Alvin Toffler) and a few older titles are included because of some of the ideas they present.

Useful Titles—The Future

American Academy of Arts and Sciences, Boston. Commission on the Year 2000. *The Future of the United States Government Toward the Year 2000: A Report.* Edited by Harvey S. Perloff. Englewood Cliffs, N.J.: Prentice-Hall, 1972.

Anticipatory Democracy: People in the Politics of the Future. Edited by Clement Bezold. New York: Random House, 1978.

Book of Predictions. The People's Almanac Presents the Book of Predictions. New York: Morrow, 1981.

Calder, Nigel. *1984 and After: Changing Images of the Future.* London: Century Pub., 1983.

Cetron, Marvin J. *Encounters with the Future: A Forecast of Life into the Twenty-First Century.* New York: McGraw-Hill, 1982.

Cities in the 21st Century. Edited by Gary Gappert and Richard V. Knight. Beverly Hills: Sage, 1982.

Communications Tomorrow: The Coming of the Information Society. Edited by Edward Cornish. Bethesda, Md.: World Future Society, 1982.

The Computerized Society: Living and Working in the Electronic Age. Edited by Edward Cornish. Bethesda, Md.: World Future Society, 1985.

Dickson, Paul. *The Future File: A Guide for People with One Foot in the 21st Century.* New York: Rawson Associates, 1977.

Global 2000 Study. United States. *The Global 2000 Report to the President—Entering the Twenty-First Century: A Report.* Prepared by the Council on Environmental Quality and the Department of State. Wash., D.C.: Government Printing Office, 1980–1981.

Habitats Tomorrow: Homes and Communities in an Exciting New Era. Selections from *The Futurist.* Edited by Edward Cornish. Bethesda, Md.: World Future Society, 1984.

Handbook of Futures Research. Edited by Jib Fowles. Westport, Conn.: Greenwood, 1978.

Keegan, John, and Wheatcroft, Andrew. *Zones of Conflict: An Atlas of Future Wars.* London: Cape, 1986.

Living in the Future. Edited by Isaac Asimov. New York: Beaufort Books, 1985.

Macrae, Norman. *The 2025 Report: A Concise History of the Future 1975–2025.* New York: Macmillan, 1984.

Morgan, Chris. *Future Man.* London: David & Charles, 1980.

The Omni Future Almanac. Edited by Robert Weil. New York: Harmony Books, 1982.

Scanzoni, John H. *Shaping Tomorrow's Family: Theory and Policy for the 21st Century.* Beverly Hills: Sage, 1983.

Stavrianos, Leften S. *The Promise of the Coming Dark Age.* San Francisco: Freeman, 1976.

Toffler, Alvin. *Future Shock.* New York: Random House, 1970.

———. *Previews and Premises: An Interview with the Author of Future Shock and the Third Wave.* New York: Morrow, 1983.

———. *The Third Wave.* New York: Bantam Books, 1981.

Possible LCSH Subject Headings—The Future

Be very careful here. In this case you don't want "futures" as in economics, and FUTURE LIFE as used by the LCSH headings, means life after death, in the religious sense. FUTURISM refers to an artistic movement in art and literature, and its followers were FUTURISTS, though the term today often refers to those involved in future studies. Popular indexes may use some of these headings in different ways, so be aware of the distinctions. If you look up "Future studies," you are referred to a heading you can use: FORECASTING—STUDY AND TEACHING, under the heading FORECAST-

ING. FORECASTING is also a subdivision under subjects (FASHION—FORECASTING) AND FORECASTS is a subdivision under specific centuries (TWENTY-FIRST CENTURY—FORECASTS). "Prediction" can mean logic or psychology. PROPHECIES is not necessarily religious and can be used as a subdivision under subjects, such as BIBLE—PROPHECIES, or under countries and cities, such as UNITED STATES—HISTORY—PROPHECIES.

CIVILIZATION, MODERN—1950–
FORECASTING
FORECASTING—HISTORY
FORECASTING—RESEARCH
FORECASTING—SOCIETIES, ETC.
FORECASTING—STUDY AND TEACHING
FUTURE IN LITERATURE
FUTURE IN POPULAR CULTURE
FUTURE INTERESTS
FUTURE INTERESTS—UNITED STATES
INTERNATIONAL RELATIONS—FORECASTING (example; see note above)
PROPHECIES
REGRESSION (CIVILIZATION)
TWENTY-SECOND CENTURY—FORECASTS (example; see note above)
UNITED STATES—HISTORY—PROPHECIES (example)
WARNINGS
WORLD WAR, 1939–1945—PROPHECIES (example of PROPHECIES as subdivision)

Guides/Directories—The Future

The Futures Directory: An International Listing and Description of Organizations and Individuals Active in Future Studies and Long-Range Planning. Compiled by John McHale and others. Guildford, Surrey, Eng.: IPC Science and Technology Press; Boulder, Col.: Westview Press, 1977.

World Future Society. *The Future: A Guide to Information Sources.* 2d ed. Wash., D.C.: World Future Society, 1979.

Useful Titles—Science Fiction

Anatomy of Wonder: A Critical Guide to Science Fiction. 2d ed. Edited by Neil Barron. New York: Bowker, 1981.

Bleiler, Everett Franklin. *The Checklist of Science Fiction and Supernatural Fiction.* Glen Rock, N.J.: Firebell Books, 1978.

————. *The Guide to Supernatural Fiction.* Kent, Ohio: Kent State Univ. Press, 1983.

Garber, Eric, and Paleo, Lyn. *Uranian Worlds: A Reader's Guide to Alternative Sexuality in Science Fiction and Fantasy.* Boston: G. K. Hall, 1983.

The Science Fiction Encyclopedia. Edited by Peter Nicholls. Garden City, N.Y.: Dolphin Books, Doubleday, 1979.

Tuck, Donald H. *The Encyclopedia of Science Fiction and Fantasy Through 1968: A Bibliographic Survey of the Fields of Science Fiction, Fantasy, and Weird Fiction Through 1968.* Chicago: Advent Publishers, 1974–1982.

Possible LCSH Subject Headings—Science Fiction

BIBLIOGRAPHY—BEST BOOKS—SCIENCE FICTION
FANTASTIC FICTION
FANTASTIC FICTION, AMERICAN (RUSSIAN, etc.)
FUTURE IN LITERATURE
INTERPLANETARY VOYAGES
INTERSTELLAR TRAVEL
SCIENCE FICTION
SCIENCE FICTION—BIBLIOGRAPHY
SCIENCE FICTION—HISTORY AND CRITICISM
SCIENCE FICTION—PSYCHOLOGICAL ASPECTS
SCIENCE FICTION—RELIGIOUS ASPECTS
SCIENCE FICTION—BRITISH (AMERICAN, ITALIAN, etc.)

Indexes—Science Fiction

Many general indexes cover the subject, but those listed below are specific to science fiction.

Contento, William. *Index to Science Fiction Anthologies and Collections.* Boston: G. K. Hall, 1978.

Fletcher, Marilyn P. *Science Fiction Story Index, 1950–1979.* 2d ed. Chicago: American Library Association, 1981.

Index to Stories in Thematic Anthologies of Science Fiction. Edited by Marshall B. Tymn and others. Boston: G. K. Hall, 1978.

Guide—Science Fiction

Tymn, Marshall, and others. *A Research Guide to Science Fiction Studies: An Annotated Checklist of Primary and Secondary Sources.* New York: Garland, 1977.

Part V
Other Sources

Statistics

Statistics can help authors as well as readers develop a sense of a place or a problem—the land area and population, the number of deaths in a given war—and though the statistics may never get into the story, in the course of research they may enter the writer's head and help in the visualization and creation of the plot. Historical statistics, of course, help to establish the past.

Useful Titles

Demographic Yearbook: Annuaire Demographique. New York: United Nations, 1949– . Annual.

Handbook of Economic Statistics. Wash., D.C.: National Foreign Assessment Center, 1975– . Annual.

Kurian, George. *The New Book of World Rankings*. Rev. ed. New York: Facts on File, 1984.

United Nations Statistical Office. *Statistical Yearbook; Annuaire Statistique*. New York: United Nations, 1948– . Annual.

Statesman's Yearbook: Statistical and Historical Annual of the States of the World. London: Macmillan, 1864– . Annual.

The World in Figures. 4th ed. London: The Economist, 1981.

World Tables. 3d ed. 2 vols. Baltimore: Publ. for the World Bank, by Johns Hopkins Univ. Press, 1984.

Useful Titles—United States

American Year Book: A Record of Events and Progress. Vols. 1–36. New York: Nelson, 1911–1950.

Andriot, John L. *Population Abstract of the United States.* Enl. and rev. ed. McLean, Va.: Andriot Associates, 1983.

Bogue, Donald J. *The Population of the United States: Historical Trends and Future Projections.* New York: Free Press, 1985.

Marlin, John T., and Avery, James S. *The Book of American City Rankings.* New York: Facts on File, 1983.

The New Book of American Rankings. FYI Information Services. New York: Facts on File, 1984.

Social Indicators I–, 1976–: Selected Data on Social Conditions and Trends in the United States. Wash., D.C.: U.S. Dept. of Commerce, Office of Federal Statistical Policy and Standards, and Bureau of the Census, 1977–   . Triennial.

U/S: A Statistical Portrait of the American People. Edited by Andrew Hacker. New York: Viking, 1983.

U.S. Bureau of the Census. *Statistical Abstracts of the United States.* Wash., D.C.: Government Printing Office, 1879–   . Annual.

————. *County and City Data Book.* Wash., D.C.: Government Printing Office, 1952–   . Irregular.

————. *Historical Statistics of the United States, Colonial Times to 1970.* 2 vols. Wash., D.C.: U.S. Dept. of Commerce, 1975.

Vital Statistics of the United States. Wash., D.C.: U.S. Bureau of the Census, 1939–   . Annual.

Possible LCSH Subject Headings

This is another field where it is important to remember the possible *subdivisions* for statistics under other subjects and the names of cities, countries, etc. They are STATISTICS, STATISTICAL SERVICES, STATISTICAL METHODS, STATISTICS, VITAL, and STATISTICS, MEDICAL. For example:

AGRICULTURE—STATISTICS
ENGINEERING—STATISTICAL METHODS
FRANCE—STATISTICS, MEDICAL
ITALY—STATISTICS, VITAL
UNITED STATES—STATISTICAL SERVICES

Some other direct headings are:

CENSUS
CRIMINAL STATISTICS
ECONOMETRICS
EDUCATIONAL STATISTICS
GAMBLING SYSTEMS
INDUSTRIAL STATISTICS
JUDICIAL STATISTICS
MILITARY STATISTICS
POLITICAL STATISTICS
STATISTICS
STATISTICS—CHARTS, DIAGRAMS, ETC.
STATISTICS—DATA PROCESSING
STATISTICS—GRAPHIC METHODS
STATISTICS—STANDARDS
STATISTICS—TABLES
VITAL STATISTICS

Indexes

American Statistics Index . . . A Comprehensive Guide and Index to the Statistical Publications of the U.S. Government. Wash., D.C.: Congressional Information Service, 1973–   . Annual, with monthly cumulations.

Index to International Statistics: A Guide to the Statistical Publications of International Intergovernmental Organizations. Wash., D.C.: Congressional Information Service, 1973–   . Monthly, with quarterly and annual cumulations.

Population Index. Princeton, N.J.: Office of Population Research, Princeton Univ., and the Population Assoc. of America, 1935–   . Quarterly.

Schulze, Suzanne. *Population Information in Nineteenth Century Census Volumes.* Phoenix, Ariz.: Oryx Press, 1983.

Statistical Reference Index: A Selective Guide to American Statistical Publications from Sources Other than the U.S. Government. Wash., D.C.: Congressional Information Service, 1980–   . Monthly with quarterly and annual cumulations.

Bibliographies and Guides

Andriot, Donna, et al., eds. *Guide to U.S. Government Statistics.* 1986 ed. McLean, Va.: Documents Index, 1986.

Statistics Sources. 9th ed. Edited by Paul Wasserman and Jacqueline O'Brien. Detroit: Gale, 1984.

U.S. Bureau of the Census. *Bureau of the Census Catalog.* Wash., D.C.: Government Printing Office, 1947–   . Frequency varies; annual beginning 1980.

————. *Guide to Recurrent and Special Governmental Statistics.* State and Local Government Special Studies, no. 78. Wash., D.C.: Government Printing Office, 1976.

Manuscripts, Archives, and Special Collections

This is primarily an area for serious research, certainly not the path for finding quick information or facts. Locating and searching archives and manuscripts can be painstaking but very rewarding because original material has a reality and vividness not found in secondary sources. Reading the personal papers and letters of historical figures can contribute much detail and background to a novel based on a certain time period, or such material can serve as the basis for a fictional character. (See also the segment "Diaries, Memoirs, and Biographical Tools" in part 2, especially the Matthews title *American Diaries in Manuscript, 1580–1954,* and his *British Diaries,* as well as the Batts title, *British Manuscript Diaries.* . . .) The original documents surrounding a historical event frequently offer more than a history book can, and there is also a wealth of archival information on the very recent past. Because special collections are indeed special, this material is carefully preserved, and often its use is restricted. Using the guides to manuscripts and collections listed below, writers can determine the location and description of certain collections. If you must travel to another location, *call or write the library or archive beforehand* to make sure the material is there as described and available for use on the days and times you wish.

With a couple of exceptions, the works listed below are general American and British sources. For specific topics and other countries use the suggested subject headings. Probably of most use to authors is the work by Ash, *Subject Collections,* which identifies special collections (not necessarily manuscripts) in the United States and Canada. For example, Ash will identify a library (or museum, university, etc.) that has a collection on early railroading or on clowns and will identify what institution houses the papers of Truman or of Hemingway. The library directories, especially the *Directory of Special Libraries and Information Centers,* which has a subject index, also describe the collections of libraries in the United States and Canada. The titles below are individually annotated to distinguish the use of each bibliography or index.

Useful Titles

Annuaire Internationale des Archives. International Directory of Archives. (As of January 1975.) Paris: Presses Universitaires de France, 1975. Directory information on "those archives repositories open to the public and having materials of value for historical research."

Ash, Lee, and Miller, William G., comps. *Subject Collections.* 6th ed., rev. and enl. 2 vols. New York: Bowker, 1985. Subtitled: A guide to special book collections and subject emphases as reported by university, college, public and special libraries and museums in the United States and Canada. (See note above.)

British Library. Dept. of Manuscripts. *Index of Manuscripts in the British Library.* Vols. 1–4. Cambridge, Eng.: Chadwyck-Healey, 1984– . In progress. To be 11 vols. An alphabetical personal-and place-name index to manuscript collections acquired by the library up to 1950.

British Museum Dept. of Manuscripts. *The Catalogues of the Manuscript Collections.* Rev. ed. By T. C. Skeat. London: Trustees of the British Museum, 1962. An annotated list of 176 printed and handwritten catalogs of the museum's various collections of Western manuscripts.

Commager, Henry S. *Documents in American History.* 9th ed. Englewood Cliffs, N.J.: Prentice-Hall, 1973. A selection of basic source documents from the age of discovery to 1973.

Downs, Robert Bingham. *American Library Resources: A Bibliographical Guide.* Chicago: American Library Assoc., 1951.

————. Supp. 1950–1961. 1962.

————. Supp. 1961–1970. 1972.

————. Supp. 1971–1980. 1981.

Rather than a description of resources, this is a bibliography of bibliographies. Bibliographies, union lists, checklists, surveys, and catalogs of particular libraries and special collections from all parts of the country are included. There is a full index by library, subject, and author. (Library collections for which there are no lists available do not appear in the work.)

Downs, Robert Bingham. *British and Irish Library Resources: A Bibliographic Guide.* London: Mansell, 1981. Records "all published library catalogs—general and special; all checklists of specialized collections in libraries; calendars of manuscripts and archives; . . ."

English Historical Documents. Edited by David C. Douglas. 12 vols. London: Eyre & Spottiswoode, 1953–77. A comprehensive selection of source documents covering 500–1914. Each volume contains an introductory survey of the period and a general selected bibliography. Documents are arranged by topic.

————. 2d ed. Edited by David C. Douglas. London: Eyre Methuen; New York: Oxford, 1979– . In progress.

Foster, Janet, and Sheppard, Julia. *British Archives: A Guide to Archive Resources in the United Kingdom.* Detroit: Gale, 1982. Intends to provide directory information on "where archives, in the widest sense of the word, are held and made relatively accessible." Has a general index to collections (mainly personal names and institutions) and a key "subject word index."

Great Britain. Public Record Office. *Guide to the Contents of the Public Record Office.* 3 vols. London: HMSO, 1963–1968. Revised ed. of *Guide to the Manuscripts Preserved in the Public Record Office.* Presents information essential to use of documents with an introduction to the source of records, dates, and organization of records. Notes printed guides to special parts of collections. Indexes of persons, places, and subjects.

Meckler, Alan M., and McMullin, Ruth. *Oral History Collections.* New York: Bowker, 1975. Has a name and subject index of oral history centers.

National Union Catalog of Manuscript Collections, 1959/61– . Hamden, Conn.: Shoe String, 1962–   . Annual. Compiled and edited by the Descriptive Cataloging Division of the Library of Congress. Publisher varies. Each volume includes reproductions of catalog cards for collections reported to the Library of Congress by libraries and repositories throughout the United States. Entry information gives description of the collection, location (library, etc.), finding tools, access, etc.

U.S. Library of Congress. *Special Collections in the Library of Congress: A Selective Guide.* Compiled by Annette Melville. Wash., D.C.: Library of Congress, 1980. About 300 collections are described—"thematically related groups of material maintained as separate units within the general holdings of the Library of Congress."

U.S. National Archives and Records Service. *Catalog of National Archives Microfilms Publications.* Wash., D.C.: National Archives and Records Service, 1974. With *Supplementary List of National Archives Microfilms Publications 1974–82.* (1982) Lists the source materials and unpublished documents housed in the National Archives that are now available for purchase on positive microfilm.

U.S. National Archives and Records Service. *Guide to the National Archives of the United States.* Wash., D.C.: For sale by the Supt. of Documents, 1974. Briefly describes and lists the various collections of official records as of June 30, 1970, regardless of where the records are located.

U.S. National Historical Publications and Records Commission. *Directory of Archives and Manuscript Repositories.* Wash., D.C.: National Archives and Records Service, 1978. This directory serves as a companion to the Hamer's *Guide* below. Arranged by state or other political unit, then by city and repository, gives brief description of historical source material. Index of subjects and repositories.

U.S. National Historical Publications Commission. *A Guide to Archives and Manuscripts in the United States.* Edited by Philip M. Hamer. New Haven: Yale Univ. Press, 1961. The work above is a more current companion to this volume. A guide to "source materials for the study of the history of the United States and its relations with other nations and peoples."

LIBRARY DIRECTORIES

American Library Directory: A Classified List of Libraries in the United States and Canada with Personnel and Statistical Data. New York: Bowker, 1923– . Annual.

Directory of Special Libraries and Information Centers. 9th ed. 1985: 3 vols. Detroit: Gale, 1963– .

Subject Directory of Special Libraries and Information Centers. Detroit: Gale, 1975– . Irregular.

ANCIENT, MEDIEVAL, AND RENAISSANCE MANUSCRIPTS

Though some of the titles above cover this material, there are titles specific to the subject:

Braswell, Laurel Nichols. *Western Manuscripts from Classical Antiquity to the Renaissance: A Handbook.* New York: Garland, 1981.

Ker, Neil Ripley. *Medieval Manuscripts in British Libraries.* Vols. 1–3. Oxford: Clarendon Press, 1969–1983. In progress.

Possible LCSH Subject Headings

There are some subdivisions worth noting in this area. ARCHIVAL RESOURCES is a heading and can be used as a subdivision under topics and countries; e.g. TELEVISION BROADCASTING—ARCHIVAL RESOURCES and UNITED STATES—ARCHIVAL RESOURCES. MANUSCRIPTS is also both a heading and a subdivision under subjects and the names of authors and individual works. The same is true of ARCHIVES, which can be divided geographically and can be a subdivision under subjects; PRESIDENTS—UNITED STATES—ARCHIVES.

AFRO-AMERICANS—HISTORY—MANUSCRIPTS (example of use)
ARCHIVAL MATERIAL

ARCHIVAL RESOURCES (also a subdivision—see above note)
ARCHIVES (also a subdivision—see above note)
ARCHIVES—HISTORY
ARCHIVES—HISTORY—TO 500
ARCHIVES—REFERENCE SERVICES
ARCHIVES—UNITED STATES
MANUSCRIPTS (also a subdivision—see above note)
MANUSCRIPTS—COLLECTIONS
MANUSCRIPTS—FACSIMILES
MANUSCRIPTS, AMERICAN (and CLASSICAL, IRISH, ORIENTAL, etc.)
THEATER—UNITED STATES—ARCHIVES (example of use)

Guides

Brooks, Phillip Cooledge. *Research in Archives: The use of Unpublished Primary Sources.* Chicago: Univ. of Chicago Press, 1969.

Hockett, Homer Carey. *The Critical Method in Historical Research and Writing.* New York: Macmillan, 1955. Repr. Westport, Conn.: Greenwood, 1977.

Thorpe, James. *The Use of Manuscripts in Literary Research: Problems of Access and Literary Property Rights.* 2d ed. New York: Modern Language Assoc. of America, 1979.

Government Publications

What the government publishes in a given year certainly reflects that society and its concerns and, of course, is historically interesting. There is a wealth of original and primary source material in the form of government documents. Going back to read the transcripts of, for example, the McCarthy hearings in the fifties and subsequent congressional concern about McCarthy himself gives new meaning to the words "stranger than fiction." Looking at the concerns of Congress as viewed through its publications (or just looking at the subject headings in the *Monthly Catalog* index) for a given year will give you lots of information about that time in our history, and reading the text of hearings and committee meetings will reveal language, attitudes, and offer other insights into an age. The terms *government documents* and *government publications* are used interchangeably, but the word *document* might be too heavy for some of the popular publications put out by the government—things like cookbooks, houseplant advice, and park and recreation material.

Governments, especially that of the United states, publish extensively, so extensively that it is sometimes difficult to get through the mass of material to the document you want. There are, however, some very good guides to locating and using documents. Usually what people find difficult is the way documents are numbered and filed since, with some exceptions, they are not cataloged in the usual way and *often do not appear in the library's main catalog.* Most libraries have separate departments for the records, reports, bulletins, and other publications issued by various national, state, and municipal governments, and documents librarians can help you locate this material. These publications are called *public documents* or *government publications,* and you need to remember that they exist and ask where they are located in the library simply because much, if not most, of the material is not in general catalogs. There is much general and statistical information published by governments, *so make a consideration of documents a step in your research process.* The "government documents" section of your library usually has the documents not only of the United States but also of other governments and of international government agencies such as the United Nations. United Nations publications are discussed at the end of this segment.

Some libraries are called *depository libraries,* which means they receive, free of charge, publications from the U.S. government designated for general distribution to depository libraries in return for making them available to the general public. Some depository libraries are regional (at least one per state) and must accept all publications distributed; others are selective and may choose which items they wish to receive. In the indexes to U.S. documents, a black dot as part of an entry means this is a depository item, so if you're in a depository library, you'll know they may have selected that item.

U.S. government material is identified according to the Superintendent of Documents (SuDocs) classification system—an alphanumeric system used by many libraries to arrange government publications. The basic elements are a letter based on the issuing department (A—Agriculture) followed by numbers assigned for subagencies, series, and individual publications. So when you're using the indexes to government material, you will be making note of a different kind of classification and "call number" than you find in library catalogs, but one which works the same way by indicating the location of material as filed in the library. The librarians will assist you with this process. If you identify material in indexes that your library does not own, you can usually get it through interlibrary loan or purchase it if it is for sale and still in print through the Government Printing Office (GPO). (Sales publications do not stay in print for long unless they are truly best-sellers.) The *GPO Sales Publications Reference File* (PRF), on microfiche, is an index to what is currently available for sale by the Government Printing Office. Addresses and information on agencies can be found in the *United States Organization Manual.*

If you think you have a quick and easy question (or a difficult one), a librarian can guide you, but with government publications, if your search is even slightly difficult, it is a good idea to *start* with a research guide, since the possibilities are vast and you can easily miss important items. The guides are listed first below. The Sears and Moody *Using Government Publications* is an excellent two-volume guide with chapters on specific topics—foreign policy, foreign governments, occupations, business, copyright, elections, health, agriculture, education, genealogy, regulations, and administrative code in volume 1 and statistics for specific topics such as population, vital statistics, economics, business, income, employment, foreign trade, crime, and defense in volume 2. This guide also offers search strategies for special studies like treaties, technical reports, and patents. The Morehead book is an excellent *Introduction to United States Public Documents*, and the Andriot book provides a comprehensive listing of series and periodicals by SuDoc number and by agency with information about the authority and creation of government agencies and those agencies that have been abolished. The Schmeckebier is old but useful, as is the Brown guide for international publications. The Wynkoop *Subject Guide . . .* is kept up-to-date by *Government Reference Books.* The Palic title covers U.S. documents, foreign countries, and the publications of international government organizations. The Parish work has state information on Blue Books, legislative manuals, directories, statistical sources, tourist guides, etc. The Municipal Government Reference Sources and the *Monthly Checklist of State Publications* are bibliographies that also serve as guides and the checklist as a kind of subject index. See segment "Politics and Government," in part 3, for information on *Congres-*

sional Quarterly publications, which cover the activities of Congress and the government.

Research Guides

Andriot, John L. *Guide to U.S. Government Publications.* McLean, Va.: Documents Index, 1984. Vol. 1, *Current Agencies,* published annually; vol. 2, *Non-Current Agencies,* published every five years.

————. *Guide to U.S. Government Statistics.* 4th ed. McLean, Va.: Document Index, 1973.

Leidy, William Philip. *A Popular Guide to Government Publications.* 4th ed. New York: Columbia Univ. Press, 1976.

Morehead, Joe. *Introduction to United States Public Documents.* 3d ed. Littleton, Col.: Libraries Unlimited, 1983.

Newsome, Walter L. *New Guide to Popular Government Publications for Libraries and Home Reference.* Littleton, Col.: Libraries Unlimited, 1978.

Schmeckebier, Laurence Frederick, and Eastin, Roy B. *Government Publications and Their Use.* 2d rev. ed. Wash., D.C.: Brookings Institute, 1969.

Sears, Jean L., and Moody, Marilyn K. *Using Government Publications.* Vol. 1, *Searching by Subjects and Agencies;* vol. 2, *Finding Statistics and Using Special Techniques.* Phoenix, Ariz.: Oryx Press, 1985.

Subject Guide to Major United States Publications. 2d ed. Expanded and revised by Wiley J. Williams. Chicago: American Library Assoc., 1987.

Wynkoop, Sally. *Subject Guide to Government Reference Books.* Littleton, Col.: Libraries Unlimited, 1972. *Government Reference Books* serves as a continuing supplement. Littleton, Col.: Libraries Unlimited 1970–   . Biennial.

Research Guides for State and Municipal Publications

Municipal Government Reference Sources: Publications and Collections. Edited for the American Library Assoc. Government Documents Round Table by Peter Hernon and others. New York: Bowker, 1978.

Parish, David W. *State Government Reference Publications: An Annotated Bibliography.* 2d ed. Littleton, Col.: Libraries Unlimited, 1981.

State Government Research Directory. Edited by Kay Gill and Susan E. Tufts. Detroit: Gale, 1987.

U.S. Library of Congress. Exchange and Gift Division. *Monthly Checklist of State Publications.* Wash., D.C.: Government Printing Office, 1910–   . Monthly.

International Guides

(See also United Nations sources on page 245.)

Brown, Everett Somerville. *Manual of Government Publications: United States and Foreign.* New York: Appleton, 1950. Repr. New York: Johnson, 1964.

A Guide to Official Gazettes and Their Contents. Compiled by John E. Roberts. Wash., D.C.: Library of Congress, Law Library, 1985.

Palic, Vladimir M. *Government Publications: A Guide to Bibliographic Tools.* Wash., D.C.: Library of Congress, 1975.

Bibliographies

Subject Bibliographies are issued by the Government Printing Office—more than 250 bibliographies on different topics. This is a selected list of sales publications and does not include every bibliography done by the government, though these bibliographies are available free of charge. The *Subject*

Bibliographies cover topics, agencies, single titles, or series, and are revised and reissued on a continuing basis. Example titles are *Federal Communications Commission Publications, Recreational and Outdoor Activities,* and *Space, Rockets and Satellites.* An index to the subjects covered is issued as *Subject Bibliography #888.* This can be searched by subject to determine if a bibliography is available on a certain topic.

Another useful title for subject bibliographies is the one listed below, which lists bibliographies found in the *Monthly Catalog,* several hundred Tennessee Valley Authority bibliographies, and bibliographies from the *Subject Bibliographies.*

Scull, Roberta A. *A Bibliography of United States Government Bibliographies, 1968–1973.* Ann Arbor, Mich.: Pierian Press, 1975.

———. *1974–1976.* Ann Arbor, Mich.: Pierian Press, 1979.

Indexes

Listed below are the main access points to government publications. Most of these indexes are available for on-line searching through BRS, DIALOG, or SDC. *There are checklists and indexes going back to about 1774 and covering the first Congresses; check the Morehead and other guides listed above for those sets.*

Though the *Monthly Catalog* was for some time the basic, "Readers' Guide"–type index to government publications, since the appearance of the *CIS* and *ASI* indexes, it is no longer necessarily the best place to begin to search, depending on the question. For a question discussed in Congress, use *CIS,* and if the question is statistical, use *ASI. If in doubt, consult a librarian or check the guides.*

The *Monthly Catalog* index has several access points—an author index, a title index, a title keyword index, and a subject index (which uses the Library of Congress Subject Headings [LCSH]). It also has a series/report index and a contract index. This is a two-step process: (1) Find the author, title, keyword, subject, etc., in one of the indexes and get the *Monthly Catalog* entry number; then (2) find the entry number in the bibliographic section to obtain the complete bibliographic citation and the SuDocs number for the document. The majority of the publications in the *Monthly Catalog* are depository items and available in depository libraries. (See sample *Monthly Catalog* entry.)

American Statistics Index (ASI). Wash., D.C.: Congressional Information Service, 1973–   . Monthly. Annual cumulations. A comprehensive index to government statistics.

CIS Index. Index to Publications of the United States Congress. Wash., D.C.: Congressional Information Service, 1970–   . Monthly. Annual cumulations. Abstracts of hearings and documents. Has an index volume and an abstracts volume. Goes farther back under other titles.

Index to U.S. Government Periodicals. Chicago: Infodata International Inc., 1970–   . Quarterly. An index to over 180 government periodicals. A wide range of subjects and agencies. Major coverage of the military and the Defense Department.

U.S. Superintendent of Documents. *Catalog of the Public Documents of Congress and of Other Departments of the Government of the United States for the Period March 4, 1893–Dec. 31, 1940.* 25 vols. Wash., D.C.: Government Printing Office, 1896–1945. (Referred to by its binder's title *Document Catalog*.)

U.S. Superintendent of Documents. *Monthly Catalog of United States Government Publications, 1895–* . Wash., D.C.: Government Printing Office, 1895–   . Monthly.

Some general indexes lead readers to information about government publications and to government documents themselves, most notably the *Public Affairs Information Service*.

Useful Titles

Some of the most used titles are listed here. These standard titles are often cataloged and appear in main library catalogs, but that does not necessarily mean that other government publications appear in the catalog. See the "Politics"

Monthly Catalogue of
U.S. Government Publications

SAMPLE ENTRY

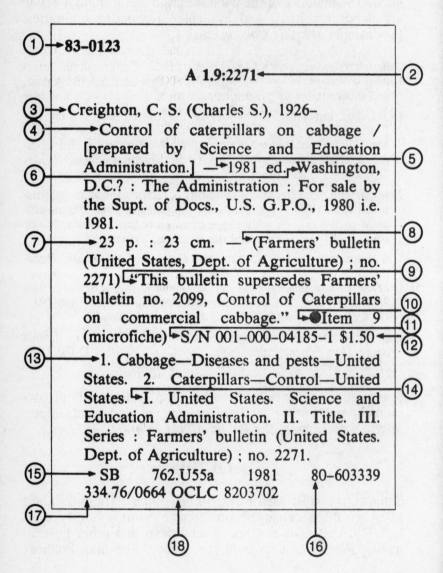

(1) → **83–0123**

A 1.9:2271 ← (2)

(3) → Creighton, C. S. (Charles S.), 1926–

(4) → Control of caterpillars on cabbage / [prepared by Science and Education Administration.] — 1981 ed. Washington, D.C.? : The Administration : For sale by the Supt. of Docs., U.S. G.P.O., 1980 i.e. 1981. (5)

(6)

(7) → 23 p. : 23 cm. — (Farmers' bulletin (United States, Dept. of Agriculture) ; no. 2271) "This bulletin supersedes Farmers' bulletin no. 2099, Control of Caterpillars on commercial cabbage." Item 9 (microfiche) S/N 001–000–04185–1 $1.50 ← (8) (9) (10) (11) (12)

(13) → 1. Cabbage—Diseases and pests—United States. 2. Caterpillars—Control—United States. I. United States. Science and Education Administration. II. Title. III. Series : Farmers' bulletin (United States. Dept. of Agriculture) ; no. 2271. (14)

(15) → SB 762.U55a 1981 80–603339 334.76/0664 OCLC 8203702 (16)

(17)

(18)

1. MONTHLY CATALOG ENTRY NO.—The entry number is assigned after the records are arranged alphanumerically by the Superintendent of Documents classification number. The first two digits establish the year; the last four digits locate the record in the Catalog.
2. SUPT. OF DOCS. CLASS NO.—This is the number assigned by the GPO Library to identify the document cataloged.
3. MAIN ENTRY—A main entry may be a personal author, a corporate author, a conference, uniform title, or the document title, as established by the Anglo-American Cataloging Rules.
4. TITLE PHRASE/STATEMENT OF RESPONSIBILITY—Title phrase and author statement are recorded from the title page or its substitutes. Material in brackets is supplied from other prominent sources.
5. EDITION—The edition is recorded from information in the document.
6. IMPRINT—The imprint contains place of publication, issuing agency, and date of issue. Includes name of distributor if different from issuing agency.
7. COLLATION—Collation notes pages, illustrations, and size.
8. SERIES STATEMENT—This identifies the series title and number.
9. NOTES—Notes include additional bibliographic information about the publication, including funding information for technical reports.
10. ITEM NO.—This document was distributed to depository libraries requesting this item number. Microfiche indicates the document was distributed as such.
11. STOCK NO.—This is a Government Printing Office sales stock number. It is used only in ordering from the Superintendent of Documents.
12. PRICE—GPO sales price.
13. SUBJECT HEADINGS (Arabic numerals)—Headings are selected from the Library of Congress subject headings. Some Natl. Agricultural Library and Natl. Library of Medicine subjects may be used. Natl. Libr. of Med. subjects will be indicated by an asterisk(*). Natl. Agri. Lib. subjects will be indicated by a dagger (†).
14. ADDED ENTRIES (Roman numerals)—When the Government publisher is not a main entry, it is included with added entries.
15. LIBRARY OF CONGRESS CLASS NO.—This is given when it is available from the Library of Congress.
16. LIBRARY OF CONGRESS CARD NO.—Included when it is available from the Library of Congress.
17. DEWEY CLASS NO.—Dewey class is given when it is available from the Library of Congress.
18. OCLC NO.—This is the number assigned by the OCLC to identify this record in the data base.

segment, part 3, for details on *Congressional Quarterly Weekly Report* and other CQ publications that are essential sources for following the activity of Congress.

U.S. Bureau of the Census. *Statistical Abstracts of the United States.* Wash., D.C.: Government Printing Office, 1879– . Annual. Summary statistics on political, social, and economic matters. Vital statistics, crime, etc.

———. *Historical Statistics of the United States, Colonial Times to 1970.* Bicentennial ed. 2 vols. Wash., D.C.: U.S. Dept. of Commerce, 1975.

U.S. Congress. *Official Congressional Directory.* Wash., D.C.: Government Printing Office, 1809– . Irregular. Biographical information on current members of Congress, committee membership, terms, congressional maps, etc.

United States Government Organization Manual. Wash., D.C.: Government Printing Office, 1935– . Annual. Describes the creation and activity of government agencies and quasi-official agencies. Names key people and gives addresses and other pertinent information.

Vital Statistics of the United States, 1937– . Wash., D.C.: U.S. Bureau of the Census, 1939– . Annual.

STATE AND MUNICIPAL TITLES

The Book of States. Lexington, Ky.: Council of State Governments, 1935– . Biennial. State information from mottoes and flowers to legislatures.

Municipal Year Book. Chicago: International City Managers Association, 1934– . Annual?

State and Metropolitan Databook, 1979– . Wash., D.C.: Government Printing Office, 1980– . A *Statistical Abstract* Supplement.

U.S. Bureau of the Census. *County and City Data Book, 1949–* . Wash., D.C.: Government Printing Office, 1952– . Irregular.

———. *City Government Finances, 1909–* . Wash., D.C.: Government Printing Office, 1913– . Annual.

———. *State Government Finances, 1915–* . Wash., D.C.: Government Printing Office, 1916.

Possible LCSH Subject Headings

There are subject headings for government publications that usually lead to information about this kind of publishing: how it is acquired, cataloged, and handled. For information on a particular government's publications remember that GOVERNMENT PUBLICATIONS is a subdivision under the names of countries; e.g. IRELAND—GOVERNMENT PUBLICATIONS.

GAZETTES
GOVERNMENT PUBLICATIONS (and GOVERNMENT PUBLICATIONS as a subdivision under names of countries.)
INTERNATIONAL ORGANIZATIONS
LOCAL GOVERNMENT DOCUMENTS
MUNICIPAL DOCUMENTS
PRINTING, PUBLIC
UNITED NATIONS

UNITED NATIONS

Guides

Brimmer, Brenda, et al. *A Guide to the Use of United Nations Documents*. Dobbs Ferry, N.Y.: Oceana, 1962.

Hajnal, Peter I. *Guide to United Nations Organization, Documentation, and Publishing for Students, Researchers, Librarians*. Dobbs Ferry, N.Y.: Oceana, 1978.

Winton, Harry N. M., comp. *Publications of the United Nations System: A Reference Guide*. New York: Bowker, 1972.

Indexes

United Nations. Dag Hammarskjold Library. *United Nations Documents Index*. Vols. 1–24. Jan. 1950–Dec. 1973. New York:

1950–1975. Superseded for 1950–62 by Cumulated Index, vols. 1–13, 1950–1962. 4 vols. Millwood, N.Y.: Kraus, 1974.

————. UNDEX. *United Nations Documents Index.* vol. 1– , Jan. 1970– ; Series B: *Country Index;* vol. 1– , Jan. 1970– ; Series C: *List of Documents Issued;* vol. 1– , Jan. 1974. New York: United Nations, 1970, 1974– . Monthly except July/Aug.

Titles/Yearbooks

A Comprehensive Handbook of the United Nations: A Documentary Presentation in Two Volumes. Compiled by Min-Chuan Ku. 2 vols. New York: Monarch Press, 1978.

Everyone's United Nations. 9th ed. New York: United Nations, 1979– . Irregular.

Osmanczyk, Edmund Jan. *The Encyclopedia of the United Nations and International Agreements.* Philadelphia: Taylor & Francis, 1985.

United Nations Statistical Office. *Demographic Yearbook; Annuaire Demographique.* New York: United Nations, 1949– . Annual.

United Nations. Statistical Office. *Statistical Yearbook; Annuaire Statistique.* New York: United Nations, 1948– . Annual.

United Nations. *Yearbook of the United Nations.* New York: UN Dept. of Information, 1947– . Annual.

Locating Experts

There are times when either the easiest or the only solution to a research problem is to talk to an expert. An expert is said to be someone who knows more and more about less and less, but they certainly are useful. The ideal route to take is to have someone you know refer you to the expert so you have a certain identity and don't have to call or write someone "cold," without an introduction. Try to get your doctor or your lawyer or your professor to refer you to an expert in their fields. But there are ways to locate a subject authority without "knowing somebody."

Even if you're planning to talk to an expert, *it is important for you to do some basic research so you know what questions to ask and so you'll understand the answers*. As an intelligent writer you will be less irritating to the specialist, who is not like a book that you can refer to over and over until you understand. If you can, though, it's a good idea to *tape the interview. And remember to ask the experts what reading and reference books they would recommend to a novice in the subject.*

One international title covers learned societies, research institutions, libraries, museums, universities, and other institutions of higher education, listing administrators and faculties, and is arranged alphabetically by country. This is *World of Learning* (London: Europa Pubns., 1947– . Annual.)

The list below, briefly annotated, should help locate experts in various fields through organizations, research institutions, colleges, museums, libraries, and biographical directories.

247

ORGANIZATIONS

Directory of Directories: An Annotated Guide to Business and Industrial Directories, Professional and Scientific Rosters, and Other Lists and Guides of All Kinds. Detroit: Information Enterprises, 1980– . Biennial. Directories arranged in broad subject fields with title and subject indexes.

Encyclopedia of Associations. Detroit: Gale, 1956– . Annual. Vol. 1, *National Organizations of the United States; vol. 2, Geographic and Executive Guides; vol. 3, New Associations and Projects; vol. 4, International Organizations; vol. 5, Research Activities and Funding Programs.* The subtitle on vol. 1 is "A guide to national and international organizations including: trade, business and commercial; agriculture and commodity; governmental and public administration; legal and military; scientific, engineering and military; educational; cultural; social welfare; health and medical; public affairs; fraternal, foreign interest, nationality and ethnic; religious; veteran, hereditary and patriotic; hobby and avocational; athletic and sports; labor unions, associations and federations; chambers of commerce; and Greek letter related organizations." Associations are grouped according to categories and there is an alphabetical and keyword index. Volume 4 is the *International Organizations* part of the works, with name, keyword, geographic, and executive indexes.

Government Research Centers Directory. Detroit: Gale, 1980–82– Biennial. A guide to U.S. government research and development centers, institutes, bureaus, data collection, and analysis centers, in fields such as art, business, medicine, environment, etc.

International Organizations: A Dictionary and Directory. 2d ed. Edited by Giuseppe Schiavone. London: Macmillan, 1986. This work lists organizations and identifies terms, treaties, etc.

Research Centers Directory. Detroit: Gale, 1960– . Biennial. A guide to university-related and other nonprofit research organizations. A classified arrangement with an alphabetical index, an index of sponsoring institutions, and a subject index.

Yearbook of International Organizations. Annuaire des Organizations Internationales. Brussels: Union of Internat. Assoc., 1948– . Irregular. 23d ed. New York: Saur, 1986/87. Volume 1 has organization descriptions and index; volume 2 is a geographic volume, describing country participation in organizations, with a directory of secretariats.

LIBRARIES, MUSEUMS, AND SPECIAL COLLECTIONS

American Art Directory. New York: Bowker, 1952–   . Triennial. Title and frequency vary. Part 1 lists art organizations, museums, associations; part 2 lists art schools; part 3 covers art information (art councils, magazines, critics, scholarships, and so on). With some exceptions in section 3, this directory covers the United States and Canada.

American Library Directory: A Classified List of Libraries in the United States and Canada with Personnel and Statistical Data. New York: Bowker, 1923–   . Annual. Gives the names of librarians and, usually, department heads and is arranged by state and city. Useful in many ways, one of which might be to find information about a small American town by calling the local library.

Ash, Lee, comp. *Special Collections.* 6th ed., rev. and enl. New York: Bowker, 1985. An extremely useful work that locates collections such as presidential papers, authors' works, and collections on various subjects such as railroads, the circus, theater subjects, sports, business, famous people, movies, science, ethnic groups, and many, many more.

Directory of Museums and Living Displays. 3d ed. Edited by Kenneth Hudson and Ann Nicolls. New York: Stockton Press, 1985. It is often useful to visit a "living display" of, for example, a re-created early American town or an Indian camp.

Directory of Special Libraries and Information Centers. Detroit: Gale, 1963–   . (10th ed. 1987) A guide to special libraries, research libraries, information centers, archives, and data centers maintained by government agencies, business, industry, newspapers, educational institutions, nonprofit organizations, and societies in the field of science, technology, law, art, religion, history, medicine, social sciences, and humanistic studies. This guide to libraries in the United States and Canada has an alphabetical arrangement with an index by subject.

Evinger, William R. *Directory of Federal Libraries.* Phoenix, Ariz.:

Oryx Press, 1987. Lists libraries in branches and departments of the federal government such as housing, agriculture, education, etc., in Washington, D.C. and the states. Gives the names of administrators and available services in reference and circulation. Has a subject index.

Guide to Ethnic Museums, Libraries, and Archives in the United States. Compiled by Łubomyr Wynar and Lois Buttlar. Kent. Ohio: Kent State Univ., 1978. Provides addresses, personnel names, publications, etc., under groups such as Turkish-Americans, Slavic-Americans, Tibetan-Americans, etc.

Museums of the World. 3d rev. ed. New York: Saur, 1981. An international list.

The Official Museum Directory. New York: American Association of Museums and Crowell-Collier Educ., 1971–   . Annual. Gives information on over 6000 museums of art, history, and science with personnel, lists of special collections, publications, hours.

INDIVIDUALS

If you know the name and just want to locate the person, use the standard biographical tools such as *Who's Who in America, Biography and Genealogy Master Index, Contemporary Authors, Contemporary Artists, Who's Who in the Theatre,* etc. Check guides to biographical sources such as Slocum's *Biographical Dictionaries and Related Works* and *ARBA Guide to Biographical Dictionaries* listed in segment "Diaries, Memoirs, and Biographical Tools," part 2.

Various membership directories can be found in library catalogs under the name of the organization, and the *Directory of Directories,* listed above, will also reveal directories of members of various societies and organizations (most have geographic indexes) such as:

American Psychiatric Association. *Biographical Directory of the Fellows and Members of the American Psychiatric Association.* Wash., D.C.: American Psychiatric Press, 1983.

American Psychological Association. *Directory of the Members of the American Psychological Association.* Wash., D.C.: The Association, 1985.

There is an *American Medical Directory,* a *Directory of Medical Specialists,* and an *ABMS Compendium of Certified Medical Specialists* (see the "Medicine" section in this guide) listing doctors by their specialty. There is a *Martindale-Hubbell Law Directory,* arranged geographically by state and city, listing firms and lawyers, but it has no alphabetical list of lawyers and no list by special expertise. You might seek the help of the local Bar Association. Be careful you don't get charged for help (that's why a referral from someone who knows the expert is a better idea). In both these areas calling a medical school or a law school for a faculty expert might be the most productive road to take.

American Men and Women of Science. Physical and biological sciences. 16th ed. Edited by Jacques Cattell Pr. 7 vols. New York: Bowker, 1986.

American Men and Women of Science. Social and behavioral sciences. 13th ed. New York: Jacques Cattell Pr./Bowker, 1978. Lists contemporary scientists by specialty.

Directory of American Scholars: A biographical directory. 8th ed. New York: Bowker, 1982. Lists currently active U.S. and Canadian scholars in volumes for (1) history; (2) English, speech, and drama; (3) foreign languages, linguistics, and philology; and (4) philosophy, religion, and law.

The Faculty Directory of Higher Education. 12 vols. Detroit: Gale, 1987– . Annual. Each volume is a discipline directory—Business & Economics, Computer Science, Education, Engineering, Fine Arts, etc.—identifying faculty and courses taught. Index volume has an alphabetical list of faculty.

National Faculty Directory. Detroit: Gale, 1970– . Annual. An alphabetical list, with addresses, of teaching faculty at colleges and universities in the United States and selected Canadian institutions. This does not list faculty by subject expertise, but if you have the names of authors of articles and books, this will sometimes locate them at a college or university. College catalogs list faculty by subject (most large libraries have a set of these on microfiche), and so does the title above, *The Faculty Directory of Higher Education.*

Researcher's Guide to Washington Experts. By Washington Researchers. Wash., D.C.: The Researchers, 1981. Annual. Continues *Researcher's Guide to Washington*, 1977–1980.

The *Subject Guide to Books in Print* will give you a list of current nonfiction books by subject so you can both read the book and possibly contact the author by using biographical dictionaries or writing the publisher.

YELLOW PAGES

Remember the yellow pages of your local telephone book can be very useful for locating a nearby specialist in everything from computers to tree trimming.

Locating Pictures and Photographs

Well, writers usually express doubts about whether or not one picture is really worth a thousand words, but perhaps one picture can help authors write a thousand words . . . or set a scene. If you can't visit a place or see a person, sometimes a picture will save the day. In addition to the sources listed here, many libraries will have lists and directories of local sources for photographs (for example, *Sources for Photographs in the Los Angeles Metropolitan Area,* published by the Southern California Answering Network of the Los Angeles Public Library, 1980).

Remember, too, that the abbreviation "ill." or "il." on a catalog card or in a periodical or newspaper index means that the book or article is accompanied by at least one illustration. "Por." means there is a portrait of a person. Noticing this kind of information can save time if you're just looking for pictures.

Looking at pictures and portraits is especially useful for details, and details are often better than generalities for quickly conveying a convincing setting. What kind of eyeglasses did a person wear in 1910? What did an art deco kitchen look like? What does Versailles look like today? It's a good idea to take photographs or pick up postcards when you travel, in case you later use that place as a setting for a play or novel. Of course, *you* are not the "ugly American," but traveling can sometimes be a rush through palaces and Left Banks so that the places and cultures are not fully appreciated. One can stare at a picture for a long time, taking in the small, intimate details.

Paintings and fine art from other times and places can also help authors "see" a time and place, so some indexes to reproductions of famous art are included here. Also listed below are a few indexes to periodicals like *Life* and the *National Geographic,* which are obvious sources for pictures and serve here as examples of the kind of works to remember. Most magazines of this type, however, are also indexed in periodical indexes, so there is usually a way of getting at pictures and articles in journals that do not have their own index. Frequently journals of various historical societies also have their own indexes. Some of the sources below will lead you to commercial photograph dealers.

Sometimes material written for children or young people can help you visualize places and things. For example, the Warwick Press publishes a "See Inside Series" letting you see inside a castle, a Norman town, a TV studio, a space station, and an oil rig and tanker.

Useful Titles/Research Guides

Evans, Hilary. *The Art of Picture Research: A Guide to Current Practice, Procedure, Techniques and Resources.* Newton Abbot, Devon: Davis & Charles, 1979.

Evans, Hilary, and Evans, Mary. *The Picture Researcher's Handbook: An International Guide to Picture Sources and How to Use Them.* Van Nostrand Reinhold (UK), 1986.

Robl, Ernest. *Picture Sources 4.* 4th ed. New York: Special Libraries Association, 1983.

Smith, Lyn Wall, and Moure, Nancy Dustin Wall. *Index to Reproductions of American Painting Appearing in More Than 400 Books, Mostly Published Since 1960.* Metuchen, N.J.: Scarecrow, 1977.

Stock Photo and Assignment Source Book: Where to Find Photographs Instantly. 2d ed. Edited by Fred W. McDarrah. New York: Photographic Arts Center, 1984.

World Photography Sources. Edited by David N. Bradshaw. New York: Directories, 1982.

Possible LCSH Subject Headings

PICTORIAL WORKS is a subdivision under subjects, for example, TWENTIETH CENTURY—PICTORIAL WORKS. PORTRAITS is a heading that can be divided geographically and can also be used as a subdivision under headings, for example, BIOGRAPHY—20TH CENTURY—PORTRAITS. PHOTOGRAPHS FROM SPACE is a subdivision under countries, cities, and other headings; CLOUDS—PHOTOGRAPHS FROM SPACE.

AERIAL PHOTOGRAPHS
CARICATURES AND CARTOONS
INTERIOR ARCHITECTURE
ITALY—PHOTOGRAPHS FROM SPACE (see note above)
PHOTOGRAPHS
PHOTOGRAPHS—PSYCHOLOGICAL ASPECTS
PHOTOGRAPHS IN INTERIOR DECORATION
PORTRAITS
PORTRAITS, BRITISH (example: PORTRAITS, AMERICAN, etc.)
WIT AND HUMOR, PICTORIAL
[Subject]—PICTORIAL WORKS (as a subdivision under other headings; see note above.)

Indexes

A.L.A. Portrait Index to Portraits Contained in Printed Books and Periodicals. Edited by W. C. Lane and N. E. Browne. Wash., D.C.: Library of Congress, 1906.

Cirker, Hayward, and Cirker, Blanche. *Dictionary of American Portraiture: 4045 Pictures of Important Americans from the Earliest Times to the Beginning of the Twentieth Century.* New York: Dover, 1967.

Clapp, Jane. *Art in Life.* New York: Scarecrow, 1959. Supp. New York: Scarecrow, 1965.

Ellis, Jesse Croft. *Index to Illustrations*. Boston: Faxon, 1966.

———. *Nature and Its Applications: Over 200,000 Selected References to Nature Forms and Illustrations of Nature as Used in Every Way*. Boston: Faxon, 1949.

———. *Travel Through Pictures: References to Pictures, in Books and Periodicals, of Interesting Sites All over the World*. Boston: Faxon, 1935.

Illustration Index. 2d ed. 1966. (Incorporates 1st ed. 1957 and supp. 1961) 3d ed. 1973. 4th ed. 1980. 5th ed. 1984. Metuchen, N. J.: Scarecrow Pr.

Monro, Isabel Stevenson, and Monro, Kate M. *Index to Reproductions of American Paintings; A Guide to Pictures Occurring in More than 800 Books*. New York: Wilson, 1948. First Supp. 1964.

———. *Index to Reproductions of European Paintings; A Guide to Pictures in More than 300 Books*. New York: Wilson, 1956.

National Geographic Index 1888–1946. Wash., D.C.: National Geographic Society, 1984.

National Geographic Index 1947–1983. Wash., D.C.: National Geographic Society, 1984.

Parry, Pamela Jeffcott. *Contemporary Art and Artists: An Index to Reproductions*. Westport, Conn.: Greenwood, 1978.

Smith, Lyn Wall, and Moure, Nancy Dustin Wall. *Index to Reproductions of American Paintings Appearing in More than 400 Books, Mostly Published Since 1960*. Metuchen, N.J.: Scarecrow Press, 1977.

Remember that various periodical indexes such as the *Readers' Guide, Business Periodicals Index, Art Index, Social Science Index,* etc., indicate illustrations and portraits accompanying articles with "ill.," or "il.," and "por."

Finding Other Fiction by Subject

Writers often have mixed emotions about looking at other fiction written on the same subject they have chosen. Reading other work can give you ideas, but of course, one worries about stealing ideas or copying styles either consciously or unconsciously. On the other hand, reading "good" books and studying "great" ones must surely have good consequences and enhance your own abilities. Just plain curiosity about how another author handled a scene in ancient Rome or the nineteen-twenties can motivate you to look at the work of others. Subject approaches to nonfiction abound, but finding fiction by subject is a bit more difficult.

Library catalogs—with their subject headings—and the *Subject Guide to Books in Print* (available in bookstores as well as libraries [see "Books," part 3] lead readers to nonfiction sources by subject, not usually fiction by subject. With the exception of catalogs for children's literature, library catalogs usually show fiction only by author and title unless it is clearly defined and finds its way under a special subject heading like GHOST STORIES. There are, however, some excellent ways to locate fiction by subject, and the titles below either have subject indexes or are arranged by subject. The *Fiction Catalog* includes a generous representation of foreign fiction that has been translated into English in its over five thousand titles of the best fiction in English. It has author, title, and subject approaches. The *Play Index* and other indexes listed below all have subject indexes. *The Book Review Digest* lists fiction by subject under the heading "Fiction Themes" in its Title and Subject Index.

Useful Titles

Baker, Ernest Albert. *Guide to Historical Fiction.* London: Routledge; New York: Macmillan, 1914. (Reprinted, New York: Argosy-Antiquarian, 1968.)

————, and Packman, James. *Guide to the Best Fiction, English and American, Including Translations from Foreign Countries.* New and enl. ed. London: Routledge; New York: Macmillan, 1932.

Burns, Grant. *The Sports Pages: A Critical Bibliography of Twentieth Century American Novels and Stories Featuring Baseball, Basketball, Football, and Other Athletic Pursuits.* Metuchen, N.J.: Scarecrow, 1987.

Cumulated Fiction Index, 1945/60– . London: Assoc. of Assist. Librarians, 1960– . Irregular.

Fiction Catalog. 10th ed. Edited by Juliette Yaakov and Gary L. Bogart. New York: Wilson, 1981.

Hanna, Archibald. *A Mirror for the Nation: An Annotated Bibliography of American Social Fiction, 1901–1950.* New York: Garland, 1985.

Irwin, Leonard Bartram. *A Guide to Historical Fiction for the Use of Schools, Libraries, and the General Reader.* 10th ed. New and rev. Brooklawn, N.J.: McKinley, 1971.

McGarry, Daniel D., and White, Sarah Harriman. *World Historical Fiction Guide: An Annotated, Chronological, Geographical, and Topical List of Selected Historical Novels.* 2d ed. Metuchen, N.J.: Scarecrow, 1973.

Neild, Jonathan. *A Guide to the Best Historical Novels and Tales.* New York: Macmillan, 1929.

Crime and Mystery Stories

Hagen, Ordean A. *Who Done It? A guide to Detective, Mystery and Suspense Fiction.* (With sections on mystery films and plays.) New York: Bowker, 1969.

Hubin, Allen J. *Crime Fiction 1749–1980: A Comprehensive Bibliography.* New York: Garland, 1984.

Menendez, Albert J. *The Subject Is Murder: A Selective Subject Guide to Mystery Fiction.* New York: Garland, 1986.

Olderr, Stephen. *Mystery Index: Subjects, Settings, and Sleuths of 10,000 Titles.* Chicago: American Library Assoc., 1987.

Science Fiction, Fantasy, and Gothic Stories

Bleiler, Everett Franklin. *The Checklist of Science Fiction and Supernatural Fiction.* Glen Rock, N.J.: Firebell Books, 1978.

———. *The Guide to Supernatural Fiction.* Kent, Ohio: Kent State Univ. Press, 1983.

Frank, Frederick S. *Guide to the Gothic: An Annotated Bibliography of Criticism.* Metuchen, N.J.: Scarecrow, 1984.

The Science Fiction Encyclopedia. Edited by Peter Nicholls. Garden City, N.Y.: Dolphin Books, Doubleday, 1979.

Tuck, Donald H. *The Encyclopedia of Science Fiction and Fantasy Through 1968; a Bibliographic Survey of the Fields of Science Fiction, Fantasy, and Weird Fiction Through 1968.* Chicago: Advent Publishers, 1974–1983.

Indexes

Book Review Digest. New York: Wilson, 1905– . Monthly with annual cumulations. Includes subject index.

Contento, William. *Index to Science Fiction Anthologies and Collections.* Boston: G. K. Hall, 1978.

Fletcher, Marilyn P. *Science Fiction Story Index, 1950–1979.* 2d ed. Chicago: American Library Association, 1981.

Play Index. 6 vols. New York: Wilson, 1953–1983. Irregular.

Short Story Index. New York: Wilson, 1953– . Annual with five-year cumulations.

Thomson, Ruth Gibbons. *Index to Full Length Plays, 1895–1925.* Supplement *1926–1944.* Boston: Faxon, 1946, 1956.

Continued by:

Ireland, Norma O. *Index to Full Length Plays, 1944–1964*. Boston: 1965.

Subject Headings

Some headings have "fiction" as a subdivision for individual or collected works on identifiable topics:

CHILDREN—FICTION
FATHERS AND SONS—FICTION

The subject heading FICTION leads primarily to works *about* fiction in various centuries, as well as history, technique, etc. There are subject headings for types of fiction:

ADVENTURE STORIES
DETECTIVE AND MYSTERY STORIES
GHOST STORIES
HISTORICAL FICTION
RELIGIOUS FICTION
SCIENCE FICTION
SPY STORIES
WAR STORIES
WESTERN STORIES

Knowing When to Stop

In your heart of hearts you know when to stop . . . when you have enough. Remember the mystery of storytelling. There's no point in piling it on or your research will be visible through your story. Research is a two-sided coin—it can boost imagination or it can be a way of procrastinating. Of course, one thing does lead to another, something found in a bibliography that one simply must see—the trail can be endless. Graduate students everywhere, stricken with a sort of research virus, spend years scrambling through book stacks and filling out interlibrary loan requests to look at just one more item. It is astonishing that any dissertation ever gets written. But you will know when to stop, especially if you have followed the advice given earlier to use research as you go along, not postponing the writing until you have "all" the information.

Your research is done in *support* of your writing; it is not the most important part of the process. The facts and background are used to flesh out characters and their behavior, events, connections, transitions, and dialogue. Good fiction *reveals* truth; it is not all true. The creative process and imagination are only strengthened by research, never replaced by it. Even Einstein said the imagination is more important than knowledge.

Bring in your own "deus ex machina" and simply stop, no matter how impossible it seems. Chances are, if the search for time and place is too prolonged, it has become too complex and, again, will show through the seam of the play or novel. More is not necessarily better. Emily Dickinson created a place with such economy:

> To make a prairie it takes a clover and a bee,
> One clover, and a bee,
> And revery.
> The revery alone will do,
> If bees are few.

Read your text or script aloud as a test to see if your research is neatly tucked away. This is often a recommendation of creative writing teachers anyway. Read aloud to see (or hear) if the work flows and sounds right. Research clichés need weeding just as language clichés do. Reading a manuscript out loud will help you notice when you have used a fact or detail artificially, when your investigation of time and place interrupts the story rather than being woven into it.

The process can cease when you know you have carefully and accurately established the time and place so your readers will not have the slightest suspicion of bamboozlement. Authors decide how much influence time and place will have on characters—whether these aspects are merely background, however authentic, or whether they determine the characters. In "Adagia," Wallace Stevens confesses:

> Life is an affair of people not of places.
> But for me life is an affair of places and
> that is the trouble.

Fiction writers have the job of recreating a world but one still within our world. John Gardner writes in *The Art of Fiction* (Knopf, 1984):

> Somehow the endlessly recombining elements that make up works of fiction have their roots hooked, it seems, into the universe, or at least into the hearts of human beings. Somehow the fictional dream persuades us that it's a clear, sharp, edited version of the dream all around us. Whatever our doubts, we pick up books at train stations, or withdraw into our studies to write them; and the world—or so we imagine—comes alive.

Bibliographies

Time and Place in Fiction Writing

Bachelard, Gaston, *The Poetics of Space*. Translated from the French by Maria Jolas. Boston: Beacon Press, 1969.

Brooks, Cleanth, and Warren, Robert Penn. *Understanding Fiction*. 3d ed. Englewood Cliffs, N.J.: Prentice-Hall, 1979.

Cassill, R. V. *Writing Fiction*. Englewood Cliffs, N.J.: Prentice Hall, 1975.

Chamberlain, Anne. "When Scenery Becomes Character." *The Writer* 95 (August 1982): 12–15.

Clark, Kenneth. *Landscape Into Art*. New York: Harper & Row, 1976.

"Fictional History." *Times Literary Supplement,* 3 November 1961, 789.

Field, Syd. *Screenplay: The Foundations of Screenwriting*. New exp. ed. New York: Delacorte Press, 1982.

Fryer, Judith. *Felicitous Space: The Imaginative Structures of Edith Wharton and Willa Cather*. Chapel Hill, N.C.: Univ. of North Carolina Press, 1986.

Gardner, John. *The Art of Fiction: Notes on Craft for Young Writers*. New York: Knopf, 1984.

———. *On Becoming a Novelist*. New York: Harper & Row, 1983.

Hanna, Archibald. *A Mirror for the Nation: An Annotated Bibliography of American Social Fiction, 1901–1950*. New York: Garland, 1985.

Hillard, Robert L. *Writing for Television and Radio*. 4th ed. Belmont, Cal.: Wadsworth, 1984.

Hinojosa-Smith, Rolando. "The Writer's Sense of Place." In *The Texas Tradition: Fiction, Folklore, History*. Edited by Don Graham, et al. Austin: Univ. of Texas, 1983.

Leneman, Leah. "History as Fiction." *History Today* 30 (January 1980): 52–55.

Lowery, Marilyn M. *How To Write Romance Novels That Sell*. New York: Rawson, 1983.

Lutwack, Leonard. *The Role of Place in Literature*. Syracuse, N.Y.: Syracuse Univ. Press, 1984.

McConnell, Malcolm. *The Essence of Fiction: A Practical Handbook for Successful Writing*. New York: Norton, 1986.

Madden, Davis, *A Primer of the Novel for Readers and Writers*. Metuchen, N.J.: Scarecrow Press, 1980.

Marcus, Stephen. "Historical Novels. If it didn't happen that way, it should have, and besides, it sells." *Harper's* 248 (March 1974): 85–90.

Morse, Samuel French. "A Sense of Place." In *The Motive for Metaphor: Essays on Modern Poetry*. Edited by Francis C. Blessington. Boston: Northeastern Univ., 1983.

Nairn, Ian. *The American Landscape*. New York: Random House, 1965.

Person, Leland S. "Playing House: Jane Austen's Fabulous Space." *Philological Quarterly* 59 (Winter 1981): 62–75.

Pike, Frank, and Dunn, Thomas G. *The Playwright's Handbook: For Beginning and Professional Playwrights—the First Complete Guide to Writing a Full-Length Play and Getting It Produced*. New York: New American Library, 1985.

Relph, Edward. *Place and Placelessness*. London: Pion, 1976.

Renault, Mary. "The Fiction of History." *London Magazine* 18 (March 1979): 52–57.

———. "History in Fiction." *Times Literary Supplement*, 23 March 1973, 315–316.

———. "Imagining the Past." *Times Literary Supplement*, 23 August 1974, 893–894.

Robinson, Brian S. *Geography as Stillness*. Occasional Papers in Geography. Halifax, N.S., Canada: St. Mary's University, 1980.

Salter, Christopher L., and Lloyd, William J. *Landscape in Literature*. Resource Papers for College Geography. Wash., D.C.: Association of American Geographers, 1977.

Simmons, James C. *The Novelist as Historian: Essays on the Victorian Historical Novel*. The Hague: Mouton, 1973.

Tuchman, Barbara W. "The Historian as Artist." *The Writer* 81 (February 1968): 15–17.

Vidal, Gore. "Vidal, to Vidal: On Misusing the Past." *Harper's*, October 1965, 162–164.

Weber, Ronald. *The Literature of Fact: Literary Nonfiction in American Writing*. Athens, Ohio: Ohio Univ. Press, 1980.

Welty, Eudora. *Place in Fiction*. New York: House of Books, 1957.

———. "Some Notes on Time in Fiction." *Mississippi Quarterly* 66 (Fall 1973): 483–492.

Wilson, Colin. *The Craft of the Novel*. London: Victor Gollancz, 1975.

Wolff, Robert Lee. "Present Uses for the Past." *Times Literary Supplement*, 13 December 1974, 1404.

Reference Sources

ARBA Guide to Subject Encyclopedias and Dictionaries. Edited by Bohdan S. Wynar. Littleton, Col.: Libraries Unlimited, 1986.

Chan, Lois Mai; Richmond, Phyllis A.; and Svenonius, Elaine, eds. *Theory of Subject Analysis: A Sourcebook*. Littleton, Col.: Libraries Unlimited, 1985.

Cheney, Francis N., and Williams, Wiley J. *Fundamental Reference Sources*. 2d ed. Chicago: American Library Assoc., 1980.

Daniells, Lorna M. *Business Information Sources*. 2d ed. Berkeley: Univ. of California Press, 1985.

Fenichel, Carol H., and Hogan, Thomas F. *Online Searching: A Primer*. 2d ed. Medford, N.J.: Learned Information, 1984.

Gates, Jean Key. *Guide to the Use of Libraries and Information Sources*. 5th ed. McGraw-Hill, 1983.

Handlin, Oscar. "Libraries and Learning." *American Scholar* (Spring 1987): 205–218.

Kister, Kenneth F. *Best Encyclopedias: A Guide to General and Specialized Encyclopedias.* Phoenix, Ariz.: Oryx, 1986.

Leidy, William P. *A Popular Guide to Government Publications.* 4th ed. New York: Columbia Univ. Press, 1976.

Library of Congress. *Library of Congress Subject Headings.* 10th ed. Wash., D.C.: Library of Congress, 1986.

McCormick, Mona. *New York Times Guide to Reference Materials.* 2d ed. New York: New American Library, 1986.

McIlvaine, Betsy. *A Consumers', Researchers', and Students' Guide to Government Publications.* New York: Wilson, 1983.

Morehead, Joe. *Introduction to United States Public Documents.* 3d ed. Littleton, Col.: Libraries Unlimited, 1983.

Sears, Jean L., and Moody, Marilyn K. *Using Government Publications.* Vol. 1, *Searching by Subjects and Agencies;* vol. 2, *Finding Statistics and Using Special Techniques.* Phoenix, Ariz.: Oryx Press, 1985.

Sheehy, Eugene P., ed. *Guide to Reference Books.* 10th ed. Chicago: American Library Association, 1986.

Wasserman, Paul, ed. *Encyclopedia of Business Sources.* 5th ed. Detroit: Gale, 1983.

Webb, William H., and Associates. *Sources of Information in the Social Sciences.* 3d ed. Chicago: American Library Assoc., 1986.

Index

Buikatra, J. E., and Rathbun, T. A.:
  Human Identification, 205
Bulfinch, T.: *Bulfinch's Mythology*,
  90
Bulfinch's Mythology, 90
Buranelli, V., and Buranelli, N.:
  Spy/Counterspy, 168
Burchfield, R. W., ed.: *Oxford
  English Dictionary*, supplement
  to, 76
Bureau of the Census Catalog, 228
Burke, J. H., and Hackett, A. P.: *80
  Years of Best Sellers, 1895–1975*,
  108
Burns, A. R.: *Money and Monetary
  Policy in Early Times*, 208
Burns, G.: *The Sports Pages*, 258
Burns, R. D., ed.: *Guide to
  American Foreign Relations
  Since 1700*, 148
———, and Leitenberg, M.:. *The
  Wars in Vietnam, Cambodia and
  Laos, 1945–1982*, 198
Burr, S.: *Money Grows Up in
  America*, 208
Business, 208–12
Business Information, 212
Business Information Sources, 212
Business Periodicals Index, 40, 211
Business Periodicals Literature, 256
Buttlar, L., and Wynar, L., comps.:
  *Guide to Ethnic Museums,
  Libraries, and Archives in the
  United States*, 250
Byler, M. G., Dorris, M. A., and
  Herschfelder, A. B.: *Guide to
  Research on North American
  Indians*, 98

Cable, T. A.: *A Companion to
  Baugh and Cable's History of the
  English Language*, 79
Cable, T. A., and Baugh, A. C.: *A
  History of the English Language*, 79
Cabot, P. S. de Q.: *Juvenile
  Delinquency*, 165
Caitlin, E.: *The Complete Spy*, 169
Calder, N.: *1984 and After*, 217
Calendars, 32–33
Calinescu, M.: *Faces of Modernity*,
  103

Cambridge Ancient History, 57, 58
*Cambridge History of American
  Literature*, 107, 108
*Cambridge History of English
  Literature*, 107, 108
Cambridge Medieval History, 58
Campbell, J.: *The Masks of God*, 90
Canby, C.: *A History of Weaponry*,
  199
Card catalog. *see* Library catalog
Carroll, B. A., et al.: *Peace and War*,
  198
Carruth, G., and Associates: *The
  Encyclopedia of American Facts
  and Dates*, 31
*Cassell's Encyclopedia of World
  Literature*, 107, 108
Cassidy, F. G., ed.: *Dictionary of
  American Regional English
  (DARE)*, 76
*Catalog of National Archives
  Microfilms Publications*, 232
*Catalog of the Public Documents of
  the Congress and Other
  Departments of the Goverment . . .*,
  241
*Catalogues of the Manuscript
  Collections* of the British
  Museum Department of Manu-
  scripts, 230
Catholic Encyclopedia, 83, 86
*Catholic Periodical and Literature
  Index*, 40, 88
Catholic Periodical List, 88
Catoe, L. E.: *UFOs and Related
  Subjects*, 158
Cavendish, R., ed.: *Mythology: An
  Illustrated Encyclopedia*, 90
Celebonovic, A.: *Some Call It Kitsch*,
  103
Cetron, M. J.: *Encounters with the
  Future*, 217
Chamberlain, Anne: *The Writer*, 263
Chambers, R.: *Books of Days*, 190
Chambers Biographical Dictionary, 71
Chambers of commerce, 176
Chambers's Encyclopedia, 12
Chandler, L. V.: *America's Greatest
  Depression, 1929–1941*, 210
Chapman, R., ed.: *Dictionary of
  American Slang*, 77

GOOD WRITING—AS EASY AS A-B-C

☐ **HOW TO WRITE LIKE A PRO by Barry Tarshis. Foreword by Don McKinney, Managing Editor, *McCall's* Magazine.** Proven, successful techniques for writing nonfiction for magazines, newspapers, technical journals and more by one of this country's top writing pros and a well-known writing teacher. You'll learn not only *how* professional writing works, but *why* it works.
(254116—$7.95)

☐ **HOW TO WRITE WITHOUT PAIN by Barry Tarshis.** This books is designed to help everyone stricken with writer's cramp. In this easy to follow, practical guide Tarshis shows you how to turn an intimidating task into a manageable process.
(256860—$8.95)

☐ **FICTION WRITERS RESEARCH HANDBOOK by Mona McCormick.** The comprehensive, easy-to-use guide to finding the facts fiction writers need most. Whether you write romance novels or historical sagas, westerns or mysteries, it's important to have reliable facts about a date, a historical era, a famous event. This essential volume not only saves time and limits frustration, it also triggers ideas.
(261570—$8.95)

☐ **THE SONGWRITER'S RHYMING DICTIONARY by Sammy Cahn.** Contains more than 50,000 rhyme words—arranged in terms of sounds and syllables—for the writer of songs, jingles, and light verse, by the great Academy Award-winning lyricist, plus Sammy's memorable anecdotes about his collaboration with the likes of Bing Crosby, Frank Sinatra, and others. There is no better guide if you have a song in your heart but trouble finding the words.
(009545—$9.95)

☐ **WRITING ON THE JOB: A Handbook for Business & Government by John Schell and John Stratton.** The clear, practical reference for today's professional, this authoritative guide will show you how to write clearly, concisely, and coherently. Includes tips on memos, manuals, press releases, reports, editing and proofreading and much more.
(255317—$9.95)

Prices slightly higher in Canada

To order use coupon on next page.